ATM
Networks

Concepts, Protocols, Applications

ELECTRONIC SYSTEMS ENGINEERING SERIES

Consulting editors

E L Dagless
University of Bristol

J O'Reilly
University College of Wales

OTHER TITLES IN THE SERIES

SECOND EDITION

ATM
Networks

Concepts, Protocols, Applications

**Rainer Händel, Manfred N. Huber
and Stefan Schröder**

Siemens AG, Munich

ADDISON-WESLEY
PUBLISHING
COMPANY

Wokingham, England · Reading, Massachusetts · Menlo Park, California · New York
Don Mills, Ontario · Amsterdam · Bonn · Sydney · Singapore
Tokyo · Madrid · San Juan · Milan · Paris · Mexico City · Seoul · Taipei

© 1994 Addison-Wesley Publishers Ltd.
© 1994 Addison-Wesley Publishing Company Inc.

The programs in this book have been included for their instructional value. They have been tested with care but are not guaranteed for any particular purpose. The publisher does not offer any warranties or representations, nor does it accept any liabilities with respect to the programs.

Many of the designations used by manufacturers and sellers to distinguish their products are claimed as trademarks. Addison-Wesley has made every attempt to supply trademark information about manufacturers and their products mentioned in this book.

Cover designed by Chris Eley incorporating photograph
© Telegraph Colour Library
and printed by The Riverside Printing Co. (Reading) Ltd.
Typeset by the authors using TeX
Printed in Great Britain at the University Press, Cambridge

First printed 1994. Reprinted 1995.

ISBN 0-201-42274-3

British Library Cataloguing in Publication Data applied for
A catalogue record for this book is available from the British Library.

Library of Congress Cataloguing-in-Publication Data applied for

Foreword

There are few technical topics as difficult to explain as asynchronous transfer mode (ATM). And yet ATM seems so easy once one explains that it isn't about banking. After all, what could be so hard about a protocol that just transmits data as fixed-sized packets?

But ATM is hard to explain. A large part of the difficulty is due to those 'fixed-sized packets', generally known as cells. The cell size is small, just 53 bytes, which has led some experts to think of ATM cells as just bigger bits (i.e. bigger time-division multiplexed data units). But the cells include a basic packet header, and have a variety of transmission modes (unicast, multicast, best-effort delivery, guaranteed delivery) that allow the cells to act like small packets.

The truth seems to be that ATM should be thought of as both big bits and small packets, and which description is more accurate depends on the context. For instance, at high bandwidths (a few 100 Mbit/s or faster), ATM cells look very much like bits. Each cell takes a neglible amount of time to send, and is too small for a sending or receiving computer to handle efficiently. But at low bandwidths (64 kbit/s or slower), cells start to look big. A cell takes over 6 ms to transmit, a long time in a world where processors perform an instruction every few nanoseconds.

The big bits versus packets issue has echoes in some of the efforts to model the performance of ATM networks. If one assumes that cells for a given conversation on an ATM network will be nicely spread out, then one can model ATM performance in a fashion similar to the way we currently model telephone network performance. However, if one assumes that related cells clump together as they tend to do in data networks – then the telephony models generally fall apart. Data traffic appears to follow fractal models rather than the more comfortable Poisson models.

ATM lies in this middle ground because it is an attempt to combine the best features of telephone and data networks into a coherent link-layer protocol. What makes ATM so exciting to many people is that it has apparently partially succeeded in merging the two approaches. And one of the things that makes ATM so challenging is that, to understand it, one needs an appreciation of both telephone and data networking (and possibly cable networking too!).

If ATM is challenging to the student, I hope it is clear by now that it is almost equally challenging to anyone trying to write about it. The authors have succeeded in viewing ATM simultaneously from different perspectives, and in finding a good balance between the various views. I felt one of the great strengths of the first editon of this book was the balanced presentation that Rainer Händel and Manfred Huber achieved, and it is my pleasure to introduce this, the updated second edition, written in conjunction with Stefan Schröder.

Craig Partridge

May 1994

Preface

Preface to the Second Edition

The ATM standards available for implementation have matured in the past two years. Though still not complete, a considerable number of new issues have been tackled and at least partly resolved. This covers mainly operation and maintenance of ATM-based networks, signalling scenarios and procedures, resource management, ATM adaptation layer type 5 etc. The promotion of ATM standards is currently being pushed not only by the conventional standards bodies such as International Telecommunications Union T (ITU-T), formerly named Comité Consultatif International Télégraphique et Téléphonique (CCITT), European Telecommunication Standard Institute (ETSI) and American National Standard Institute (ANSI), but also in the ATM Forum which, founded in North America in 1991, has meanwhile spread all over the world.

The first ATM-based trial networks and, immediately afterwards, commercial ATM networks are about to be realized in Europe, America, Asia and Australia. In Europe many network operators have signed a Memorandum of Understanding by which they commit themselves to the implementation of a pan-European ATM network.

Manufacturers are offering ATM equipment such as switches, cross-connects, hubs, multiplexers and terminal interfaces.

Deployment strategies and the usage of ATM over the next couple of years are becoming clearer:

- customer premises networks evolve from shared medium (ring/bus) local area networks (LANs) to star-configured ATM-LANs;
- corporate networks (private or shared or virtual private network) employ ATM as a 'seamless' wide-area technique;
- public network operators realize ATM based data backbone networks.

Moreover, ATM technology is penetrating the terminal market; not only ATM interfaces are implemented but also internal control of terminals, such as workstations, will more and more be based on ATM, and desk-area networks (DANs), assembled with ATM components (ATM-DANs), will evolve.

ATM is now an established technique, and the term ATM is well known to the public, so we decided to give the book the new title *ATM Networks – Concepts, Protocols, Applications*.

The following new features have been included in this second edition:

- data services, such as connectionless services and frame relay, to be supported by ATM;
- ATM-LANs;
- new ATM interfaces;
- interim local management interface;
- new ATM adaptation layer type 5;
- higher-layer protocols and interworking issues (for example, frame relay and connectionless service on top of ATM; interworking between ATM-based services and others);
- signalling protocols;
- ATM switching and transmission equipment (for example, realization of ATM nodes, ATM passive optical networks);
- ongoing ATM network projects all over the world: objectives, network features, applications, schedules;
- outlook towards optical networks and their relationship to ATM.

This second edition is a completely revised up-to-date version of our book on ATM-based broadband networks.

The ITU-T standards references have been updated and information on specifications issued by ANSI, ETSI, ATM Forum and Bellcore has been added. However, the overall structure remains unchanged; we hope the reader already acquainted with the book will appreciate this. We have tried to keep the book 'readable', so emphasis was again put on generally applicable ATM features supplemented by illustrative examples relating to ATM networking. The comprehensive reference list will help readers to find more detailed information on available standards, network concepts, products etc.

The authors would like to thank Professor J. Eberspächer and Professor C. Partridge for reviewing the manuscript and I. Pfaffinger and U. Utri for their efficient technical support in preparing the second edition.

R. Händel
M.N. Huber
S. Schröder

June 1994

Preface to the First Edition

Virtually everyone uses the phone nowadays as a (more or less) efficient communication tool. It provides us with the capability of exchanging information between different places around the world; it is quick because of its real-time operation and it is easy to use. These assets, namely global availability, short response times and user-friendliness, have made telephony the communication evergreen that is listened to by millions of people around the world every minute.

Engineers developing integrated broadband network concepts and products are dreaming that their ideas will be as successful as plain old telephony was. Of course, not all experts are yet convinced that this will actually happen, nor are potential customers, who often do not even know what powerful communication tools the future will offer them.

Integrated broadband networks are being conceived as an extension of 64 kbit/s based integrated services digital networks (ISDNs). These themselves incorporate telephony as one of their main applications; in fact, ISDN is based on the digitized telephone network.

ISDN is an all-digital network; all source information (irrespective of its meaning to the user) is transmitted and switched as digital signals end to end. Thus a common signal transfer mechanism can be employed in the network to serve several applications that are quite different in nature, such as voice and data transmission.

ISDN seems to be a natural development of plain telephony with good prospects of success as well.

Broadband integrated services digital networks (B-ISDNs) will add a tremendous new feature to ISDNs: considerably higher bit rates will be available for fast data or moving picture transmission, for example, and these bit rates may be demanded per connection with great flexibility in choosing the value actually needed.

How this will be achieved is described in this book. It introduces the idea of integrated broadband networks, gives a survey of the current situation concerning B-ISDN and provides a detailed technical discussion of broadband networks based on the emerging international standards.

The book will address the following items:

- What broadband capabilities are and where they are needed.

- 'Integrated broadband networks': the original approach to add broadband channels to the 64 kbit/s ISDN and what really happened with B-ISDN.

- The main ingredients of B-ISDN: asynchronous transfer mode (ATM) and optical transmission (synchronous digital hierarchy).

- ATM networking (virtual paths and virtual channels; resource allocation; traffic management; network performance etc.).

- User–network access configurations and interfaces/protocols.

- B-ISDN network equipment: ATM switches, cross-connects and transmission systems.

- How to evolve towards B-ISDN.

- How to integrate existing networks and networks that will probably be implemented before B-ISDN, such as metropolitan area networks (MANs).

- B-ISDN trials.

- Possible future development (Gbit/s systems, optical switching).

Some other ATM-specific problems will also be covered, including voice delay and echo in ATM networks, connectionless service provision and tariffing in ATM networks.

An overview of the current standardization situation is annexed. Reference to the standards documents is made whenever appropriate so that the reader can easily find further information.

The book addresses people involved in the planning, development, implementation and sale of telecommunication networks and terminals. The material presented may also be used for an introductory course into broadband networks in the academic field.

The authors appreciate the stimulating and fruitful discussions with all their colleagues. We would also like to express our thanks to A. Biersack, U. Branczik and R. Trox for technical support.

R. Händel
M.N. Huber

June 1991

Contents

Chapter 1

Introduction

1.1 The Current Situation

At present, most networks are dedicated to specific purposes like telephony, TV distribution, circuit-switched or packetized data transfer.

Some applications, such as facsimile, make use of the widespread telephone network. Using pre-existing networks for new applications may lead to characteristic shortcomings, however, as such networks are not usually tailored to the needs of services that were unknown when the networks were implemented. So data transfer over the telephone network is confined by a lack of bandwidth, flexibility and quality of analogue voice transmission equipment. Telephone networks were engineered for a constant bandwidth service, therefore using them for variable bit rate data traffic requires costly adaptation.

Since in general the public telephone network was not able effectively to support non-voice services to the extent that was required by the customer, other dedicated networks arose, such as public data networks or private data networks connecting, say, a big company's plants or several research institutes. An example of a large data network is the Internet.

Private networks often deploy equipment, interfaces and protocols which are unable to offer access to other networks and users. If in such an environment gateways are required to the outside world, their implementation may be tedious and costly.

Table 1.1 illustrates the variety of existing data transmission schemes. Note that this table contains only standardized user classes according to ITU-T Recommendation X.1 [149]. ITU-T is a sector of the International Telecommunications Union (ITU), which is in charge of setting network standards for public telecommunication. ITU-T is the new name for the well-known CCITT, which is the acronym for *Comité Consultatif International Télégraphique et Téléphonique*.

1

Table 1.1: *User classes within public data networks*

Class	Bit Rate	Characteristics
1	300 bit/s	Start/Stop mode
2	50 ... 200 bit/s	Start/Stop mode
3	600 bit/s	Synchronous operation mode
4	2400 bit/s	Synchronous operation mode
5	4800 bit/s	Synchronous operation mode
6	9600 bit/s	Synchronous operation mode
7	48000 bit/s	Synchronous operation mode
8	2400 bit/s	CCITT Recommendation X.25 [150]
9	4800 bit/s	CCITT Recommendation X.25
10	9600 bit/s	CCITT Recommendation X.25
11	48000 bit/s	CCITT Recommendation X.25
12	1200 bit/s	CCITT Recommendation X.25
13	64000 bit/s	CCITT Recommendation X.25
19	64000 bit/s	Synchronous operation mode
20	50 ... 300 bit/s	CCITT Recommendation X.28 [151]
21	75 ... 1200 bit/s	CCITT Recommendation X.28
22	1200 bit/s	CCITT Recommendation X.28
23	2400 bit/s	CCITT Recommendation X.28
30	64000 bit/s	ISDN

1.2 The Idea of the Integrated Services Digital Network

In 1984, the Plenary Assembly of the CCITT adopted the I series recommendations dealing with integrated services digital network (ISDN) matters. The CCITT stated that 'an ISDN is a network ... that provides end-to-end digital connectivity to support a wide range of services, including voice and non-voice services, to which users have access by a limited set of standard multipurpose user–network interfaces' [78]. Such an ISDN standard interface was defined and called **basic access**, comprising two 64 kbit/s B channels and a 16 kbit/s signalling D channel. Another type of interface, the **primary rate access**, with a gross bit rate of about 1.5 Mbit/s or 2 Mbit/s offers the flexibility to allocate high-speed H channels or mixtures of B and H channels and a 64 kbit/s signalling channel (see Table 1.2).

The ISDN concept laid down in the 1984 recommendations has since been further elaborated; its evolution is documented in the 1988 CCITT Blue Books, and later CCITT/ITU-T recommendations.

This original ISDN is based on the digitized telephone network which is charac-

Table 1.2: *ISDN channels and interface structures*

ISDN Channels		
Channel	**Bit Rate**	**Interface**
B	64 kbit/s	Basic access
H0	384 kbit/s	Primary rate access
H11	1536 kbit/s	Primary rate access
H12	1920 kbit/s	Primary rate access
D16	16 kbit/s	Basic access
D64	64 kbit/s	Primary rate access

Interface Structures		
Interface	**Gross Bit Rate**	**Structure**
Basic access	192 kbit/s	2B + D16
Primary rate access	1544 kbit/s	23B + D64
		3H0 + D64
		H11
		etc.
Primary rate access	2048 kbit/s	30B + D64
		5H0 + D64
		H12 + D64
		etc.

terized by the 64 kbit/s channel. The channel bit rate of 64 kbit/s is derived from 3.4 kHz voice transmission requirements (8-bit sampling with a frequency of 8 kHz).

The 64 kbit/s ISDN is basically a circuit-switched network but it can offer access to packet-switched services [21].

ISDNs are being implemented in this decade. Their benefits for the user and network provider include [21]:

- common user–network interface for access to a variety of services
- enhanced (out-of-band) signalling capabilities
- service integration
- provision of new and improved services.

1.3 B-ISDN

The highest bit rate a 64 kbit/s based ISDN can offer to the user is about 1.5 Mbit/s or 2 Mbit/s, that is, the H1 channel bit rates (see Table 1.2). Connection of local area networks (LANs), however, or transmission of moving images with good resolution may, in many cases, require considerably higher bit rates (cf. Chapter 2). Consequently, the conception and realization of a broadband ISDN (B-ISDN) was desirable.

1.3.1   What is B-ISDN?

ITU-T Recommendation I.113 [99] ('Vocabulary of Terms for Broadband Aspects of ISDN') defines **broadband** as:

> '... a service or system requiring transmission channels capable of supporting rates greater than the primary rate.'

B-ISDN thus includes 64 kbit/s ISDN capabilities but in addition opens the door to applications utilizing bit rates above 1.5 Mbit/s or 2 Mbit/s. The bit rate available to a broadband user is typically from about 50 Mbit/s up to hundreds of Mbit/s (see Section 5.2.2).

This definition of broadband does not indicate anything about its technical concept. Whereas this definition was settled from the beginning, the final technical concept for B-ISDN, as described in the following chapters, only emerged after long and controversial discussions within the standardization bodies, reflecting the differing backgrounds and intentions of the participants.

The first concrete idea of B-ISDN was simply to:

- add new high-speed channels to the existing channel spectrum

- define new broadband user–network interfaces

- rely on existing 64 kbit/s ISDN protocols and only to modify or enhance them when absolutely unavoidable.

So in the dawn of B-ISDN, channel bit rates of 32–34 Mbit/s and around 45 Mbit/s, 70 Mbit/s and 135–139 Mbit/s were foreseen. The corresponding channels were denominated H2, H3, H4.

These bit rates (and also the interface bit rate of about 140 Mbit/s) were oriented towards the bit rates of the plesiochronous hierarchy (ITU-T Recommendation G.702 [85]) so that the H channels could be transmitted within the signals of the corresponding hierarchical level. (The plesiochronous hierarchy is defined by a set of bit rates and multiplexing schemes for the multiplexing of several, not necessarily synchronous, 64 kbit/s ISDN channels into higher bit rate signals.)

These broadband channels would have provided a rigid bit rate scheme to be applied to all future broadband services which then were not yet fully described. This led to some concern about the suitability of the H channel concept.

Moreover, a decision regarding which and how many H and B channels should be incorporated into the broadband interface could not be achieved at all. There were proposals such as:

$$H4 + 4H1 + n \times B + \text{signalling channel} \qquad (\text{e.g. } n = 30)$$

to which a lot of critical questions were immediately raised:

- Is this the only interface option or will other channel combinations be allowed?

- Can the H4 channel be subdivided into smaller pieces (e.g. into $4 \times$ H2 or into B/H1/H2 combinations) and can the four H1 channels be combined to yield a 6 Mbit/s or 8 Mbit/s entity?

- If several channel structures can be used as options at the interface, do they have to be fixed at subscription time or can they be dynamically changed?

These issues were never completely resolved, as other ideas entered the discussion.

As another intermediate step, so-called hybrid interface structures were proposed comprising channels for both circuit-oriented (or stream) traffic and capacity to be used for burst-type traffic. Obviously, such structures would have been more flexible than merely channel-oriented ones.

Again, there were never-ending talks about where to draw the border between the stream and burst parts of the interface, whether to allow it to change dynamically, and the steps (in terms of bit rate) by which changes could be made.

This deadlock was finally overcome by adopting an interface model based on a complete breakdown of its payload capacity into small pieces called *cells*, each of which can serve any purpose. Each cell may be employed to carry information relating to any type of connection.

In the following chapters, this principle, embodied by the **asynchronous transfer mode** (ATM), and its impact on B-ISDN will be considered in more detail.

Chapter 2

ATM-Based Services and Applications

2.1 B-ISDN Services

B-ISDN development can be justified and will be successful only if it meets the needs of potential customers. Therefore, a brief outline of foreseeable broadband applications will be given before entering into a discussion of network aspects.

In principle, B-ISDN should be suitable for both business and residential customers. Thus as well as data communication, the provision of TV programme distribution and other entertainment facilities has to be considered.

B-ISDN will support services with both constant and variable bit rates, data, voice (sound), still and moving picture transmission and, of particular note, multimedia applications which may combine, say, data, voice and picture service components.

Some examples may be used to illustrate the capabilities of B-ISDN. In the business area, videoconferencing is already a well-established, but still not commonly used, method which facilitates the rapid exchange of information between people. As travelling can be avoided, videoconferencing helps to save time and costs. B-ISDN may considerably improve the current situation and allow videoconferencing to become a widespread telecommunication tool, as it allows for high-picture quality (at least today's TV quality or even better), which is crucial for its acceptance, and is able to provide connections between all potential users via standard interfaces.

Another salient feature of B-ISDN is the (cost-effective) provision of high-speed data links with flexible bit rate allocation for the interconnection of customer networks.

The residential B-ISDN user may appreciate the combined offer of text, graphics, sound, still images and films giving information about such things as holiday resorts, shops or cultural events, as well as interactive video services and video on demand.

7

Tables 2.1, 2.2, 2.3, 2.4 and 2.5 (based on [103]) give an overview of possible broadband services and applications as presented by ITU-T.

Table 2.1: *Messaging services*

Type of information	Examples of broadband services	Applications
Moving pictures (video) and sound	Video mail service	Electronic mailbox service for the transfer of moving pictures and accompanying sound
Document	Document mail service	Electronic mailbox service for mixed documents[1]

[1]   Mixed document means that a document may contain text, graphics, still and moving picture information as well as voice annotations.

Table 2.2: *Retrieval services*

Type of information	Examples of broadband services	Applications
Text, data, graphics, sound, still images, moving pictures	Broadband videotex	• Videotex including moving pictures • Remote education and training • Telesoftware • Tele-shopping • Tele-advertising • News retrieval
	Video retrieval service	• Entertainment purposes • Remote education and training
	High-resolution image retrieval service	• Entertainment purposes • Remote education and training • Professional image communications • Medical image communications
	Document retrieval service	Mixed documents[1] retrieval from information centres, archives, etc.
	Data retrieval service	Telesoftware

[1]   Mixed document means that a document may contain text, graphics, still and moving picture information as well as voice annotations.

Table 2.3: *Conversational services*

Type of information	Examples of broadband services	Applications
Moving pictures and sound	Broadband videotelephony	Communication for the transfer of voice (sound), moving pictures, and video-scanned still images and documents between two locations (person-to-person) • Tele-education • Tele-shopping • Tele-advertising
	Broadband videoconference	Multipoint communication for the transfer of voice (sound), moving pictures, and video-scanned still images and documents between two or more locations (person-to-group, group-to-group) • Tele-education • Business conference • Tele-advertising
	Video-surveillance	• Building security • Traffic monitoring
	Video/audio information transmission service	• TV signal transfer • Video/audio dialogue • Contribution of information
Sound	Multiple sound programme signals	• Multilingual commentary channels • Multiple programme transfers

Data	High-speed unrestricted digital information transmission service	• High-speed data transfer
		  – LAN interconnection
		  – MAN interconnection
		  – Computer–computer interconnection
		• Transfer of video information
		• Transfer of other information types
		• Still image transfer
		• Multi-site interactive computer aided design
		• Multi-site interactive computer aided manufacturing

	High-volume file transfer service	• Data file transfer
	High-speed teleaction	• Real-time control • Telemetry • Alarms
Document	High-speed telefax	User-to-user transfer of text, images, drawings, etc.
	High-resolution image communication service	• Professional images • Medical images • Remote games
	Document communication service	User-to-user transfer of mixed documents[1]

[1]   Mixed document means that a document may contain text, graphics, still and moving picture information as well as voice annotations.

Table 2.4: *Distribution services without user-individual presentation control*

Type of information	Examples of broadband services	Applications
Data	High-speed unrestricted digital information distribution service	• Distribution of unrestricted data
Text, graphics, still images	Document distribution service	• Electronic newspaper • Electronic publishing
Moving pictures and sound	Video information distribution service	• Distribution of video/audio signals
Video	Existing quality TV distribution service (NTSC, PAL, SECAM)	TV programme distribution
	Extended quality TV distribution service • Enhanced definition TV distribution service • High-quality TV	TV programme distribution
	High-definition TV distribution service	TV programme distribution
	PayTV (pay-per-view, pay-per-channel)	TV programme distribution

Table 2.5: *Distribution services with user-individual presentation control*

Type of information	Examples of broadband services	Applications
Text, graphics, sound, still images	Full channel broadcast videography	• Remote education and training • Tele-advertising • News retrieval • Telesoftware

According to ITU-T Recommendation I.211 [103], services are classified into **interactive** and **distribution** services. Interactive services comprise conversational, messaging and retrieval services; distribution services can be split into services with or without user-individual presentation control.

B-ISDN messaging services include mailbox services for the transfer of sound, pictures and/or documents (Table 2.1). Retrieval services (Table 2.2) can be used, for example, to obtain video films at any time or to access a remote software library. Conversational services allow the mutual exchange of data, whole documents, pictures and sound. Examples are given in Table 2.3. Finally, examples of distribution services (Tables 2.4 and 2.5) are electronic publishing and TV programme distribution with existing and, in the future, enhanced picture quality, for example, high-definition TV (HDTV).

To be able to derive the network requirements to be met by B-ISDN from potential broadband services, Armbrüster and Rothamel [7] tried to compile technical characteristics for major B-ISDN applications. The results are given in Table 2.6.

This table illustrates the following remarkable properties of broadband applications:

- Not all services require very high bit rates, although some do, especially moving picture services with high resolution. In Table 2.6, bit rates of 30 to 130 Mbit/s for TV distribution and 130 Mbit/s for HDTV distribution are given. Even though these values are steadily decreasing – for example, as a result of ongoing research into encoding TV video signals with much less than 10 Mbit/s – the resulting bit rates will still be far above those employed for conventional ISDN services. The most demanding service will be HDTV, which will require a bit rate of about 30 to 50 Mbit/s per channel.

- Several types of communication are highly bursty in nature. If this feature were adequately reflected in network design, considerable economizing on network resources might be achieved (statistical multiplexing gain). In the case of TV and HDTV distribution, the statistical multiplexing gain is hard to realize because of the nature of the source signals, so in Table 2.6 the burstiness is set to 1.

The variety of possible B-ISDN services and applications shown in the table obviously requires a network with universal transfer capabilities to:

- cater for services which may employ quite different bit rates
- support burst-type traffic
- take into account both delay and loss-sensitive applications.

Table 2.6: *Characteristics of broadband services*

Service	Bit rate (Mbit/s)	Burstiness
Data transmission (connection-oriented)	1.5 to 130	1 – 50
Data transmission (connectionless)	1.5 to 130	1 – 50
Document transfer/retrieval	1.5 to 45	1 – 20
Videoconference/videotelephony	1.5 to 130	1 – 5
Broadband videotex/video retrieval	1.5 to 130	1 – 20
TV distribution	30 to 130	1
HDTV distribution	130	1

Burstiness = peak bit rate/average bit rate

The network concept which is assumed to meet all these requirements will be presented in the following chapters.

2.2 Initial ATM Network Services

The full set of possible B-ISDN services listed in the Section 2.1 cannot be offered from the very beginning of ATM networking for several reasons. First, most of the envisaged services are not completely defined. Second, an implementable subset of network services has to be identified that will attract customers. These services must include existing applications (and similar services evolving in parallel). However, new ATM-specific features should be visible for marketing reasons.

The basic service of an ATM network is the transport and routing (i.e. multiplexing, transmission and switching) of ATM cells. This ATM (bearer) service is also named **cell relaying**. The network does not need to know anything about the end-to-end application which is running on an ATM connection. Users can employ this ATM service to exchange data, voice, pictures, or a combination thereof, across the network. This will stimulate users to experiment with new applications, such as multimedia, via ATM. The practical experience gained from such trials will assist in eventually defining appropriate service characteristics.

Early ATM implementations serve as backbone networks mainly for data communications. Therefore existing or upcoming data services, such as X.25, frame relay, and **switched multi-megabit data service** (SMDS) [15] have to be supported. (This support, in terms of adaptation/interworking equipment and interworking protocols, will be specified in more detail in Section 5.7.)

Frame relay is an enhanced packet-type service. Higher throughputs and less delay are achieved by reducing error control and forgoing end-to-end flow control (in contrast to X.25 [150]). Frame relay is a connection-oriented service offering bit rates of from some kbit/s up to 2 Mbit/s or possibly higher.

SMDS was introduced by Bellcore as a high-speed, connectionless packet-type data service at bit rates up to 45 Mbit/s and, subsequently 155 Mbit/s. SMDS uses the ITU-T-defined address scheme of Recommendation E.164 [81] to support global addressing. SMDS will first be run on top of a distributed queue dual bus (DQDB) metropolitan area network (see Section 9.4.1.2), but later on can also use an ATM network. (The European version of SMDS is called **connectionless broadband data service** (CBDS), see Section 5.7.2.4.)

Another service to be offered initially to customers is the constant bit rate leased line service operating, for example, at 1.5/2 Mbit/s or 34/45 Mbit/s (**circuit emulation**). As in the case of frame relay and SMDS, such a leased line service can, of course, also be provided by conventional networks. The merit of an ATM backbone network for the network operator is that a common, unique network infrastructure can be deployed flexibly to support all the existing and future services.

The first ATM implementations only offer **permanent virtual connections**
(PVCs) established/released by network management, whereas at a later stage
switched virtual connections established/released via signalling procedures
will follow.

Chapter 3

Principles and Building Blocks of B-ISDN

3.1 B-ISDN Principles

The motivation behind incorporating broadband features into ISDN is neatly documented in ITU-T Recommendation I.121 ('Broadband Aspects of ISDN') [101]:

The B-ISDN recommendations were written taking into account the following:

- The emerging demand for broadband services (candidate services have been listed in Chapter 2).

- The availability of high-speed transmission, switching and signal processing technologies (bit rates of hundreds of Mbit/s are being offered).

- The improved data and image processing capabilities available to the user.

- The advances in software application processing in the computer and telecommunication industries.

- The need to integrate interactive and distribution services and circuit and packet transfer modes into a universal broadband network. In comparison to several dedicated networks, service and network integration has major advantages in economic planning, development, implementation, operation and maintenance. While dedicated networks require several distinct and costly customer access lines, the B-ISDN access can be based on a single optical fibre for each customer. The large-scale production of highly integrated system components of a unique B-ISDN will lead to cost-effective solutions.

- The need to provide flexibility in satisfying the requirements of both user and operator (in terms of bit rate, quality of service etc.).

ISDN is conceived to support 'a wide range of audio, video and data applications in the same network' [101]. B-ISDN thus follows the same principles as 64 kbit/s

15

based ISDN (cf. ITU-T Recommendation I.120 [100]) and is a natural extension
of the latter [101]:

> 'A key element of service integration is the provision of a
> wide range of services to a broad variety of users utilizing a
> limited set of connection types and multipurpose user–
> network interfaces.'

Whereas most pre-ISDN telecommunication networks have been specialized networks (e.g. for telephony or data) with rather limited bandwidths or throughput and processing capabilities, the future B-ISDN is conceived as a universal
(standardized) network supporting different kinds of applications and customer
categories. ITU-T Recommendation I.121 [101] presents an overview of B-ISDN
capabilities:

> 'B-ISDN supports switched, semi-permanent and permanent,
> point-to-point and point-to-multipoint connections and pro-
> vides on-demand, reserved and permanent services. Connec-
> tions in B-ISDN support both circuit mode and packet mode
> services of a mono- and/or multimedia type and of a connec-
> tionless or connection-oriented nature and in a bidirectional
> or unidirectional configuration.
> A B-ISDN will contain intelligent capabilities for the purpose
> of providing advanced service characteristics, supporting pow-
> erful operation and maintenance (OAM) tools, network con-
> trol and management.'

We believe the reader of this list of intended B-ISDN capabilities must be deeply
impressed; B-ISDN is designed to become *the* universal future network!

B-ISDN implementations will, according to the ITU-T, be based on the asynchronous transfer mode. This transfer mode will be briefly introduced in the next
section (and its technical details will be discussed later, see Chapters 4 and 5).

3.2   Asynchronous Transfer Mode

The asynchronous transfer mode is considered the ground on which B-ISDN is to
be built [101]:

> 'Asynchronous transfer mode (ATM) is the transfer mode for
> implementing B-ISDN ...'

The term *transfer* comprises both transmission and switching aspects, so a *transfer
mode* is a specific way of transmitting and switching information in a network.

In ATM, all information to be transferred is packed into fixed-size slots called
cells. These cells have a 48 octet information field and a 5 octet header. Whereas

the information field is available for the user, the header field carries information that pertains to the ATM layer functionality itself, mainly the identification of cells by means of a label (see Figure 3.1).

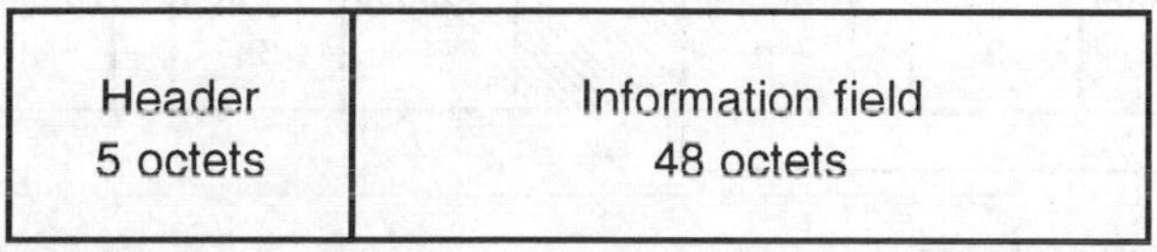

Header 5 octets	Information field 48 octets

Figure 3.1: *ATM cell structure*

A detailed description of the ATM layer functions and ATM header structure and coding will be given in Section 5.5. The protocol reference model for ATM-based networks will be addressed in Section 5.1; the boundaries between the ATM layer and other layers are discussed in Chapter 5.

ATM uses a label field inside each cell header to define and recognize individual communications. In this respect, ATM resembles conventional packet transfer modes. Like packet switching techniques, ATM can provide a communication with a bit rate that is individually tailored to the actual need, including time-variant bit rates.

The term **asynchronous** in the name of the new transfer mode refers to the fact that, in the context of multiplexed transmission, cells allocated to the same connection may exhibit an irregular recurrence pattern as they are filled according to the actual demand. This is shown in Figure 3.2(b).

In the **synchronous transfer mode** (STM) (see Figure 3.2(a)), a data unit associated with a given channel is identified by its position in the transmission frame, while in ATM (Figure 3.2(b)) a data unit or cell associated with a specific virtual channel may occur at essentially any position. The flexibility of bit rate allocation to a connection in STM is restricted as it uses predefined channel bit rates (e.g. B, H2; cf. Chapter 1) and the conventional transmission frames have a rigid structure. These normally will not permit individual structuring of the payload or will only permit a quite limited selection of channel mixes at the corresponding interface at subscription time. Otherwise the network provider would have to manage a host of different interface types, a situation that the designer would try to avoid for obvious reasons (for example, STM switching of varying B and H channel mixes per interface requires switching equipment that can simultaneously handle all sorts of channels potentially used by customers at any time).

In ATM-based networks the multiplexing and switching of cells is independent of the actual application. Thus the same piece of equipment can, in principle, handle

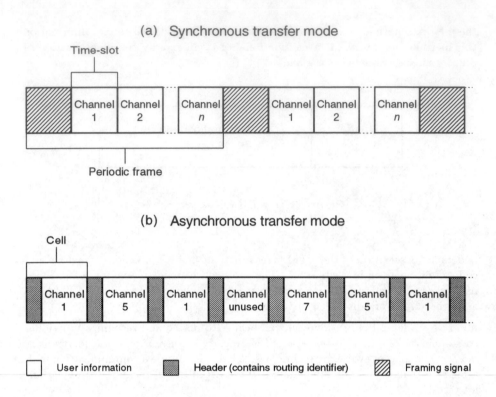

Figure 3.2: *STM and ATM principles*

a low bit rate connection as well as a high bit rate connection, be it of stream or burst nature. Dynamic bandwidth allocation on demand with a fine degree of granularity is provided. Consequently the definition of high-speed channel bit rates is now, in contrast to the situation in a STM environment, a second-rank task.

The flexibility of the ATM-based B-ISDN network access resulting from the cell transport concept strongly supports the idea of a unique interface which can be employed by a variety of customers with quite different service needs. However, the ATM concept requires many new problems to be solved. For example, the impacts of possible cell loss, cell transmission delay and cell delay variation on service quality need to be determined (cf. Section 4.4). Other ATM-inherent difficulties – voice echo and tariffs – will be addressed in Sections 10.1 and 10.2.

To sum up, whereas today's networks are characterized by the coexistence of circuit switching and packet switching, B-ISDN will rely on a single new method called ATM which combines advantageous features of both circuit- and packet-oriented techniques. The former requires only low overhead and processing, and, once a circuit-switched connection is established, the transfer delay of the information being carried is low and constant. The latter is much more flexible in terms of the bit rate assigned to individual (virtual) connections. ATM is a circuit-oriented, hardware-controlled, low-overhead concept of virtual channels which (in contrast to X.25 access [150]) have no flow control or error recovery. The implementation of these virtual channels is done by fixed size (relatively short) cells and provides the basis for both switching and multiplexed transmission. The use of short cells in ATM and the high transfer rates involved (e.g. 150 Mbit/s, see Section 3.3) result in transfer delays and delay variations which are sufficiently small to enable it to be applied to a wide range of services, including real-time services such as voice and video. The ability of ATM to multiplex and switch on the cell level supports flexible bit rate allocation, as is known from packet networks.

The overall protocol architecture of ATM networks comprises:

- A single link-by-link cell transfer capability common to all services.

- Service-specific adaptation functions for mapping higher layer information into ATM cells on an end-to-end basis. Examples are packetization/depacketization of continuous bit streams into/from ATM cells, and segmentation/reassembly of larger blocks of user information into/from ATM cells (core-and-edge concept).

Another important feature of ATM networks is the possibility of grouping several virtual channels into one so-called virtual path. The impact of this technique on the B-ISDN structure will be addressed in the following chapter.

3.3 Optical Transmission

The development of powerful and economic optical transmission equipment was a major driving force behind B-ISDN. Optical transmission is characterized by:

- low fibre attenuation (allowing for large repeater distances)

- high transmission bandwidths (up to several hundred Mbit/s)

- small diameter (low weight and volume)

- high mechanical flexibility of the fibre

- immunity against electromagnetic fields

- low transmission error probability

- no crosstalk between fibres

- tapping much more difficult.

The high bandwidth of optical transmission systems – currently up to 2.5 Gbit/s can be transported on one optical link – has led to early implementations in public networks to support existing services like telephony. Fibre-based local area networks are also widely in use nowadays, providing bit rates of the order of some hundred Mbit/s to the users. Thus for B-ISDN the use of optical fibre-based transmission systems is straightforward from a technical viewpoint, at least in the trunk network and in the local access part of the network where considerable distances have to be bridged. (Technical details on optical transmission to be deployed in B-ISDNs will be discussed in Chapter 8.)

In B-ISDN a bit rate of about 150 Mbit/s will typically be offered to the user across the broadband user–network interface (cf. Section 5.2). Although much higher bit rates could comfortably be transmitted on optical fibre links, the cost of the electronics involved in the transmission equipment (sender/receiver in network terminations, terminals etc.) together with considerations on expected service needs – that is, the bit rates simultaneously required at the interface – led to the conclusion that a B-ISDN 'basic' interface at about 150 Mbit/s would be sufficient in many cases.

In addition, a second interface type operating at about 600 Mbit/s, at least in the direction from the network to the user, is also foreseen (see Section 5.2), and ATM cell transport on even higher bit rate systems has been defined. Handling of such ATM signals is technically feasible; their implementation may, however, be an economic challenge.

Driven by such economic considerations, additional (not necessarily optical) lower bit rate ATM interfaces – in the range of 1.5 or 2 Mbit/s up to 150 Mbit/s – will be quite important for the introduction of ATM (see Section 5.5).

The deployment of highly reliable (mainly optical) transmission systems with low bit error probabilities benefits a simplified network concept with, for example, potentially reducible data link layer functionality.

Chapter 4

B-ISDN Network Concept

4.1 General Architecture of the B-ISDN

The architectural model of the B-ISDN is described in ITU-T Recommendation I.327 [108]. According to this recommendation, the information transfer and signalling capabilities of the B-ISDN comprise:

- broadband capabilities
- 64 kbit/s ISDN capabilities
- user-to-network signalling
- inter-exchange signalling
- user-to-user signalling.

This is depicted in Figure 4.1.

Broadband information transfer is provided by ATM. The ATM data unit is the cell, a fixed-size block of 53 octets (cf. Section 5.5). The 5 octet cell header carries the necessary information to identify cells belonging to the same virtual channel. Cells are assigned on demand, depending on source activity and the available resources.

ATM guarantees (under normal fault-free conditions) **cell sequence integrity**. This means that nowhere in the network can a cell belonging to a specific virtual channel connection overtake another cell of the same virtual channel connection that has been sent earlier.

ATM is a **connection-oriented technique**. A connection within the ATM layer consists of one or more links, each of which is assigned an identifier. These identifiers remain unchanged for the duration of the connection.

Signalling information for a given connection is conveyed using a separate identifier (out-of-band signalling).

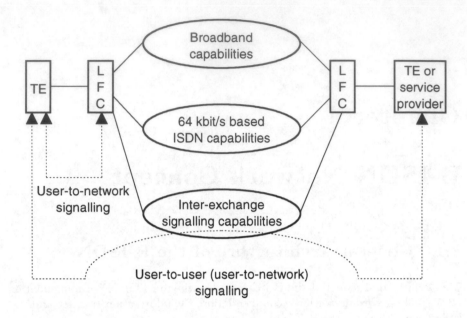

LFC   Local function capabilities
TE   Terminal equipment

Figure 4.1: *Information transfer and signalling capabilities*

Although ATM is a connection-oriented technique, it offers a flexible transfer capability common to all services, including connectionless data services. The proposed provision of connectionless data services via the ATM-based B-ISDN will be discussed in Section 5.7.2.

4.2   Networking Techniques

4.2.1   Network Layering

ITU-T Recommendation I.311 [105] presents the layered structure of the B-ISDN depicted in Figure 4.2 (see also Section 5.1).

In this section, we only address the ATM transport network for which the functions are split into two parts, namely physical layer transport functions and ATM layer transport functions. Both the physical layer and the ATM layer are hierarchically structured. The physical layer consists of:

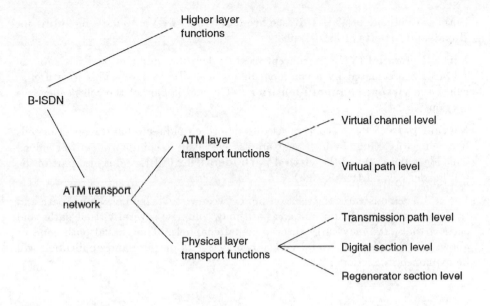

Figure 4.2: *B-ISDN layered structure*

- transmission path level
- digital section level
- regenerator section level.

These are defined in the following way:

Transmission path: The transmission path extends between network elements that assemble and disassemble the payload of a transmission system (the payload will be used to carry user information; together with the necessary transmission overhead it forms the complete signal).

Digital section: The digital section extends between network elements which assemble and disassemble continuous bit or byte streams.

Regenerator section: The regenerator section is a portion of a digital section extending between two adjacent regenerators.

The ATM layer has two hierarchical levels, namely:

- virtual channel level
- virtual path level.

Both are defined in ITU-T Recommendation I.113 ('Vocabulary of Terms for Broadband Aspects of ISDN') [99]:

Virtual channel (VC): 'A concept used to describe unidirectional transport of ATM cells associated by a common unique identifier value.' This identifier is called the **virtual channel identifier** (VCI) and is part of the cell header (see Section 5.5.2.4).

Virtual path (VP): 'A concept used to describe unidirectional transport of cells belonging to virtual channels that are associated by a common identifier value.' This identifier is called the **virtual path identifier** (VPI) and is also part of the cell header (see Section 5.5.2.3).

Figure 4.3 demonstrates the relationship between virtual channel, virtual path and transmission path. A transmission path may comprise several virtual paths and each virtual path may carry several virtual channels. The virtual path concept allows the grouping of several virtual channels. Its purpose and application will be explained in Section 4.2.3.

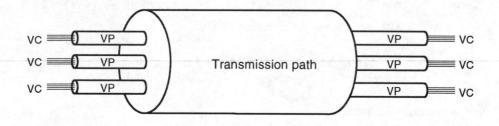

VC   Virtual channel
VP   Virtual path

Figure 4.3: *Relationship between virtual channel, virtual path and transmission path*

Concerning the levels of the ATM layer (virtual channel and virtual path), it is helpful to distinguish between links and connections [99]:

Virtual channel link: 'A means of unidirectional transport of ATM cells between a point where a VCI value is assigned and the point where that value is translated or removed.'

Similarly, a **virtual path link** is terminated by the points where a VPI value is assigned and translated or removed.

A concatenation of VC links is called a **virtual channel connection** (VCC), and likewise, a concatenation of VP links is called a **virtual path connection** (VPC).

The relationship between different levels of the ATM transport network is shown in Figure 4.4.

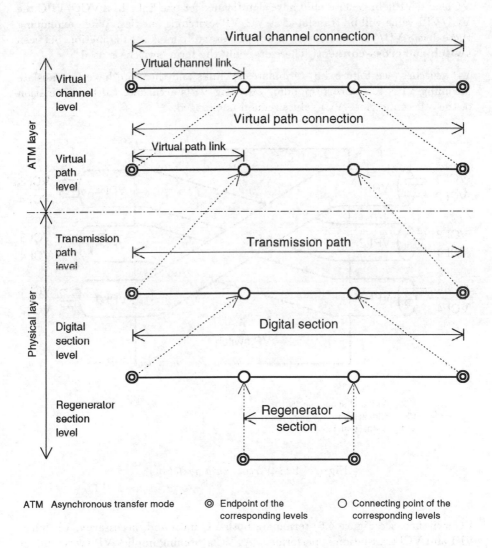

Figure 4.4: *Hierarchical layer-to-layer relationship*

A VCC may consist of several concatenated VC links, each of which is embedded in a VPC. The VPCs usually consist of several concatenated VP links. Each VP link is implemented on a transmission path which hierarchically comprises digital sections and regenerator sections.

4.2.2   Switching of Virtual Channels and Virtual Paths

VCIs and VPIs in general only have significance for one link. In a VCC/VPC the VCI/VPI value will be translated at VC/VP switching entities. When explaining these basic VC/VP concepts it is not necessary to make a distinction between **switch** and **cross-connect**. Therefore, only the term 'switch' is used.

VP switches (see Figure 4.5) terminate VP links and therefore have to translate incoming VPIs to the corresponding outgoing VPIs according to the destination of the VP connection. VCI values remain unchanged.

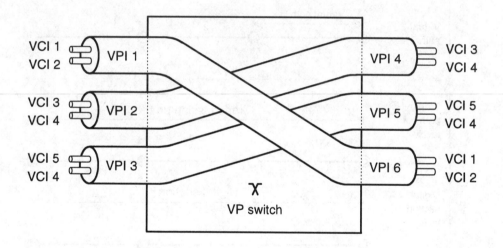

VCI	Virtual channel identifier
VP	Virtual path
VPI	Virtual path identifier

Figure 4.5: *Virtual path switching*

VC switches (see Figure 4.6) terminate both VC links and, necessarily, VP links. VPI and VCI translation is performed. As VC switching implies VP switching, in principle a VC switch can also handle mere VP switching.

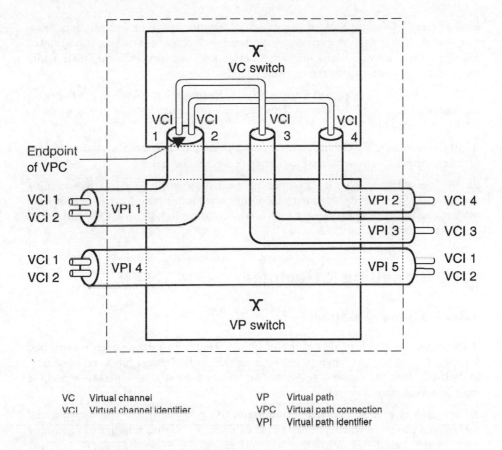

VC	Virtual channel	VP	Virtual path
VCI	Virtual channel identifier	VPC	Virtual path connection
		VPI	Virtual path identifier

Figure 4.6: *Virtual channel/virtual path switching*

4.2.3 Applications of Virtual Channel/Path Connections

VCCs/VPCs can be employed between:

- user and user
- user and network
- network and network.

All cells associated with an individual VCC/VPC are transported along the same route through the network. Cell sequence is preserved (first sent–first received) for all VCCs and VPCs.

User-to-user VCCs are able to carry user data and signalling information, user-to-network VCCs may, for instance, be used to access local connection-related functions (user-network signalling), and network-to-network VCC applications include network traffic management and routeing.

A VPC between users provides them with a transmission 'pipe', the VC organization of which is up to them. This concept may, for example, be applied to LAN–LAN coupling.

A user-to-network VPC can be used to aggregate traffic from a customer to a network element such as a local exchange or a specific server.

Finally, network-to-network VPCs can be used to organize user traffic according to a predefined routeing scheme or to define a common path for the exchange of routeing or network management information. (More details on VCCs and VPCs can be found in Section 5.5.3.)

4.3   Signalling Principles

4.3.1   General Aspects

B-ISDN follows the principle of out-of-band signalling that has been established for the 64 kbit/s ISDN where a physical signalling D channel has been specified. In B-ISDN the VC concept provides the means logically to separate signalling channels from user channels.

A user may now have multiple signalling entities connected to the network call control management via separate ATM VCCs. The actual number of signalling connections and the bit rates allocated to them can be chosen in B-ISDN in a way that optimally satisfies a customer's need.

4.3.2   Capabilities Required for B-ISDN Signalling

B-ISDN signalling must be able to support:

- 64 kbit/s ISDN applications
- new broadband services.

This implies that existing ISDN signalling functions according to ITU-T Recommendation Q.931 [135] must be included in B-ISDN signalling capabilities; on the other hand, the nature of B-ISDN – the ATM transport network – and the increasing desire for advanced communication forms, such as multimedia services, requires specific new signalling elements. In the following, an overview of necessary B-ISDN signalling capabilities is given. (More details on such functions will be discussed in Chapter 6.)

ATM network-specific signalling capabilities have to be realized in order to:

- establish, maintain and release ATM VCCs for information transfer;
- negotiate (and perhaps renegotiate) the traffic characteristics of a connection.

Other signalling requirements are basically not ATM related but reflect the fact that more powerful service concepts have become feasible. Examples are the support of multi-connection calls and multi-party calls.

For a multi-connection call, several connections have to be established to build up a 'composite' call comprising, for example, voice, image and data. It must also be possible to remove one or more connections from a call or to add new connections to the existing ones. Thus the network requires a means of correlating the connections of a call. In any case, it must be possible to release a call as a whole. These correlation functions should be performed in the origination and destination B-ISDN switches only, since transit nodes should not be burdened with such tasks.

A multi-party call consists of several connections between more than two endpoints (conferencing). Signalling to indicate establishment/release of a multi-party call and adding/removing one party is required. (A communication that is part of a multi-party call may also be of the multi-connection type.)

In a broadband environment, asymmetric connections (that is, low or zero bandwidth in one direction and high bandwidth in the other) will become important, so it is necessary to establish signalling elements to support such connections.

Another broadband issue affecting signalling is **interworking**, for example, B-ISDN with non B-ISDN services, or between video services with different coding schemes.

4.3.3 Signalling Virtual Channels

In B-ISDN, signalling messages will be conveyed out-of-band in dedicated **signalling virtual channels** (SVCs). Different types of SVC are provided [105] as shown in Table 4.1.

Table 4.1: *Possible signalling virtual channels at B-ISDN user–network interface*

SVC type	Directionality	Number of SVCs
Meta-signalling channel	Bidirectional	1
General broadcast SVC	Unidirectional	1
Selective broadcast SVC	Unidirectional	Several possible
Point-to-point SVC	Bidirectional	One per signalling endpoint

There may be one **meta-signalling virtual channel** (MSVC) per interface. This channel is bidirectional and permanent. It is a sort of interface management channel used to establish, check and release point-to-point and selective broadcast SVCs.

Whereas the meta-signalling virtual channel is permanent, a point-to-point signalling channel is allocated to a signalling endpoint only while it is active. Point-to-point signalling channels are bidirectional. They are used to establish, control and release VCCs to carry user data (VPCs as well as VCCs may also be established without using signalling procedures, for example by subscription).

Broadcast SVCs (BSVCs) are unidirectional (network-to-user direction only). They are used to send signalling messages either to all signalling endpoints in a customer's network or to a selected category of signalling endpoints. The general broadcast SVC reaches all signalling endpoints; it is always present. Selective broadcast SVCs may be provided as a network option so that all terminals belonging to the same service profile category can be addressed (a B-ISDN service profile contains information which is maintained by the network to characterize the services offered by the network to the user).

In **point-to-point** signalling access configurations, one pre-established signalling virtual channel can be used. In contrast, in a **point-to-multipoint** signalling access configuration, meta-signalling is required for managing the signalling virtual channels. More details on these configurations are described in Section 6.2.

Meta-signalling is not used for network-to-network signalling. In the case of a network–network VP containing signalling VCs, additional VCI values for signalling in this VP are pre-established. The method of pre-establishment is for further study.

To illustrate the SVC concept of B-ISDN, an example (based on ITU-T Recommendation I. 311 [105]) is given in Figure 4.7. This highlights different possibilities for carrying signalling information from the customer to the network and vice versa.

Four different VP links/connections are depicted in the figure. The first (a) is a signalling VP link which transports all the signalling information to be exchanged between the customer and the local exchange, including meta-signalling. When a signalling capability to a point in the network other than the local exchange is required (for example, to communicate with a special service provider located elsewhere), such signalling can be done on an extra VPC (c) which may carry signalling and user data. This VPC goes through the local exchange and is terminated at the appropriate place. (The other two VPs (b) and (d) are shown for completeness; they only carry user data. In case (b), the corresponding VCs are switched in the local exchange while in case (d) the VP as a whole passes transparently through the local exchange.)

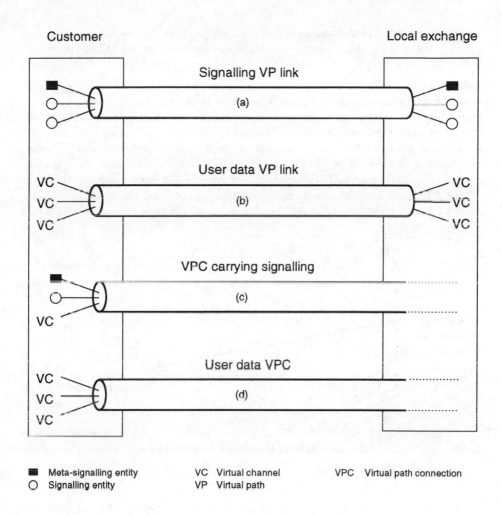

Figure 4.7: *Allocation of signalling virtual channels to a customer*

4.4 Broadband Network Performance

Broadband networks based on ATM cell transfer must meet certain performance requirements in order to be accepted by both potential users and network providers. ATM-related performance parameters and measures need to be specified in addition to the performance parameters already introduced for existing networks. In this section, we only deal with ATM layer-specific network performance. The quality of service as perceived by the user may be influenced not only by the ATM transport network performance but also by higher layer mechanisms. In some cases, these will be able to compensate for shortcomings in the ATM transport network.

Cells belonging to a specified virtual connection are delivered from one point in the network to another, for example, from A to B. A and B may denote the very endpoints of a virtual connection, or may delimit a certain portion of the cell transport route (for example, A and B may indicate national network boundaries of an international ATM connection). Because there is some transfer delay, cells sent from A arrive at B within $\Delta t > 0$ (see Figure 4.8). Note that the cell exit event occurs according to ITU-T Recommendation I.356 [109] when the first bit of the ATM cell has completed transmission across A, and the cell entry event occurs when the last bit of the ATM cell has completed transmission across B.

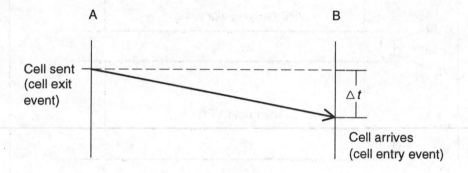

Figure 4.8: *Cell transfer (schematic)*

In order adequately to describe the quality of ATM cell transfer, ITU-T Recommendation I.356 [109] first defines the following outcome categories:

- successfully transferred cell

- errored cell

- lost cell

- misinserted cell

- severely errored cell block.

If Δt is less than a maximum allowed time T (the exact value is not yet specified) and the cell is not affected by bit errors, then the cell has been successfully transferred.

If the cell arrives in due time but there are one or more bit errors in the received cell information field, the cell is errored.

A lost cell outcome occurs if the cell arrives after time T (or never reaches B). Errors in the ATM cell header that cannot be corrected (cf. Section 5.3.1.5) or cell buffer overflows in the network (for example, in an ATM switch) lead to lost cells.

If a cell that has not been sent from A on this virtual connection arrives at B, then this misdelivered cell produces a misinserted cell outcome. Header errors that are not detected or are erroneously corrected may produce misinserted cells.

A severely errored cell block occurs if more than M errored cells are observed in a block of N cells transmitted consecutively on a given connection. M and N have yet to be specified.

By making use of the above considerations, it is possible to define the performance parameters. The parameters and their definitions are listed in Table 4.2.

Table 4.2: *ATM performance parameters*

Parameter	Definition
Cell loss ratio	Ratio of lost cells to transmitted cells
Cell misinsertion rate	Number of misinserted cells per connection second
Cell error ratio	Ratio of errored cells to the number of delivered (= successfully transferred + errored) cells
Severely errored cell block ratio	Ratio of the number of severely errored cell blocks to total number of cell blocks
Cell transfer delay	Δt (see Figure 4.8)
• Mean cell transfer delay	Arithmetic average of a specified number of cell transfer delays
• Cell delay variation	Difference between a single observation of cell transfer delay and the mean cell transfer delay on the same connection

Note that in Table 4.2 cell loss and cell error *ratios* are given, whereas the cell insertion outcomes are measured by a *rate* (events per time unit). As the mechanism by which inserted cells are produced has nothing to do with the number of cells on the observed connection, this performance parameter cannot be expressed as a ratio, only as a rate.

Bit errors in errored cells can be corrected to a certain extent by error protection methods applied to the cell information field contents (see Section 5.6).

Lost and misinserted cells can cause severe problems if they are not detected. For example, when using a constant bit rate, the real-time services synchronism between sending and receiving terminals may be disturbed. Lost and misinserted cell events can be detected (in many cases) by monitoring a sequence number in the cell information field or an equivalent mechanism (see Section 5.6).

Both cell transfer delay and cell delay variation must be kept within a limited range in order to meet service requirements. Cell delay and delay variation are introduced, for example, by ATM multiplexers or ATM switches and cross-connects (see Chapters 7 and 8).

ATM network performance requirements in terms of parameter values are not specified yet. This issue will be addressed again in the following chapters whenever appropriate (for example, in Chapters 7 and 8 on ATM switching and transmission).

4.5   Traffic Control

4.5.1   Overview of Functions

To ensure the desired broadband network performance outlined in the previous section, an ATM-based network will have to provide a set of traffic control capabilities. ITU-T Recommendation I.371 [113] identifies the following:

- network resource management
- connection admission control
- usage parameter control and network parameter control
- priority control
- traffic shaping
- fast resource management
- congestion control.

Their definitions and descriptions are given in later sections.

4.5.1.1   Network Resource Management

One tool of network resource management which can be employed for traffic control is the virtual path technique (cf. Section 4.2). By grouping several virtual channels together into a virtual path, call admission control (see Section 4.5.1.2) and usage/network parameter control (see Section 4.5.1.3) can be simplified as only the aggregated traffic of an entire virtual path has to be handled. Priority control (see Section 4.5.1.4) can be supported by re-aggregating traffic types requiring different qualities of service through virtual paths. Messages for the operation of traffic control (for example, congestion indication) can more easily be distributed: a single message referring to all the virtual channels within a virtual path will suffice.

Virtual paths can play an important role in supporting statistical multiplexing by separating traffic thus preventing statistically multiplexed traffic from being interfered with guaranteed bit rate traffic.

4.5.1.2   Connection Admission Control

Connection admission control is defined as 'the set of actions taken by the network during the call set-up phase (or during the call renegotiation phase) to establish whether a VC/VP connection can be accepted' [113].

A connection can only be accepted if sufficient network resources are available to establish the connection end-to-end with its required quality of service. The agreed quality of service of existing connections in the network must not be affected by the new connection.

Two classes of parameters are foreseen to support connection admission control:

- a set of parameters describing the source traffic characteristics;
- another set of parameters to identify the required quality of service class.

Source traffic can be characterized by its:

- peak cell rate
- average cell rate
- burstiness
- peak duration
- or by an equivalent set of other parameters.

The exact definitions of burstiness and peak duration are pending issues in ITU-T. (Burstiness might be defined as the ratio of peak bit rate to average bit rate; for further information see [113].) The description of source traffic parameters and quality of service class parameters cannot be completed unless more detailed information on ATM service requirements is compiled.

4.5.1.3   Usage Parameter Control and Network Parameter Control

Usage parameter control (UPC) and network parameter control (NPC) perform similar functions at different interfaces. The UPC function is performed at the user–network interface, whereas the NPC function is performed at the network–node interface.

The use of a UPC function is recommended, and the use of an NPC function is a network option. Whether or not the operator chooses to use the NPC function, the network-edge-to-network-edge and user-to-user performance objectives need to be met.

UPC/NPC is defined as:

> 'the set of actions taken by the network to monitor and control traffic in terms of traffic offered and validity of the ATM connection, at the user access and the network access respectively. Their main purpose is to protect network resources from malicious as well as unintentional misbehaviour which can affect the quality of service of other already established connections by detecting violations of negotiated parameters and taking appropriate actions. Connection monitoring encompasses all connections crossing the user–network/network–node interface. UPC/NPC apply to both user VCCs/VPCs and signalling virtual channels.' [113]

Usage parameter monitoring includes the following functions:

- Checking of the validity of VPI/VCI values.

- Monitoring the traffic volume entering the network from all active VP and VC connections to ensure that the agreed parameters are not violated.

- Monitoring the total volume of the accepted traffic on the access link.

What is actually carried out will depend on the access network configuration.

The parameters subject to monitoring and control may be the same as those used for source traffic characterization to support connection admission control, namely average and peak bit rate, burstiness and peak duration. However, further studies are required.

Usage parameter control can simply *discard* cells that violate the negotiated traffic parameters. In addition, a 'guilty' connection may be released. Another, less rigorous, option would be *tagging* of violating cells. These cells can be transferred as long as they do not cause any serious harm to the network. Thus the overall throughput of ATM cells might possibly be raised.

When, optionally, usage parameter control and traffic shaping (see Section 4.5.1.5) are combined, cells that comply with the negotiated connection parameters may be rescheduled in order to improve network performance.

To illustrate the concept of usage parameter control, Figure 4.9 shows different access network arrangements with the appropriate usage parameter control meas-

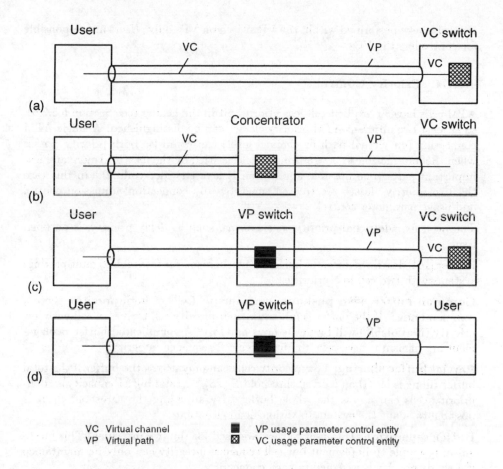

VC Virtual channel   ■ VP usage parameter control entity
VP Virtual path   ⊠ VC usage parameter control entity

Figure 4.9: *Illustration of usage parameter control*

ures applied to VCs or VPs at the point where they are first accessible. This point
may be a switch/cross-connect or a concentrator.

In case (a), a user is connected directly to a VC switch. Usage parameter control
is performed within the VC switch on VCs before they are switched.

In case (b), a user is connected to a VC switch via a concentrator. Usage parameter
control is performed within the concentrator on VCs only.

In case (c), a user is connected to a VC switch via a VP switch. Here usage
parameter control is performed within the VP switch on VPs only and within the
VC switch on VCs only.

In case (d), a user is connected to another user via a VP switch. Usage parameter

control is now performed within the VP switch on VPs only. Users are responsible
for controlling the VCs.

4.5.1.4   Priority Control

ATM cells have an explicit cell loss priority bit in the header (see Section 5.5.2.6),
so at least two different ATM priority classes can be distinguished. A single ATM
connection (on virtual path or channel level) can comprise both priority classes
when the information to be transmitted is classified by the user into more and less
important parts (one possible application is layered video-coding). In this case
the two priority classes are treated separately by connection admission control
and usage parameter control.

The need for additional priority mechanisms, such as delay priority, is an open
issue.

Kröner [161] describes different buffering mechanisms for (switching/multiplexing)
systems with two cell loss priorities:

Common buffer with pushout mechanism: Cells of both priorities share a
common buffer. If the buffer is full and a high-priority cell arrives, a cell with low
priority (if available) will be pushed out and lost. A complicated buffer management mechanism is necessary to guarantee cell sequence integrity.

Partial buffer sharing: Low-priority cells can only access the buffer if the total
buffer filling is less than a given threshold S_L (S_L < total buffer capacity). High-
priority cells can access the whole buffer. By adjusting the threshold S_L it is
possible to adapt the system to various load situations.

Buffer separation: Different buffers are used for the two priorities. This mechanism is simple to implement but cell sequence integrity can only be maintained
if a single priority is assigned to each connection.

The results given in [161] showed that the system performance can be improved
using priorities and that the partial buffer sharing mechanism is a very good
strategy (best compromise between performance and implementation complexity).

4.5.1.5   Traffic Shaping

Traffic shaping actively alters the traffic characteristics of a stream of cells on a
VPC or VCC in order to reduce the peak cell rate, limit the burst length or reduce
the cell delay variation by suitably spacing cells in time. Of course, traffic shaping
must maintain the cell sequence integrity of an ATM connection.

Traffic shaping is an option for both network operators and users. Within a
customer network it can be used to ensure conformance to the traffic contract
of the traffic across the user–network interface (UNI). For a network operator,
traffic shaping may assist in dimensioning the network more cost-effectively.

4.5.1.6   Fast Resource Management

Fast resource management is a tool that enables the immediate allocation of necessary capacity, such as bit rate or buffer space, to individual burst-type connections for the duration of a cell burst. Indication of a burst by the user and allocation acknowledgement by the network could be signalled in-band via specific ATM layer messages.

This promising technique is currently under investigation. It might support statistical multiplexing of bursty traffic without stringent real-time requirements.

4.5.1.7   Congestion Control

Congestion is a state of network elements (for example, switches, concentrators, transmission links) in which traffic and/or control resource overload means that the network is not able to guarantee the negotiated quality of service to the established connections and to new connection requests. Congestion can be caused by unpredictable statistical fluctuations of traffic flows or a network fault.

Congestion control is a network means of minimizing congestion effects and preventing congestion from spreading. It can employ connection admission and/or usage parameter control and network parameter control procedures to avoid overload situations. For example, congestion control could reduce the peak bit rate available to a user and monitor this (and react accordingly if the user exceeds the new parameter value).

Another optional congestion control mechanism is **explicit forward congestion** indication. A network element in a congested state may set an explicit forward congestion indication in the cell header (see Section 5.5.2.5). At the receiving end, the customer equipment may use this indication to implement protocols which adaptively lower the cell rate of the connection during congestion.

4.5.2   Traffic Control Procedures and Their Impact on Resource Management

Traffic control procedures for ATM networks are currently not fully standardized within ITU-T. In fact, there is a tendency not to specify complete algorithms but only the basic requirements. On the one hand, network providers may have a desire for flexible network tools to be able to react adequately to customers' needs (which speaks against standardization), while on the other hand settled network standards are indispensable for the benefit of users and especially terminal manufacturers. For instance, a terminal basically needs to know how the network handles its ATM cells under normal and fault conditions in order to shape its cell flow according to the rules of the ATM network and thus make optimum use of the transport facilities of the ATM network.

The choice of traffic control algorithms directly affects a network's resource allocation strategy. For example, if only the peak bit rate of a connection is considered for admission and usage parameter control, then this peak bit rate would have to be allocated to the connection. If this connection had a low average bit rate, then most of the time the network efficiency would be poor. Nevertheless, such simple strategies can assist in quickly introducing ATM-based networks. As long as knowledge about the management of ATM traffic flows is rather limited, because neither the source traffic characteristics nor the actual traffic mixes on a link is sufficiently clear, it might be wise to stay on safe ground even if a considerable amount of network capacity is wasted. Besides peak bit rate reservation, restricted utilization (e.g. 70 %) of the cell transport capability of a link helps to avoid congestion.

The goal is simultaneously to:

- achieve good ATM network efficiency
- meet the users' quality of service requirements

with a method that is generally applicable. Therefore, more sophisticated traffic control measures and resource management actions are being taken into account.

One example of a complex connection admission and bandwidth allocation algorithm is given in [59]. In this approach, both average and peak bit rates are evaluated and, in addition, the upper bound for the bit rate variance that is dependent on the behaviour of the source is considered. (A good representation of the bit rate variance is especially important when the source is a video codec.) The results are promising: this method has a considerable advantage compared with mere peak bit rate reservation if the peak bit rates of most of the connections on a link are small in relation to the total bit rate of the link, and if the peak-to-average bit rate ratio (burstiness) of these connections is high. A comparison of different connection admission control algorithms (including the one described above) is given in [191].

Different usage parameter control mechanisms have been proposed, namely **leaky bucket, sliding window, jumping window** and **exponentially weighted moving average**. Their modelling and performances are presented in [184]. A comparison of these mechanisms showed that the leaky bucket and the exponentially weighted moving average are the most promising with respect to flexibility and implementation complexity.

The basic problem of ATM networks is the statistical behaviour of the cell arrival process (e.g. at a buffer where cells generated by several sources are multiplexed together).

ATM traffic can be described by a three-level hierarchical model, as depicted in Figure 4.10 [67, 190].

The call level has a typical time scale of seconds up to hours, the burst level is related with the millisecond range up to seconds, and the cell level with the

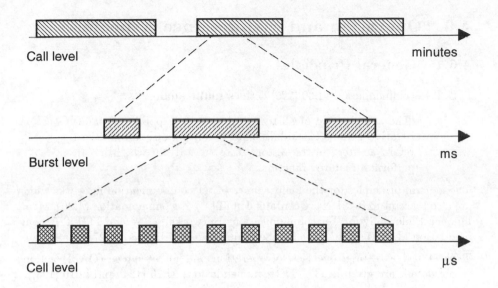

Figure 4.10: *Hierarchical modelling of ATM traffic*

microsecond range. These levels have different impacts on network implementation: whereas cell level analysis can provide information for buffer dimensioning (for example in ATM switches or multiplexers), the burst level characteristics influence mainly call admission strategies, and the call level considerations relate to ATM link dimensioning.

Based on the traffic model shown in Figure 4.10, mathematical models have been defined with different levels of abstraction [162], including:

- burstiness (peak bit rate/average bit rate)

- geometrically distributed burst lengths

- switched Poisson process

- Markov-modulated Poisson process

- generally modulated deterministic process.

It has been found that the quality of service parameters, such as jitter and loss probability, are very sensitive to the assumed source characteristic. Therefore, it is necessary to use these detailed source traffic models for performance evaluation.

4.6   Operation and Maintenance Aspects

4.6.1   General Principles

ITU-T Recommendation M.60 [125] defines **maintenance** as:

> 'The combination of all technical and corresponding administrative actions, including supervision actions, intended to retain an item in, or restore it to, a state in which it can perform a required function.'

The general principles for the maintenance of telecommunication networks which are also relevant to B-ISDN are contained in ITU-T Recommendation M.20 ('Maintenance Philosophy for Telecommunications Networks') [124] and ITU-T Recommendation M.3600 ('Principles for the Maintenance of ISDNs') [127].

Table 4.3 gives a brief overview of operation and maintenance (OAM) actions (more details are given in ITU-T Recommendations M.20 [124] and I.610 [123]).

Table 4.3: *Overview of OAM actions*

Action	Description
Performance monitoring	Normal function of the managed entity is monitored by the continuous or periodic checking of functions. As a result, maintenance event information will be produced.
Defect and failure detection	Malfunctions or predicted malfunctions are detected by continuous or periodic checking. As a result, maintenance event information or various alarms will be produced.
System protection	Effect of failure of managed entity is minimized by blocking or change-over to other entities. As a result, the failed entity is excluded from operation.
Failure or performance information	Failure information is given to other management entities. As a result, alarm indications are given to other management planes. Response to a status report request will also be given.
Fault localization	Determination by internal or external test systems of failed entity if failure information is insufficient.

Another recommendation relevant to the OAM of B-ISDN is ITU-T Recommendation M.3010 [126] entitled 'Principles for a Telecommunications Management

Network' (TMN). An example TMN architecture for B-ISDN customer access will be given in Section 5.8.

4.6.2 OAM Levels in B-ISDN

The OAM levels of the ATM transport network coincide with the levels introduced in Section 4.2.1 on network layering (see Figures 4.2 on page 23 and 4.4 on page 25). The ATM transport network comprises the physical layer (subdivided into regenerator section, digital section and transmission path level), and the ATM layer (subdivided into VP and VC levels) (cf. Figure 4.11).

The corresponding OAM information flows of each level – denominated F1 to F5 – are also shown in Figure 4.11. These OAM flows are bidirectional. As an example of an OAM flow, consider the monitoring of a VPC by supervising cells sent out at one endpoint of the VPC and mirrored at the other endpoint, to be evaluated at the sending side.

More information on these OAM information flows is presented in Section 5.8.

4.7 Customer Network Aspects

One essential block of the B-ISDN is the **customer network** (CN). Sometimes it is called the **customer premises network** (CPN) or **subscriber premises network** (SPN).

4.7.1 Reference Configuration of the B-ISDN UNI

The reference configuration for the 64 kbit/s ISDN user–network interface, which is described in ITU-T Recommendation I.411 [115], was accepted to be general enough for use in the B-ISDN environment [117]. Figure 4.12 shows the principles of the reference configuration for the B-ISDN UNI. It contains the following:

- Functional groups: Broadband network termination 1 (B-NT1), broadband network termination 2 (B-NT2) and broadband terminal equipment 1 (B-TE1).
- Reference points : T_B and S_B.

B-TE1 denotes a broadband terminal with standard interface. Physical interfaces may or may not occur at the reference points T_B and S_B. If they are realized, they must comply with the specified standard (see Section 5.2). While B-NT1 performs only line transmission termination and related OAM functions, B-NT2 may be, for example, a private branch exchange or LAN which performs multiplexing and switching of ATM cells.

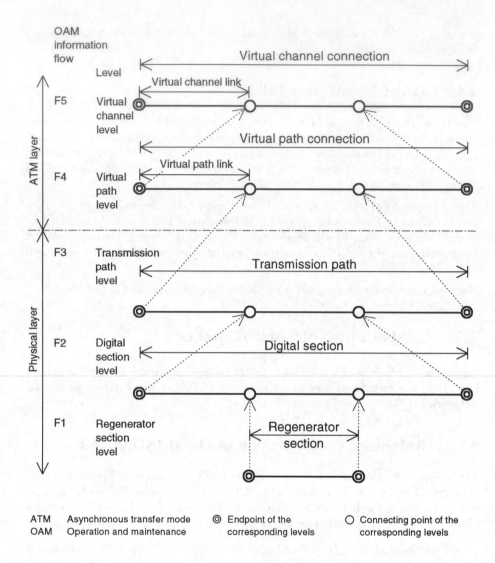

Figure 4.11: *OAM hierarchical levels*

The CN covers the area where users have access to the public network via their terminals. This is the part of the telecommunication network located at the user side of the B-NT1.

The reference configuration shown in Figure 4.12 can be used for the functional description of the CN. The interface between the CN and the public network is

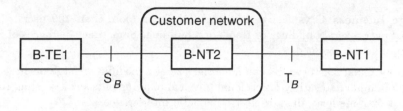

B-NT   Network termination for B-ISDN
B-TE   Terminal equipment for B-ISDN

Figure 4.12: *Reference configuration of the B-ISDN UNI*

usually at the reference point T_B. Thus the CN coincides with the functional group B-NT2 (see Figure 4.12).

4.7.2 Customer Categories

Different aspects for the classification of CNs are possible [12, 18, 36], including the environment (residential, business), number of users or topology.

The **residential** environment is characterized by a small number of people (e.g. a family) using broadband services mainly for entertainment. This category is considered to be more or less homogeneous and will be restricted to a single flat or house. In many cases, no internal switching capabilities are necessary within a residential CN.

The counterpart of the residential CNs are the **business** CNs, which are subdivided according to their size:

Small business CNs: Small business CNs have a lot in common with residential CNs. Such a CN will be installed in a small area like an office or a shop with up to about ten employees. Often the office or shop is combined with private housing and therefore the requirements of the residential CN (e.g. entertainment services) must also be met. One major difference from the residential CN is that there may be a need for internal switching.

Medium business CNs: In medium and large business CNs, as well as factory CNs, no distribution service need be supported for entertainment. Normally, only interactive services, such as telephony, videoconferencing or high-speed data transmission, will be used. One of the main characteristics is the internal switching capability. A medium business CN typically has between 10 and 100 users and spreads over several floors of a building.

Large business CNs: Large business CNs have more than 100 users. They spread over several buildings or floors of a building. Sometimes distances of up to 10 km must be spanned.

Factory CNs: Factory CNs can have the size of a medium or large business CN. They often have to satisfy exceptional physical requirements such as being robust against extreme heat, dust or electromagnetic interference.

The common characteristic of medium, large and factory CNs is the provision of internal communication. This facility is not often required in residential and small business environments.

4.7.3 General Requirements

Two types of requirement are expected to be met by a CN [198]:

- service requirements
- structural requirements.

Service requirements deal with the service mix as well as the consequences of having to support these services. The service mix depends on the customer category. This type of requirement includes the bit rate to be supported as well as the information transfer characteristics, like mean and maximum delays, delay variation, error performance and throughput. It is possible to characterize realistic service mixes for each customer category, but it is difficult to estimate the evolution of coding techniques, such as variable bit rate video-coding, which will influence the bit rate required for a specific service.

The second type of requirement are the **structural requirements**, which include aspects of flexibility, modularity, reliability, physical performance and cost.

Flexibility of the CN is the ability to cope with system changes. This can be subdivided into four parts:

1. Adaptability is the requirement which measures how the CN deals with changes that do not alter the global scale of the CN (for example, new wiring). This is very important in the terminal area for the residential as well as the business environment.

2. Expandability indicates how the CN can grow (for example, by introducing new services, increasing the bit rate to be supported, installing new terminals, or expanding the scale of the CN).

3. Mobility is the ability to interchange terminals. This requires a universal terminal interface.

4. Interworking describes how the CN can interface to other networks. This is very important in areas which are already covered by existing networks, such as LANs and private metropolitan area networks (MANs).

Modularity is the provision of a flexible structure. The network should not be limited to a few applications. Therefore, it is necessary that a modular system is used for the provision of CN capabilities.

Reliability deals with the sensitivity of the CN to errors (for example, bit errors, terminal failures and user induced errors). This requirement is extremely important when a large number of people or terminals are affected by the error, or in all cases where highly reliable operation of the CN must be guaranteed, as is the case in hospitals and fire departments. Reliability requires redundancy and therefore even the terminal connection is duplicated within large CNs.

Physical performance concerns the optimum use of the physical medium. It includes aspects of coding efficiency and cable length and influences the hardware cost. Installation and maintenance are covered by the operating performance. This must be very simple in the terminal environment so that changes can be carried out rapidly and cheaply.

Cost is one of the most important requirements influencing the acceptance of the CN. In the residential area low costs are essential, whereas in the business area it is necessary to have reasonable costs during the introduction phase. Fast system growth can only be achieved if the incremental costs can be kept low.

4.7.4   Topologies

ITU-T Recommendation I.413 illustrates different physical configurations for the realization of a CN [117]. Figure 4.13 shows a few examples of CN configurations. (Other CN configurations are not precluded.)

The first configuration is the well-known star configuration in which each terminal is directly connected to the B-NT2 by a dedicated line.

A B-NT2 can be realized as a centralized system or a distributed system. The latter can have LAN-like structures (for example, bus or ring) in which the terminals are all connected to a common medium via special medium adaptors in the general case.

However, ITU-T has also agreed to some new configurations in which terminals are directly connected to a common shared medium (e.g. dual bus), as shown in Figure 4.13(b) and (c). The major motivations for these new configurations are simplicity of deployment, economy and evolutionary aspects of B-ISDN [38]. A shared medium configuration can be extended easily by adding a new terminal. When using a star configuration, extension may result in higher costs caused by the need for an additional or larger multiplexer.

Combinations of the star and shared medium configurations are also possible (see Figure 4.13(c)). The configuration depicted in this figure is the starred bus system.

It is evident that terminals used in the shared medium configurations of Figure 4.13 have to include a medium access function. This can be supported by the generic

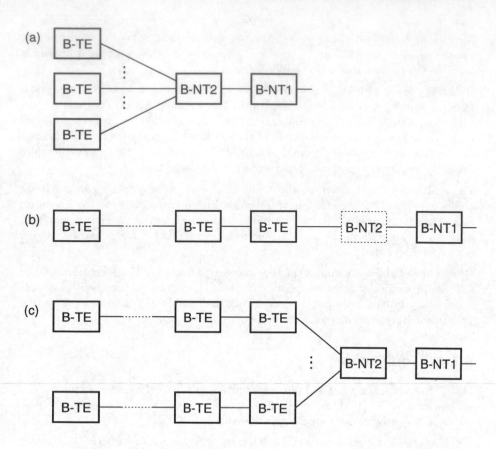

B-NT   Network termination for B-ISDN
B-TE   Terminal equipment for B-ISDN
Dashed box means the B-NT2 may or may not exist

Figure 4.13: *Physical configurations of the CN*

flow control (GFC) protocol of the ATM layer (see Section 5.5.2.2). The GFC mechanism provides orderly and fair access of terminals to the shared medium by supervising the cell streams and assigning capacity to contending terminals on a per-cell basis [55].

The influence of these new configurations on the definition of the interface between a terminal and the B-NT2 will be discussed in Section 5.2.

4.7.5 Interworking with Existing Networks

In medium and large business environments, two different types of communication system are presently used: voice and low-speed data communication like facsimile are handled by **private branch exchanges** (PBXs), while the need for pure data communication is satisfied by LANs.

LANs are primarily employed for in-house data communications. They are used for the interconnection of terminals, workstations, printers, databases, hosts and manufacturing systems. The traffic carried is characterized by short data bursts requiring high transmission speeds. Normally only connectionless services are supported by LANs.

The number of LANs used within business premises has increased dramatically in the past few years. A number of protocols are available which use different principles of operation and which have been standardized by a number of bodies, in particular the American National Standard Institute (ANSI), the Institute of Electrical and Electronic Engineers (IEEE), and the International Standard Organization (ISO).

Current LANs usually have an extent of up to 10 km and their transmission speed is in the range 1 to 16 Mbit/s. Typically, coaxial cable will be used for transmission. Most LANs use a ring or bus topology, although a star configuration is also possible.

LANs can be classified by their topology (bus, ring, star), the transmission medium (twisted pair, coaxial cable, optical fibre) and the media access control (MAC) procedure. (In higher layers, identical protocols may be used.)

Today's most frequently used LANs are:

- carrier sense multiple access with collision detection (CSMA/CD) [74]

- token bus [75]

- token ring [76].

CSMA/CD was the first standardized MAC procedure [74]. It is based on a development by Xerox called **Ethernet**. CSMA/CD uses a bus system with a specified transmission rate of 10 Mbit/s. A station having a packet to send listens to the carrier before sending. If the channel is idle the station begins sending, otherwise it waits till the channel becomes idle. Collision may occur when two or more stations begin sending at the same time. This will be detected by the sending stations and they will stop their packet transmission. The collision is resolved by the back-off algorithm (each station tries to send after a random time). In low loaded systems, this protocol works very well (low packet delay). However, the occurrence of collisions means that the performance deteriorates with increasing load.

The **token bus** system [75] uses a coaxial cable with specified transmission rates of 1, 5 or 10 Mbit/s. All stations are passively coupled to the medium. Access to the channel is controlled by a token-passing protocol. The token is delivered from one station to its neighbour, where the 'neighbour' is defined by address rather than by physical location. The number of packets which can be sent during the interval when a station possesses the token is determined by the token-passing protocol. In order to fulfil different performance requirements, each station uses four internal priority classes.

The **token ring** network [76] is made up of point-to-point unidirectional links interconnecting adjacent stations (active coupling) to form a closed loop. Transmission rates of 4 and 16 Mbit/s are specified for shielded twisted pair cables. Access to the ring is again controlled by a token-passing protocol. A station that is ready to send a packet has to wait for the token, which it receives from its physical neighbour. Different priorities can be attached to tokens but only one token can circulate at a time. During high load situations, token protocols prevent packet collisions but the delay times still increase with the network load.

Further developments in this area led to the so-called **high-speed local area networks** (HSLANs) which have a transmission rate of more than 100 Mbit/s. For example, Ethernet has been enhanced so that it can now offer transmission speeds of 100 Mbit/s. These networks are used to interconnect LANs as well as for the high-speed data communication needed by workstations and file-servers. HSLANs are not restricted to small areas. They may be installed in a metropolitan area, in which case they are called metropolitan area networks (MANs). They can cover a region of more than 100 km in diameter and up to 1000 stations can be attached to one network. The transmission medium is optical fibre. In principle LAN topologies can be used. Different types of HSLANs/MANs are discussed, for example:

- fibre-distributed data interface (FDDI) [77]

- DQDB [69].

- high-performance parallel interface (HIPPI) [196].

FDDI is already available from different suppliers, and for DQDB commercially operated networks exist. HSLANs in the Gbit/s range are currently under study (cf. Section 11.4). HIPPI offers a transmission rate of 800 Mbit/s with IEEE-based framing [68].

Increasing communication requirements demand the interconnection of LANs. This can be achieved by MANs (see Section 9.4.3.2) as well as B-ISDN. Therefore, it is necessary to interconnect LANs and private MANs with B-ISDN. An **interworking unit** (IWU) is necessary which performs protocol conversion and bit rate adaptation (necessary for the interconnection of different networks). The IWU can be attached directly to the B-NT1, as shown in Figure 4.14(a), or the

LAN/MAN can be connected by means of the IWU via S_B to a B-NT2, if present, as shown in Figure 4.14(b).

The IWU may become a bottleneck in the case of heavy traffic load. To obtain a good performance (high throughput, small delay) it is necessary that the protocols used in the LAN and in B ISDN have a lot in common. Interconnection should be done on the lowest possible level. With today's protocols, this can be achieved by the interconnection of DQDB with B-ISDN. Further details of the LAN/MAN integration into B-ISDN will be presented in Section 9.4.

4.7.6 ATM Local Area Networks

One of the most promising areas for the introduction of an ATM-based network is ATM LANs, which are also known as third generation LANs. More and more workstations, and even simple personal computers (PCs), are going to be interconnected.

Initially CSMA/CD and token ring/bus LANs were deployed. After a short period these LANs were interconnected and extended to high-speed local area networks,

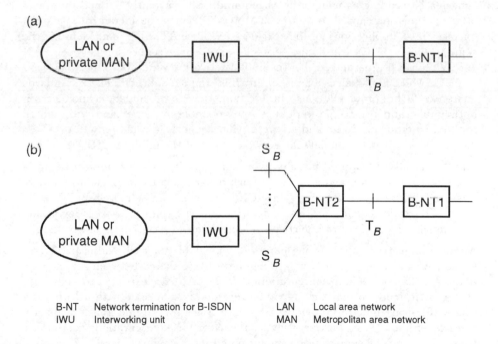

| B-NT | Network termination for B-ISDN | LAN | Local area network |
| IWU | Interworking unit | MAN | Metropolitan area network |

Figure 4.14: *Interworking LAN – B-ISDN*

such as FDDI or DQDB, which are considered to be the second generation. A third generation only has a chance to step into a competitive market if there are obvious advantages compared to the existing and well proven systems. Therefore, the major goals of a new technique for LANs are to provide:

- real-time information transfer

- scalable throughput

- high transfer capacity

- easy interworking between the LAN and **wide area networks** (WAN), such as the public network

- standards-based solution.

ATM is deemed to be the appropriate transport technique to fulfil these requirements. Besides traditional data communications, upcoming applications like multimedia or videotelephony demand a high-speed integrated network to carry all types of multiservice traffic. Thus, a mixture of different, specialized networks operating in parallel can be avoided.

ATM allows real-time transfer of information as a result of its short cells, which are normally not buffered at network elements. Scalable throughput is automatically achieved by sending as many cells as required. The currently defined interfaces offer transmission capacities up to 622 Mbit/s, which is considered to be enough for most LAN applications for the next decade. Since ATM LANs make use of the same technique as used in public networks, simple interconnection between LAN and WAN can be guaranteed. For the public network several ITU-T standards are available which are taken as a basis for any LAN implementation. These standards guarantee future-proof solutions. In addition, the use of similar technologies on both public and private networks activates possible synergies and will lead to reduced costs for hardware and software. Consequently, a rapid growth of ATM-based LANs will also stimulate faster deployment of the public B-ISDN.

ATM is usually introduced initially as a high-capacity campus **backbone network** for transmission and switching. Such a backbone network has to emulate existing LAN concepts. However, since CN equipment can be more rapidly amortized than public networks, instead of an evolutionary approach a sort of revolution may, in some cases, lead to immediate ATM implementation up to the desktop.

Another important aspect is the bandwidth available for each end-user. Traditional LANs offer up to 16 Mbit/s which have to be shared between several participants (shared medium configurations). ATM LANs are expected to be mainly **star configured**, so that the individual terminal is connected with a **hub** via a single (physical) line, thus providing the full (physically) possible transfer capacity to each terminal [173]. Moving away from ring or bus configurations has further advantages, such as simpler management functions.

Figure 4.15 shows a possible ATM-based customer network [33].

As an important step towards ATM to the desktop, the ATM Forum has specified a so-called **low-cost interface** at 52 Mbit/s (see Section 5.4) which allows the use of already installed copper cables [10]. This is crucial since the laying of new cables consumes large amounts of money.

The next step might be the ATM-based **desktop area network** (DAN), which will be used to connect several devices such as camera, telephone and PC. More and more products with a direct ATM output plug will be available, thus enabling easy interconnection [168].

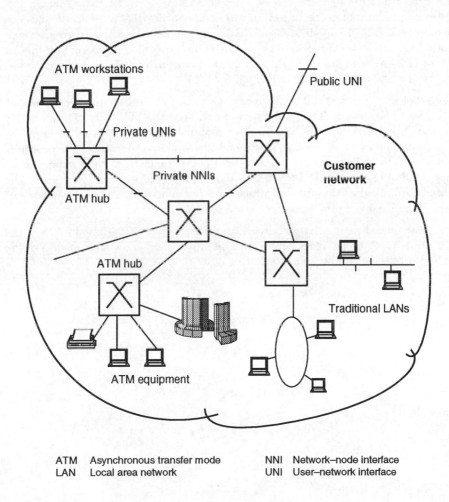

ATM	Asynchronous transfer mode	NNI	Network–node interface
LAN	Local area network	UNI	User–network interface

Figure 4.15: *ATM-based customer network*

In addition to the above, computers, workstations and PCs may employ ATM-based transmission techniques for their internal information flows.

Despite the high degree of commonality between CN equipment and public network equipment, some differences exist to allow simpler and cheaper solutions for the CN. For corporate networks, smaller switches can be used with somewhat less stringent reliability requirements for the individual end-user, thus avoiding complex and expensive redundancy concepts. Simpler solutions for OAM, signalling and management can be adopted, such as use of the **simple network management protocol** (SNMP) instead of common management information service/common management information protocol (CMIS/CMIP) (cf. Section 5.8.4.2). Tariffing and accounting mechanisms can be reduced in CNs. Traffic management processes can be simplified because terminal compliance with the network rules can be expected. (For private interfaces, UPC is not needed. Reactive congestion control schemes, which cannot be used in WANs, are possible because of the smaller extent of LANs, and the network can rely on the behaviour of the sources, that is, they will really throttle back when required [173].)

Nevertheless, there are still some open questions. The **addressing** problem for CNs has to be solved. The public network will use the ITU-T E.164 numbering scheme [81]. How can this scheme be adopted by CNs? Another strong CN-specific requirement is point-to-multipoint connections. As many CN protocols and network applications use point-to-multipoint connections they must also be supported by an ATM-based network to allow existing software and protocols to be reused [173]. Bidirectional OAM procedures for point-to-multipoint connections are still an unsolved problem.

The most crucial point that will decide on the success of ATM-based LANs is the cost per port. A modular concept has to be provided to allow later growth of the LAN combined with low first-installation costs.

Chapter 5

B-ISDN User–Network Interfaces and Protocols

This chapter deals with the B-ISDN user–network interfaces and with ATM-based protocols. In Section 5.1 the protocol reference model developed by ITU-T for B-ISDN is presented. The next sections, Sections 5.2 to 5.4, describe the user–network interfaces in general and their physical layer properties. Then in the following sections, Sections 5.5 and 5.6, functions, codings and procedures for the adjacent ATM layer and ATM adaptation layer are described. Higher layer aspects of the user plane are described in Section 5.7. A section on operation and maintenance problems of the user–network interfaces (Section 5.8) concludes Chapter 5.

5.1 B-ISDN Protocol Reference Model

5.1.1 General Aspects

In modern communication systems, a layered approach is used for the organization of all communication functions. The functions of the layers and the relations of the layers with respect to each other are described in a **protocol reference model** (PRM).

A description of the PRM for the existing ISDN is given in ITU-T Recommendation I.320 [106]. In particular it has introduced the concept of separate planes for the segregation of user, control and management functions. This PRM is the basis for the PRM of the broadband aspects of ISDN (B-ISDN PRM) which is described in ITU-T Recommendation I.321 [107]. The new recommendation takes into account the functionalities of B-ISDN. Therefore, expansion of the PRM contained in ITU-T Recommendation I.320 was necessary.

55

5.1.2   Layered Architecture

According to the **open system interconnection** (OSI) reference model of the ISO [73], each open system can be described as a set of subsystems arranged in a vertical sequence (see Figure 5.1).

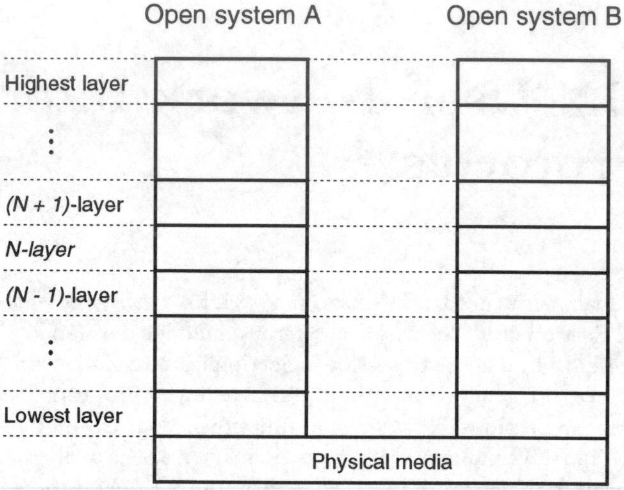

Figure 5.1: *Layered structure of the OSI reference model*

An N-subsystem which consists of one or more N-entities only interacts with the subsystem above or below. The N-entity performs functions within layer N. Communication between peer N-entities (entities of layer N) uses an N-peer-to-peer protocol. The unit of data in an N-peer-to-peer protocol is called the N-protocol data unit (N-PDU). Peer N-entities communicate using the services provided by the layer below. The services of layer N are provided to layer $(N+1)$. The point at which the N-services can be accessed by the layer above is called the N-service access point (N-SAP).

N-primitives are introduced to describe the interface between adjacent layers N and $(N + 1)$. Together with the N-primitive, the associated N-service data unit (N-SDU) is delivered from layer N to layer $(N+1)$ and vice versa. For this purpose the N-service protocol (adjacent layer protocol) is used. Figure 5.2 illustrates this service concept.

Figure 5.3 shows the relationships among the various types of data unit. An N-PDU consists of N-protocol control information (N-PCI) and N-user data. The N-PCI is the information which is exchanged between N-entities.

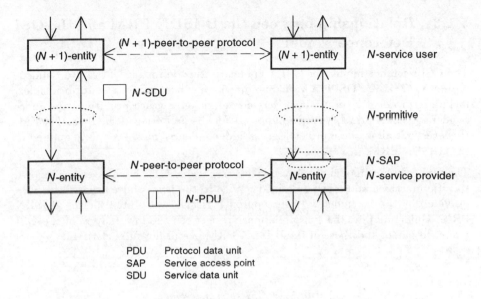

PDU   Protocol data unit
SAP   Service access point
SDU   Service data unit

Figure 5.2: *OSI service concept*

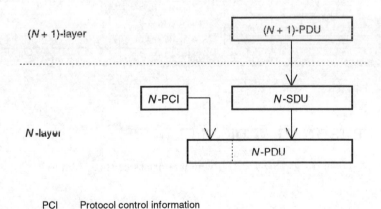

PCI   Protocol control information
PDU   Protocol data unit
SDU   Service data unit

Figure 5.3: *Relationships among the various types of data unit*

5.1.3 Relationship between the B-ISDN PRM and the OSI Reference Model

The OSI reference model for ITU-T applications is defined in ITU-T Recommendation X.200 [152]. OSI is a logical architecture which defines a set of principles, including protocol layering, layer service definition, service primitives and independence. These principles are appropriate for the definition of the B-ISDN PRM. However, not all of these principles (e.g. independence) have been fully applied in the B-ISDN PRM.

The OSI reference model uses seven layers (see Table 5.1). Each layer has its own specific functions and offers a defined service to the layer above using the service provided by the layer below. This approach is also well suited for the B-ISDN PRM. Unfortunately, the exact relationship between the lower layers of the OSI reference model and those of the B-ISDN PRM is still not fully clarified.

Table 5.1: *OSI reference model*

Layer	Name
7	Application layer
6	Presentation layer
5	Session layer
4	Transport layer
3	Network layer
2	Data link layer
1	Physical layer

5.1.4 B-ISDN PRM Description

Figure 5.4 shows the B-ISDN PRM, which consists of three planes:

- user plane
- control plane
- management plane.

The **management plane** includes two types of function called **layer management** functions and **plane management** functions. All the management functions that relate to the whole system are located in the plane management which is responsible for providing coordination between all planes. No layered structure is used within this plane.

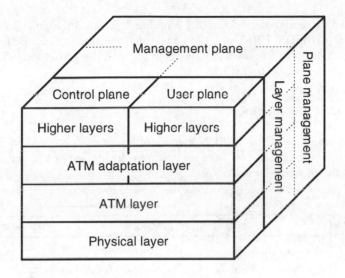

ATM   Asynchronous transfer mode

Figure 5.4: *B-ISDN protocol reference model*

Layer management has a layered structure. It performs the management functions relating to resources and parameters residing in its protocol entities (e.g. meta-signalling). Layer management handles the specific OAM information flows for each layer. More details about these management functions are presented in ITU-T Recommendation Q.940 [136].

The **user plane** provides for the transfer of user information. All associated mechanisms, like flow control and recovery from errors, are included. A layered approach is used within the user plane.

A layered structure is also used within the **control plane**. This plane is responsible for the call control and connection control functions. These are all signalling functions which are necessary to set up, supervise and release a call or connection.

The functions of the physical layer (PL) and the ATM layer are the same for the control plane and the user plane. Different functions may occur in the ATM adaptation layer (AAL) as well as in higher layers.

5.1.5   Layer Functions

The functions of the physical layer, the ATM layer and the ATM adaptation layer are described in the following subsections. These descriptions are contained in

ITU-T Recommendations I.321 [107] and I.413 [117]. In Figure 5.5 the lower layers of the B-ISDN PRM and their functions are illustrated. Different fields within the cell header are used to implement some of these functions. These fields will be described in Section 5.5.2.

5.1.5.1   Cell Terminology

Before the functions of the B-ISDN individual layers can be specified, it is necessary to clarify the notion **cell** because it is used for definitions in the ATM layer as well as the physical layer.

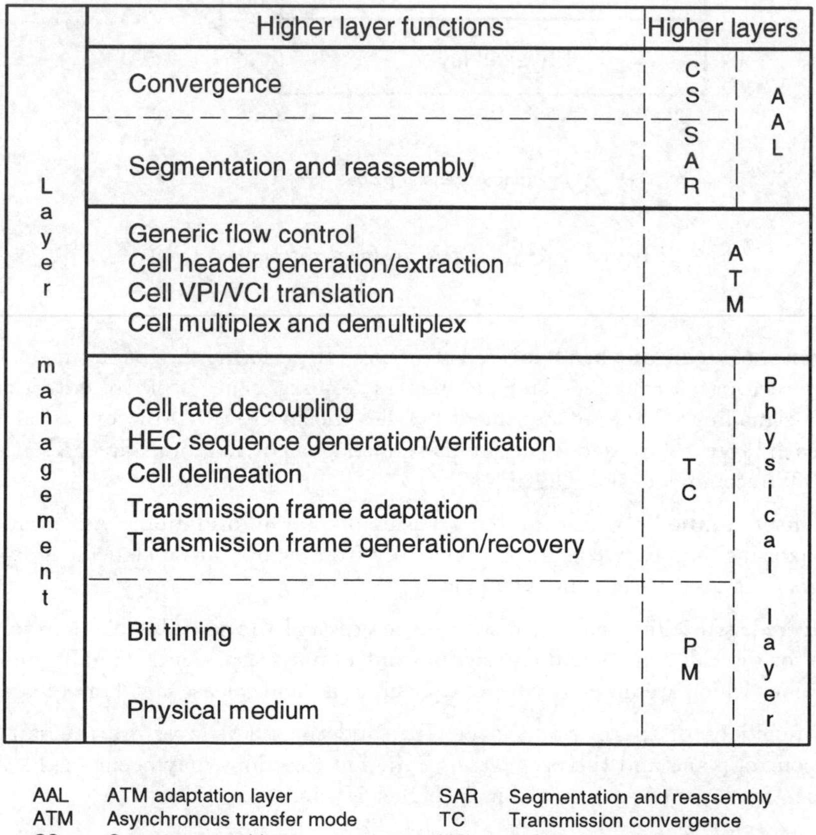

	Higher layer functions	Higher layers	
L a y e r m a n a g e m e n t	Convergence	C S	A A L
	Segmentation and reassembly	S A R	
	Generic flow control Cell header generation/extraction Cell VPI/VCI translation Cell multiplex and demultiplex	A T M	
	Cell rate decoupling HEC sequence generation/verification Cell delineation Transmission frame adaptation Transmission frame generation/recovery	T C	P h y s i c a l l a y e r
	Bit timing	P M	
	Physical medium		

AAL	ATM adaptation layer	SAR	Segmentation and reassembly
ATM	Asynchronous transfer mode	TC	Transmission convergence
CS	Convergence sublayer	VCI	Virtual channel identifier
HEC	Header error control	VPI	Virtual path identifier
PM	Physical medium		

Figure 5.5: *The functions of B-ISDN in relation to the B-ISDN PRM*

The term cell is essential for B-ISDN, and therefore it is defined in ITU-T Recommendation I.113 [99]:

> 'A cell is a block of fixed length. It is identified by a label at the ATM layer of the B-ISDN PRM.'

More detailed definitions for the different kinds of cell are presented in ITU-T Recommendation I.321 [107].

Idle cell (physical layer): A cell that is inserted/extracted by the physical layer in order to adapt the cell flow rate at the boundary between the ATM layer and the physical layer to the available payload capacity of the transmission system used.

Valid cell (physical layer): A cell whose header has no errors or has been modified by the cell header error control (HEC) verification process (for HEC mechanism see Section 5.3.1.5).

Invalid cell (physical layer): A cell whose header has errors and has not been modified by the cell HEC verification process. This cell is discarded at the physical layer.

Assigned cell (ATM layer): A cell which provides a service to an application using the ATM layer service.

Unassigned cell (ATM layer): An ATM layer cell which is not an assigned cell.

Only assigned and unassigned cells are passed to the ATM layer from the physical layer. The other cells carry no information concerning the ATM and higher layers and therefore will only be processed by the physical layer.

5.1.5.2   Physical Layer Functions

The physical layer is subdivided into the **physical medium** (PM) sublayer and the **transmission convergence** (TC) sublayer.

The PM sublayer is the lowest sublayer and includes only the physical medium dependent functions. It provides the bit transmission capability, including bit alignment. Line coding and, if necessary, electrical/optical conversion is performed by this sublayer. In many cases, the physical medium will be an optical fibre. Other media, such as coaxial and twisted pair cables, are also possible. The transmission functions are medium specific.

Bit timing functions are the generation and reception of waveforms which are suitable for the medium, insertion and extraction of bit timing information, and line coding if required.

The TC sublayer performs five functions. The lowest function is the **generation and recovery of the transmission frame**.

Transmission frame adaptation is responsible for all actions which are necessary to adapt the cell flow according to the used payload structure of the transmission system in the sending direction. In the opposite direction it extracts the cell flow from the transmission frame. This frame may be cell equivalent (no external envelope is used), a **synchronous digital hierarchy** (SDH) envelope or an envelope according to ITU-T Recommendation G.703 [86]. In the case of the B-ISDN UNI, ITU-T proposes a SDH envelope or the cell equivalent structure [120]. These alternatives are described in more detail in Section 5.3.

The functions mentioned so far are specific to the transmission frame. All other TC sublayer functions, which are presented in the following, can be common to all possible transmission frames.

Cell delineation is the mechanism that enables the receiver to recover the cell boundaries. This mechanism is described in ITU-T Recommendation I.432 [120]. The detailed procedure of the cell delineation mechanism is given in Section 5.3.1.6. To protect the cell delineation mechanism from malicious attack, the information field of a cell is scrambled before transmission. Descrambling is performed at the receiving side.

HEC sequence generation is done in the transmit direction. The HEC sequence is inserted in its appropriate field within the header. At the receiving side the HEC value is recalculated and compared with the received value. If possible, header errors are corrected, otherwise the cell is discarded. Details of the HEC mechanism are presented in Section 5.3.1.5.

In the sending direction, the **cell rate decoupling** mechanism inserts idle cells in order to adapt the rate of ATM cells to the payload capacity of the transmission system. In the receiving direction this mechanism suppresses all idle cells. Only assigned and unassigned cells are passed to the ATM layer.

5.1.5.3   ATM Layer Functions

The ATM layer is the layer above the physical layer. Its characteristic features are independent of the physical medium. Four functions of this layer have been identified.

In the transmit direction, cells from individual VPs and VCs are multiplexed into one resulting cell stream by the **cell multiplexing** function. The composite stream is normally a non-continuous cell flow. At the receiving side the **cell demultiplexing** function splits the arriving cell stream into individual cell flows appropriate to the VP or VC.

VPI and VCI translation are performed at ATM switching nodes and/or at cross-connect nodes. Within a VP node the value of the VPI field of each incoming cell is translated into a new VPI value for the outgoing cell. The values of the VPI and VCI are translated into new values at a VC switch.

The **cell header generation/extraction** function is applied at the termination points of the ATM layer. In the transmit direction, after receiving the cell information field from the AAL, the cell header generation adds the appropriate ATM cell header except for the HEC value. VPI/VCI values could be obtained by translation from the SAP identifier. In the opposite direction, the cell header extraction function removes the cell header. Only the cell information field is passed to the AAL. This function could also translate a VPI/VCI into a SAP identifier.

The **GFC** function is only defined at the B-ISDN UNI. GFC supports control of the ATM traffic flow in a customer network. It can be used to alleviate short-term overload conditions (user-to-network direction) at the UNI (more details can be found in Section 5.5.2.2). GFC information is carried in assigned or unassigned cells.

5.1.5.4 ATM Adaptation Layer Functions

The AAL is subdivided into the **segmentation and reassembly** (SAR) sublayer and the **convergence sublayer** (CS). The functions of the AAL are described in ITU-T Recommendation I.362 [111].

The AAL is between the ATM layer and higher layers. Its basic function is the enhanced adaptation of services provided by the ATM layer to the requirements of the higher layer. Higher layer PDUs are mapped into the information field of an ATM cell. AAL entities exchange information with their peer AAL entities to support AAL functions.

AAL functions are organized in two sublayers. The essential functions of the SAR sublayer are, at the transmitting side, segmentation of higher layer PDUs into a suitable size for the information field of the ATM cell (48 octets) and, at the receiving side, reassembly of the particular information fields into higher layer PDUs. The CS is service dependent and provides the AAL service at the AAL SAP.

No SAP has yet been defined between these two sublayers. The need for such SAPs needs further study. Different SAPs for higher layers can be derived using different combinations of SAR and CS. For some applications, neither a CS nor a SAR is necessary, in which case they will be empty (cf. Section 5.6.1).

To minimize the number of AAL protocols, ITU-T proposed a service classification which is specific to the AAL. This classification was made with respect to the following parameters:

- timing relation
- bit rate
- connection mode.

Figure 5.6 depicts the AAL classes. Not all possible combinations make sense and therefore only four classes are distinguished.

	Class A	Class B	Class C	Class D
Timing relation between source and destination	Required	Required	Not required	Not required
Bit rate	Constant	Variable	Variable	Variable
Connection mode	Connection oriented	Connection oriented	Connection oriented	Connection-less

Figure 5.6: *Service classification for AAL*

Some examples for the different **service classes** are listed below:

Class A: Circuit emulation (for example, transport of a 2 Mbit/s or 45 Mbit/s signal), constant bit rate video

Class B: Variable bit rate video and audio

Class C: Connection-oriented data transfer

Class D: Connectionless data transfer.

5.1.5.5   Information Flows of the Physical Layer

The following section looks at the information flows concerning the physical layer according to ITU-T Recommendation I.413 [117]. Different information flows exist:

- between the physical layer and the ATM layer
- between the physical layer and the management plane
- inside the physical layer between the sublayers.

From the PM sublayer to the TC sublayer, a flow of logical symbols (e.g. bits) and associated timing information is exchanged. This information is also transferred in the opposite direction.

The physical layer provides the ATM layer with all cells belonging to this layer, with timing information and a clock derived from the line rate of the physical layer. In the opposite direction, assigned and unassigned cells, if any are available, and their associated timing are delivered. This layer informs the management plane about loss of the incoming signal and the indication of received errors or degraded performance. Bit errors may be detected by unexpected code violations or other mechanisms. Information transfer in the opposite direction still needs further study.

5.1.6 Relationship of OAM Functions with the B-ISDN PRM

The relationship between OAM functions and the B-ISDN PRM is presented in ITU-T Recommendation I.610 [123]. A layered approach is used for the OAM functions which are allocated to the layer management. The different layer management functions are correlated with various layers. The independence requirement and the layered concept lead to the following principles:

1. OAM functions related to OAM levels are independent of the OAM capabilities of other layers and have to be introduced at each layer.

2. Each layer has its own OAM processing to obtain quality and status information. The results are delivered to the layer management or, if required, to the adjacent higher layer.

5.2 General Aspects of the User–Network Interface

5.2.1 Transfer Mode

As mentioned in Chapter 1, the B-ISDN UNI fully exploits the flexibility inherent in ATM. This means that the payload capacity of the interface (that is, the whole of the transmission capacity besides the small portion that is needed to operate the interface properly, cf. Section 5.3.1) is completely structured into ATM cells.

As at the UNI, there is no pre-assignment of cells to specific user applications; the actual use of cells for connections to be established across the interface can change dynamically. Different traffic mixes can easily be supported as long as the cell transfer capacity is not exceeded. (How this is related to the interface bit rate will be discussed later.)

5.2.2 Bit Rates

As mentioned in Section 3.3, interface bit rates of about 150 Mbit/s and 600 Mbit/s at the physical layer have been specified. The exact figures are discussed below. It should be noted that the bit rate available for the end-user's application is reduced at least by the overhead needed for operation of the physical layer, the ATM layer and the AAL.

The 150 Mbit/s interface is symmetric with respect to bit rate, offering 150 Mbit/s in both the network-to-user direction and the user-to-network direction. This sort of interface will predominantly be used for interactive services like telephony, videotelephony and data services. The extension of such an interface to a higher bit rate to meet the needs of users generating large traffic volumes seems quite natural. Thus, a bit rate-symmetric 600 Mbit/s interface was also conceived. (The reason for choosing 600 Mbit/s will soon become clearer.) Users who are expected to have a much higher traffic load from the network to themselves than in the other direction may get an asymmetric version of the 600 Mbit/s interface with a reduced upstream capacity (user-to-network direction) of only 150 Mbit/s. This would, for example, be suitable for the simultaneous transmission of several television programmes to a residential customer who only needs the standard capacity for interactive services but a higher bit rate for distribution services like TV and sound programmes.

The definition of two separate interface bit rates was a compromise between two diverging requirements, namely a very limited number of different interface types on the one hand and the cost-effectiveness of the interface on the other hand.

The exact interface bit rates at the physical layer are:

- 155.520 Mbit/s
- 622.080 Mbit/s.

These bit rates are identical to the two lowest bit rates of the SDH as defined in ITU-T Recommendation G.707 [88]. SDH is a transmission hierarchy which was adopted by ITU-T in 1988 [88, 89, 90]. It is based on the North American synchronous optical network (SONET) concept [6] which was developed to:

- set a standard for optical transmission in order to react on the upcoming variety of manufacturer-specific implementations of optical transmission systems and interfaces

- provide transmission facilities with flexible add/drop capabilities to allow for simpler multiplexing/demultiplexing of signals than in the existing plesiochronous digital hierarchy (PDH) [85]

- grant generously dimensioned transmission overhead capacity to cater for various existing and assumed network operation and maintenance applications that were not, or at least only with difficulty, realizable in PDH.

More details on SDH can be found in Sections 5.3.1 and 5.8 and Chapter 8 as well as in [24].

5.2.3   Interface Structure

SDH has the inherent flexibility to transport quite different types of signals like ISDN channels, according to ITU-T Recommendation I.412 [116], or ATM cells.

Thus SDH – being a universal transmission concept – was proposed as the B-ISDN interface structure [79]. Such a user–network interface implementation would have the advantage of full compatibility with the network–node interface. This avoids the otherwise necessary conversion of signals that are sent from the user through the network to other users. This property is extremely useful during the introductory phase of B-ISDN when a complete network infrastructure does not yet exist. Customers may easily be provided with access to a broadband network node (a cross-connect or a switch) which might be located in a place different from that of the 64 kbit/s ISDN local exchange that usually serves the customer, via SDH equipment. In some networks SDH will be implemented before B-ISDN.

However, the SDH-based B-ISDN UNI has some drawbacks. A minor one is that the large overhead capacity provided by SDH is not actually needed at the user–network interface. However, this is not a strong argument against using SDH. Generation of the byte-structured SDH frame (cf. Figure 5.7) requires interface functions that would not be necessary if the interface was completely cell structured (this is a possible solution as no 'physical' channels are foreseen, as in the case of the 64 kbit/s ISDN – cf. ITU-T Recommendation I.412 [116]).

Insertion of ATM cells from several terminals into one SDH frame in a passive bus configuration (as standardized for the 64 kbit/s ISDN, see ITU-T Recommendation I.430 [118]) is almost impossible for realistic transmission lengths because of individually varying transmission delays and the high bit rates involved. (Though

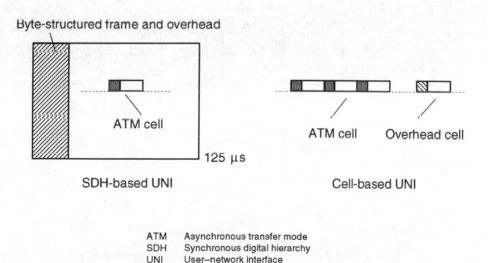

Figure 5.7: *User–network interface options*

passive configurations are no longer foreseen in ITU-T Recommendation I.413 [117], this was put forward as an argument in favour of the cell-based interfaces.)

For these reasons, two interface types were standardized [117, 120]: one based on SDH and the other based on mere cell multiplexing (see Figure 5.7).

Remarkably, although the interface bit rate of the cell-based interface is basically not determined by any frame structure but might be chosen freely, it was agreed within ITU-T to adopt the same bit rate (and payload capacity, see Section 5.3.1) for both interface types to facilitate interworking between the cell-based UNI and SDH in the network.

5.2.4   B-ISDN UNI Reference Configuration and Physical Realizations

As already mentioned in Section 4.7.1, the ISDN reference configuration for the basic access and primary rate access [115] was applied to B-ISDN with only minor modifications of notation. A reference configuration of the user-network access is a generic description based on two elements (see Figure 5.8):

- functional groups
- reference points.

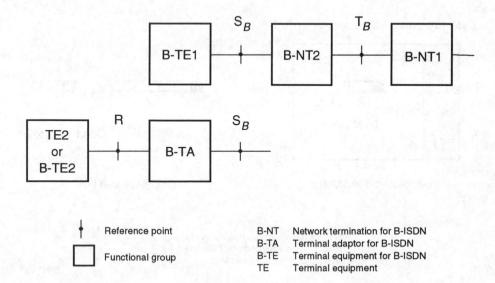

Figure 5.8: *B-ISDN UNI reference configuration*

Figure 5.8 mainly shows broadband functional groups and reference points. The corresponding entities for the 64 kbit/s ISDN are described in ITU-T Recommendation I.411 [115].

The B-NT1 includes functions broadly equivalent to layer 1 of the OSI reference model [152]. Examples of B-NT1 functions are (according to ITU-T Recommendation I.413 [117]):

- line transmission termination

- transmission interface handling

- OAM functions.

The B-NT2 includes functions broadly equivalent to layer 1 and higher layers of the OSI reference model. Examples of B-NT2 functions are [117]:

- adaptation functions for different interface media and topologies

- multiplexing/demultiplexing/concentration of traffic

- buffering of ATM cells

- resource allocation; usage parameter control

- signalling protocol handling

- interface handling

- switching of internal connections.

The generic term 'B-NT2' covers a host of actual implementations: it may not actually exist ('null B-NT2' provided that the interface definitions allow direct connection of terminals to the B-NT1), may consist solely of layer 1 connections (wires), provide concentrating and/or multiplexing functions, or be a full-blown switch (private branch exchange). The B-NT2 functions may be concentrated or distributed, for example, in a bus or ring with its access nodes (cf. Section 4.7).

S_R and T_R denote reference points between the terminal and the B-NT2, and between B-NT1 and B-NT2, respectively. Physical interfaces need not occur at a reference point in any case. As an example, B-NT1 and B-NT2 functions might be combined as shown in Figure 5.9.

It is also possible for the terminal to include B-NT2 functionality (see Figure 5.10).

If the same interface standard applies to both S_B and T_B, these reference points may coincide (see Figure 5.11), thus permitting the direct connection of a terminal to the B-NT1.

B-ISDN will also offer 64 kbit/s ISDN services and interfaces. Terminal equipments 1 (TE1 complying with ITU-T Recommendation I.430 [118], basic access) can be connected via such standard interfaces at the S reference point (as depicted in Figure 5.12).

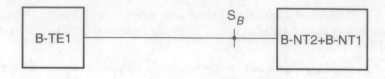

B-NT   Network termination for B-ISDN
B-TE   Terminal equipment for B-ISDN

Figure 5.9: *Configuration with physical interface at S_B only*

B-NT   Network termination for B-ISDN
B-TE   Terminal equipment for B-ISDN

Figure 5.10: *Configuration with physical interface at T_B only*

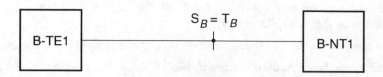

B-NT   Network termination for B-ISDN
B-TE   Terminal equipment for B-ISDN

Figure 5.11: *Coinciding S_B and T_B*

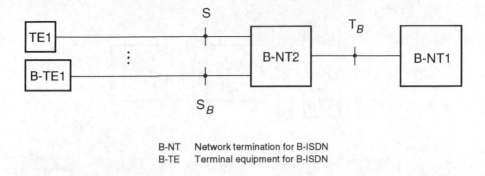

B-NT   Network termination for B-ISDN
B-TE   Terminal equipment for B-ISDN

Figure 5.12: *B-NT2 offering 64 kbit/s interfaces and broadband interfaces*

Of course B-NT2 may provide multiple interfaces of each type at the S and S_B reference points.

Finally, to complete this brief description of the B-ISDN reference configurations, let us address the lower part of Figure 5.8 showing the functional groups broadband terminal adaptor (B-TA) and TE2/B-TE2, and the R reference point between both functional groups. Whereas there must be standardized broadband interfaces at S_B and T_B (according to ITU-T Recommendation I.432 [120]; see Section 5.3), at R any other (non-ISDN) interface is used to connect a non-ISDN terminal (TE2 or B-TE2 in the figure, denoting a narrowband terminal or broadband terminal, respectively).

The provision of multiple terminal interfaces by the B-NT2, as indicated in Figure 5.12, is not restricted to a specific topology. Star, bus, ring configurations or even mixtures of those topologies, such as starred bus, are possible (see Figure 5.13).

It may have become obvious from the foregoing figures that the B-ISDN standard allows many types of implementation according to the customers' needs. However, ITU-T Recommendation I.413 [117] contains two restrictions:

1. Only one interface per B-NT1 is allowed at the T_B reference point.

2. The interfaces are point-to-point at the physical layer 'in the sense that there is only one sink (receiver) in front of one source (transmitter)' [117]. (This means that passive bus configurations are not supported. As such configurations are strongly restricted in terms of the number of connectable terminals and coverable transmission distance, they have been excluded as inappropriate for broadband.)

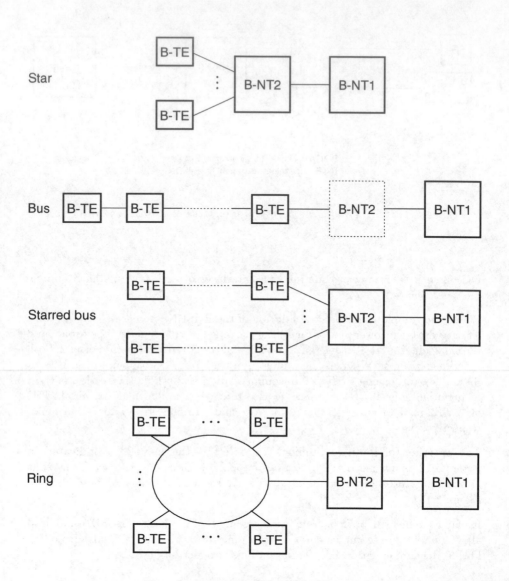

Figure 5.13: *Multiple interface arrangements*

5.2.5 Special Issues

Configurations like that in Figure 5.11 require a high degree of commonality between the interfaces at the S_B and T_B reference points. Of course the terminal interface at S_B should be unique in order to support worldwide terminal interchangeability. However, whether the last requirement can be met is not certain as there are currently two interface options at T_B (see Section 5.2.3) and there is strong support for the interfaces S_B and T_B being identical.

Another important issue is how, and to what extent, the standard interface should support shared medium configurations (bus and ring structures, as shown in Figure 5.13). Such configurations require medium access control functions which can either be part of the standard interface functionality, or otherwise have to be implemented whenever necessary in additional medium access control entities. (This problem, which affects the B-ISDN UNI definition, was introduced in Section 4.7.4.)

In a shared medium configuration, two different operation modes exist:

1. **Distributed multiplexing distributed demultiplexing** (DMDD): This is a mechanism for collecting cells from multiple terminals for service at the B-NT2 or the local exchange. In the opposite direction it provides a mechanism for the distribution of cells to multiple terminals. In the downstream direction (network towards terminal) a terminal copies all the cells it has to handle. In the upstream direction (opposite direction) the terminal waits for an idle or unassigned cell which can be used to transport information towards the network. Such a terminal is called **unidirectional** because it can only send its own cells towards the network and receive cells pertaining to it from the network direction. All cells for internal communication are served by the B-NT2 or the local exchange.

2. **LAN-like switching** (LLS): In this operation mode, **bidirectional** terminals are used. A terminal can receive and send cells in both directions. Therefore, cells used for internal communication can be served locally without involving the B-NT2 or the local exchange. This mode unburdens the B-NT2 or the local exchange from switching functions. However, LLS increases the complexity within the terminal.

In a star configuration as well as in a dual bus configuration using DMDD, only unidirectional terminals are necessary. The same type of terminal can be used as an **end terminal** in the dual bus system operating in the LLS mode. All other terminals in a dual bus with LLS are bidirectional. This does not contravene the requirement for terminal interchangeability since bidirectional terminals can also operate in the unidirectional mode. Thus the customer has a choice between the fully interchangeable bidirectional terminal and the simpler unidirectional one which has somewhat restricted functionality but may suffice in certain cases.

5.3   Physical Layer of the User–Network Interface

According to the B-ISDN protocol reference model described in Section 5.1, the physical layer is split into two sublayers. These sublayers and their functions are shown in Figure 5.14.

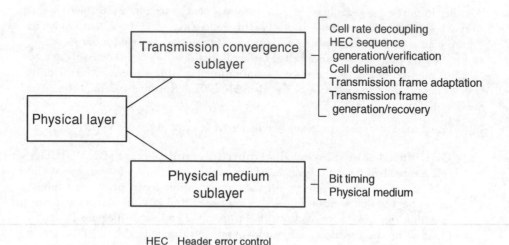

HEC   Header error control

Figure 5.14: *Physical layer structure*

The sublayer functions shown in Figure 5.14 were defined in Section 5.1. The following provides a detailed description of them based on ITU-T Recommendation I.432 [120]. OAM aspects are treated in Section 5.8.

5.3.1   Functions of the Transmission Convergence Sublayer

At the physical bit level the B-ISDN user–network interface has a bit rate of 155.520 Mbit/s or 622.080 Mbit/s. The **interface transfer capability** is defined as [120]:

> '... the bit rate available for user information cells, signalling cells and ATM and higher layer OAM information cells, excluding physical layer frame structure bytes or physical layer cells.'

Its value of 149.760 Mbit/s for the 155.520 Mbit/s interface complies with SDH. The transfer capability of the 622.080 Mbit/s interface is 599.040 Mbit/s (four times 149.760 Mbit/s).

Additional user–network interfaces (which are especially important in the introduction phase of ATM) are explained in Section 5.4.

In the following, the transmission frame generation/adaptation aspects of the two interface options (SDH based and cell-based) are described separately as they are rather different. The other transmission convergence sublayer functions can, in principle, be performed the same way in both options.

5.3.1.1 SDH-Based Interface at 155.520 Mbit/s

ITU-T Recommendations G.707-709 [88, 89, 90] specify the SDH. The transmission frame structure as given in ITU-T Recommendation G.709 is shown in Figure 5.15. This frame is byte-structured and consists of nine rows and 270 columns. The

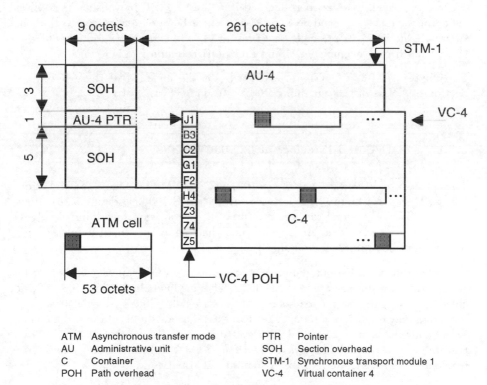

Figure 5.15: *Frame structure of the 155.520 Mbit/s SDH-based interface*

frame repetition frequency is 8 kHz (9 × 270 byte × 8 kHz = 155.520 Mbit/s). The first nine columns comprise the section overhead (SOH) and administrative pointer 4 (AU-4). Another 9 byte column is dedicated to the path overhead (POH).

This structuring of transmission overheads complies with the OAM levels already introduced in Section 4.6.2. The use of these overhead bytes will be described in Section 5.8.

Generation of the SDH-based user–network interface signal is as follows [120]. First the ATM cell stream is mapped into container 4 (C-4) (the SDH terminology is defined in ITU-T Recommendation G.708 [89]; here it is sufficient to say that C-4 is a 9 row × 260 column container corresponding to the transfer capability of 149.760 Mbit/s). Next C-4 is packed in virtual container 4 (VC-4) along with the VC-4 POH. The ATM cell boundaries are aligned with the byte boundaries of the frame. Note that an ATM cell may cross a C-4 boundary; as the C-4 capacity (2340 bytes) is not an integer multiple of the cell length (53 octets) and the C-4 capacity is entirely used for cell mapping, this will normally be the case.

Virtual container VC-4 is then mapped into the 9 × 270 byte frame (known as synchronous transport module 1, STM-1). The AU-4 pointer is used to find the first byte of VC-4. In principle, the first VC-4 byte can be located elsewhere in the STM-1 frame (excluding the first nine SOH columns).

POH bytes J1, B3, C2, G1 are activated (for the meaning of these bytes, see Section 5.8). Use of the remaining POH bytes is for further study.

5.3.1.2   SDH-Based Interface at 622.080 Mbit/s

There is a straightforward way of creating a 622.080 Mbit/s frame (STM-4) from four STM-1s according to ITU-T Recommendation G.708 (see Figure 5.16). However, the STM-4 payload can be structured in several ways, including simply as 4 × VC-4 or as one block. An advantage of the second option is the unrestricted use of about 600 Mbit/s for ATM cell mapping.

Possible future applications requiring more than the VC-4 capacity can easily be allocated bandwidth elsewhere in the 600 Mbit/s payload block. Therefore, ITU-T chose this option. The payload is exactly 4 × 149.760 Mbit/s = 599.040 Mbit/s. Although only one POH column is needed, the adjacent three columns in VC-4-4c are not usable as they are filled with stuffing octets ('fixed stuff'). This allows transmission of the STM-4 payload over four STM-1 links in cases where STM-4 transmission systems are not available in an ATM network.

Note that ATM cell mapping into STM-16 (2.5 Gbit/s) has been defined in a similar way. However, no UNI at a bit rate above STM-4 has been standardized as yet.

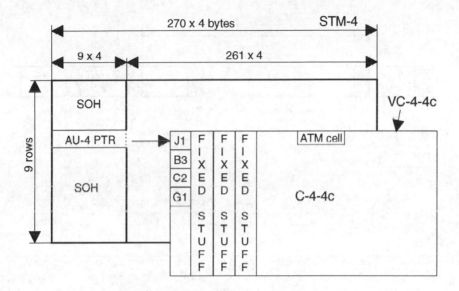

AU   Administrative unit
C-4-4c   Container 4 'concatenated'
SOH   Section overhead
STM-4   Synchronous transport module 4
VC-4-4c   Virtual container 4 'concatenated'

Figure 5.16: *Frame structure of the 622.080 Mbit/s SDH-based interface*

5.3.1.3   Cell-Based Interface

These interfaces (at both 155.520 Mbit/s and 622.080 Mbit/s) consist of a continuous stream of cells (see Figure 5.17) each containing 53 octets.

The maximum spacing between successive physical layer cells is 26 ATM layer cells. After 26 contiguous ATM layer cells the insertion of a physical layer cell is enforced in order to adapt the transfer capability to the interface rate. (The ratio 26:27 is the same as 149.760 Mbit/s to 155.520 Mbit/s or 599.040 Mbit/s to 622.080 Mbit/s.) When no ATM layer cells are available, physical layer cells are inserted.

The physical layer cells which are inserted at the transmitting side can be either idle cells (see Section 5.3.1.4 and Table 5.3) or physical layer OAM cells, depending on operation and maintenance requirements.

Physical layer OAM information (which in the SDH case is allocated to SOH and POH) is here conveyed in specific physical layer OAM cells which are identified

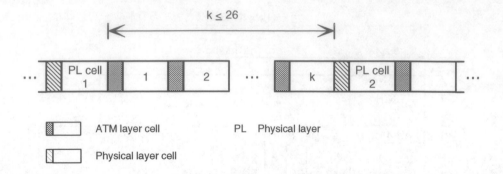

Figure 5.17: *Structure of cell-based interfaces*

by unique cell header bit patterns reserved exclusively for these cell types. (This means that the ATM layer must not use these bit combinations as code points for the corresponding cell header fields, which are shown in Figure 5.23 on page 90.) The patterns are shown in Table 5.2.

Table 5.2: *Header pattern for physical layer OAM cells*

Cell type	Octet 1	Octet 2	Octet 3	Octet 4	Octet 5
F1	00000000	00000000	00000000	00000011	HEC valid code
F3	00000000	00000000	00000000	00001001	HEC valid code

Note that at the cell-based interfaces only the F1 and F3 OAM flows of Figure 4.11 on page 44 occur. Levels F2 and F3 coincide for the cell-based interfaces, and the corresponding functions are supported by F3.

5.3.1.4   Cell Rate Decoupling

Whenever no assigned, unassigned or physical layer OAM cell is available for transmission, an **idle cell** will be inserted to adapt the cell stream to the transmission bit rate. Any idle cells will be discarded at the receiving side. The insertion and discarding of idle cells is called **cell rate decoupling**.

Idle cells are identified by a standardized pattern for the cell header, which is shown in Table 5.3. This is used throughout the ATM network to identify idle cells. Each octet of the information field of an idle cell is filled with 01101010.

Table 5.3: *Header pattern for idle cell identification*

Octet 1	Octet 2	Octet 3	Octet 4	Octet 5
00000000	00000000	00000000	00000001	HEC valid code

5.3.1.5   Header Error Control

According to the B-ISDN protocol reference model (see Section 5.1) ATM cell header error control is a physical layer function and it is described in ITU-T Recommendation I.432 [120]. It should be noted that the HEC method standardized for the user–network interface can be employed universally in the ATM network.

First the HEC generation algorithm is descried and then its capabilities.

Every ATM cell transmitter calculates the HEC value across the first 4 octets of the cell header and inserts the result in the 5th (HEC field). The HEC value is defined as 'the remainder of the division (modulo 2) by the generator polynomial $x^8 + x^2 + x + 1$ of the product x^8 multiplied by the content of the header excluding the HEC field' [120] (the transmitter device computing this remainder presets its register to all 0s before performing the division), to which the fixed pattern '01010101' will be added modulo 2.

This HEC code is capable of:

- correcting single bit errors
- detecting certain multiple-bit errors

in the ATM cell header. Both error processing capabilities will be used by the equipment receiving ATM cells according to the state–event diagram depicted in Figure 5.18.

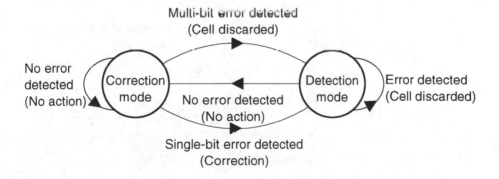

Figure 5.18: *HEC receiver actions*

After initialization the receiver is in 'correction mode'. When a single-bit error is detected, it is corrected; when a multi-bit error is detected, the cell is discarded. In both cases, the receiver switches into 'detection mode'. In this receiver state, each cell with a detected single-bit or multi-bit error is discarded. If no further errored cell is detected the receiver switches back to 'correction mode'.

The above receiver operation has been chosen to take into account the error characteristics of fibre-based transmission systems. These exhibit a mix of single-bit errors and relatively large **error bursts** (on a low error level). The specified HEC method ensures recovery from single-bit errors, and a low probability of delivering cells with errored headers under bursty error conditions.

Figure 5.19 shows the performance of the HEC mechanism as a function of bit error probability.

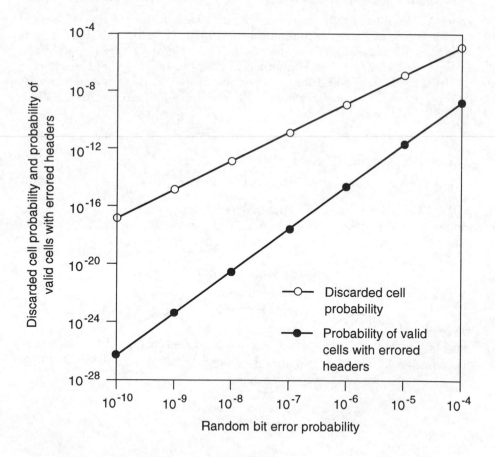

Figure 5.19: *HEC performance*

For a bit error probability of, say, 10^{-8} (a realistic value for fibre-based transmission systems) the probability that cells will be discarded (as a result of header errors which have been recognized but could not be corrected) is about 10^{-13}. The probability of valid cells with errored headers (cells with unrecognizable header errors) is about 10^{-20}.

5.3.1.6   Cell Delineation

According to ITU-T Recommendation I.432 [120] 'cell delineation is the process which allows identification of the cell boundaries'. The method recommended by ITU T [120] for cell delineation is based on the correlation between the header bits to be protected (the first 4 octets of the cell header) and the relevant control bits (1 octet HEC field, cf. Section 5.3.1.5). Figure 5.20 shows the state diagram for HEC-based cell delineation.

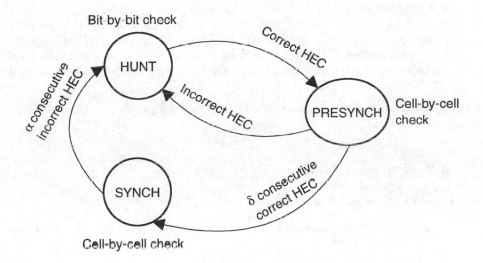

Figure 5.20: *Cell delineation state diagram*

In HUNT state, a bit-by-bit check of the assumed header field is performed. When more information is available (for example, octet boundaries), this may optionally be used. When the HEC coding law (see Section 5.3.1.5) is seen to be respected, that is, syndrome equals zero, one assumes that a header has been found and goes to PRESYNCH state. Now the HEC correlation check is performed cell by cell.

If δ consecutive correct HECs are found, the SYNCH state is entered; if not, the system goes back to HUNT state. The system leaves the SYNCH state for HUNT state if α consecutive incorrect HECs are identified.

The values for α and δ obviously influence the performance of the cell delineation process. Robustness against false misalignment caused by bit errors depends on α, while robustness against false delineation in the resynchronization phase depends on δ. The following values for α and δ have been suggested:

$\alpha = 7$, $\delta = 6$ for SDH-based interfaces
$\alpha = 7$, $\delta = 8$ for cell-based interfaces.

With $\alpha = 7$, a 155.520 Mbit/s ATM system will be in SYNCH for more than one year even when the bit error probability is about 10^{-4}. With $\delta = 6$, the same system with the same bit error probability will need about 10 cells or 28 μs to re-enter SYNCH after loss of cell synchronization [120].

This cell delineation method could fail if the header HEC correlation were imitated in the information field of ATM cells. This might be effected by a malicious user or might happen inadvertently by an application that accidentally uses the same generator polynomial. To overcome such difficulties, the information field contents will be scrambled using a self-synchronizing scrambler with the polynomial $x^{43} + 1$ in the case of SDH-based interfaces. The scrambler is effective only in PRESYNCH and SYNCH and is disabled in HUNT.

For cell-based interfaces, a distributed sample scrambler of 31st order has been specified in I.432 [120].

5.3.2   Physical Medium Characteristics

This section addresses topics such as:

- physical medium to be deployed at the user–network interface at S_B and T_B reference points;

- bit timing and interface code;

- power feeding;

- modes of operation of the interface (and necessary procedures).

5.3.2.1   Physical Medium

The future broadband integrated services digital network will be based on the deployment of optical fibre transmission (cf. Section 3.3) in the trunk network and the user access network. However, it is not so evident whether optical transmission should also be used at the interfaces at the S_B and T_B reference points.

As the interface range at S_B and T_B is usually much shorter than the distances that have to be bridged in the access network, electrical media could be employed at S_B and T_B (at least for the 155.520 Mbit/s interface). Such an electrical interface was assessed to be cheaper (at least as a short- and medium-term solution) and easier to handle in terms of installation and maintenance. For the 155.520 Mbit/s interface, a range of up to about 200 m can be covered with an electrical interface; for the 622.080 Mbit/s interface the range would decrease considerably to about 100 m [180].

Use of the same medium for 155.520 Mbit/s and 622.080 Mbit/s would support upgradability of the 155.520 Mbit/s interface to the higher bit rate. The same medium at S_B and T_B would allow for terminal portability from S_B to T_B. The optional use of both media at the interface at either reference point would require medium adaptors in all cases where equipment is to be used that does not comply with the deployed medium.

It should be noted that in the case of electrical interfaces, longer interface ranges than 100 to 200 m can be achieved by, for example, inserting an optical transmission system. This solution, however, requires electrical/optical conversion twice.

ITU-T has specified both an electrical and an optical 155.520 Mbit/s interface to be applied at T_B. The maximum range of the electrical interface depends on the attenuation of the transmission medium. A maximum range of about 100 m can be achieved for micropax (4 mm diameter) and 200 m for cable TV (CATV) type (7 mm diameter) [120]. For the optical interface, the attenuation of the optical path has been specified to be in the range of 0 to 7 dB.

ITU-T Recommendation I.432 [120] has not yet specified the physical properties of the 155.520 Mbit/s interface at the S_B reference point. Commonality between the interfaces at S_B and T_B is the objective.

The feasibility and range of application of an electrical 622.080 Mbit/s interface needs further study. For the optical 622.080 Mbit/s interface the same attenuation range of 0 to 7 dB as for the 155.520 Mbit/s interface has been specified.

Detailed information on the physical medium characteristics of the electrical 155.520 Mbit/s interface and optical interfaces (at both 155.520 Mbit/s and 622.080 Mbit/s) is presented in Tables 5.4 and 5.5.

5.3.2.2   Bit Timing and Interface Code

In normal operation, *timing* for the transmitter is locked to the timing received across the interface. Timing may alternatively be provided locally by the clock of the customer equipment in the case of the cell-based interface option. Locally provided timing will be used under fault conditions; then the interface works in free-running clock mode. For this mode, a tolerance ± 20 ppm has been defined.

Table 5.4: *155.520 Mbit/s electrical interface characteristics*

Item	Specified solution
Attenuation range	0 to 7dB
Transmission medium	two coaxial cables, one for each direction
Wiring configuration	point-to-point
Impedance	75 Ω with a tolerance of $\pm5\%$ in the frequency range 50 to 200 MHz
Attenuation of the electrical path	approximate $\sqrt{f}$ law with a maximum insertion loss of 20 dB at a frequency of 155.520 MHz
Electrical parameters	according to ITU-T Recommendation G.703 [86]

Table 5.5: *Optical interface characteristics for 155.520 Mbit/s and 622.080 Mbit/s*

Item	Specified solution
Attenuation range	0 to 7dB
Transmission medium	two single mode fibres according to ITU-T Recommendation G.652 [84], one for each direction
Operating wavelength	1310 nm (second window)
Optical parameters	according to ITU-T Recommendation G.957 [98]
Safety requirements	parameters for IEC 825 Class 1 devices shall not be exceeded even under failure conditions

Coded mark inversion (CMI) as described in ITU-T Recommendation G.703 [86] has been chosen as the interface code for the electrical 155.520 Mbit/s interface. CMI has several advantages (cf. [180]):

- Simple implementation (e.g. easy clock extraction).

- Zero direct current (DC) and low frequency content.

- Guaranteed signal transitions: the number of transitions in the encoded data stream is independent of the applied data stream. Bit sequence independence required for the interface [117] is easily achieved (and malicious attack to prevent timing extraction is made impossible).

- No bit error multiplication.

- Ability to trace discrete bit errors through code violations.

However, CMI has the drawback of doubling the transmission rate of the CMI-coded signal (baud rate = 2 × bit rate). This is not critical in the case of the

155.520 Mbit/s interface but is clearly disadvantageous for the 622.080 Mbit/s interface.

Therefore the commonly used line coding will be non-return to zero (NRZ) for the optical interfaces at 155.520 Mbit/s and 622.080 Mbit/s. The convention used for the optical logic levels is:

- emission of light for a binary ONE
- no emission of light for a binary ZERO.

The extinction ratio must be in accordance to the definitions given in [98].

5.3.2.3   Power Feeding

An optional power feeding mechanism similar to that used for the primary rate access [119] has been specified in I.432. This method is briefly described.

A separate pair of wires at the interface at the T_B reference point is to be used to power the B-NT1 via this interface. The power sink is fed:

- either by a source under the responsibility of the user when requested by the network provider;
- or by a power supply unit, under the responsibility of the network provider, connected to the mains electric supply on the customer's premises.

When power is provided by the user, the source may be an integral part of the B-NT2 or B-TE, or it may be physically separated from B-NT2 or B-TE as an individual power supply unit.

The power available at the B-NT1 via the user–network interface (at T_B) will be at least 15 W, with the feeding voltage in the range of -20 V to -57 V relative to ground.

The power source must be protected against short circuits and overload, and the power sink of B-NT1 should not be damaged by interchanging the wires.

5.3.2.4   Modes of Operation

The B-ISDN user–network interface is normally in the 'fully active' state [117]. Other modes of operation are under discussion, including an emergency mode in the case of power failure and a deactivated mode to save power. If activation/deactivation is to be implemented it will become necessary to define:

- activation/deactivation signals
- activation/deactivation procedures.

Deactivation of the interface would be used to minimize power consumption during idle periods when no connections are established. The emergency mode is necessary to guarantee minimum communication facilities in the case of power failure. For example, at least one telephone set should work. (This mode requires battery back-up in B-NT1 and/or B-NT2.)

Some considerations regarding economizing on power consumption by establishing a deactivated interface state can be found in [41]. Deactivation allows for:

- extension of the time of the battery-powered operation under power failure conditions (deactivation is especially important in the emergency state);

- reduction of the heat management problem.

These benefits could be increased if activation/deactivation of the interface were accompanied by activation/deactivation of the line. In this case the network operator would also get relief in terms of power consumption and heat management at the local exchange or remote switching/multiplexing/concentrating unit.

In [41] it is reported that in the deactivated state the power consumption of the network termination and line termination is about one-half of the corresponding value in normal (fully active) mode. The time taken to switch from the deactivated state back to the active state is estimated to be about 10 to 50 ms. The same handshake principle as described in ITU-T Recommendation I.430 [118] for the basic access could be used as a basis for the B-ISDN activation/deactivation procedure.

It should be noted that the transition of the interface from deactivated state to active state is not only a physical layer task. It also affects higher layers, such as the ATM layer where recovery procedures may be necessary.

5.4   Additional User–Network Interfaces

5.4.1   Objectives and Overview

Especially during the start-up phase of ATM-based networks, one of the main applications will be data communications between business users. In many cases the full range of possible broadband services may not be required, leading to reduced bit rate requirements at the user–network interface. ATM interfaces at the following bit rates below 155 Mbit/s have been introduced to cater for such applications:

- 100 Mbit/s (at S_B)
- 51.84 Mbit/s (at S_B)
- 34/45 Mbit/s based on PDH bit rates [85]
- 1.5/2 Mbit/s based on PDH bit rates [85] as a 'poor man's ATM interface'.

The rationale for these additional interface types is simply cost-effectiveness, and sometimes the non-availability of SDH-based transmission systems in the access network. The reason for choosing a terminal interface at 52 Mbit/s is the desire to utilize low-cost (preferably existing) in-house cabling; 1.5/2 Mbit/s ATM interfaces can be provided via ordinary copper wiring for telephony using the high-speed digital subscriber line (HDSL) technique [160]. In the following some more technical details about these interfaces are given.

5.4.2 ATM Interfaces based on PDH Bit Rates

ITU-T Recommendation G.804 [91] defines ATM cell mapping into PDH signals. In fact only the PDH bit rates of ITU-T Recommendation G.702 [85] have been retained completely; the old frame structures of the PDH signals have been partly replaced with new ones (described in ITU-T Recommendation G.832 [97]) which are capable of supporting ATM cell transport and SDH element transport.

The 1.5/2 Mbit/s signal frame of ITU-T Recommendation G.704 [87] is used for ATM cell transport by mapping ATM cells into time slots 1 to 24, or 1 to 15 and 17 to 31, respectively. Cell delineation is performed via the HEC mechanism as for the standard 155 Mbit/s interface (see Sections 5.3.1.5 and 5.3.1.6).

The frame structure for the 34 Mbit/s signal is shown in Figure 5.21.

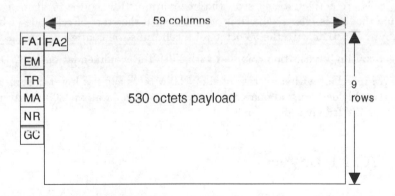

FA   Frame alignment signal
EM   Error monitoring
TR   Trail trace
MA   Maintenance and adaptation byte
NR   Network operator byte
GC   General purpose communications channel

Figure 5.21: *Frame structure at 34.368 Mbit/s*

The functions supported by the above overhead bytes are similar to the SDH functions (cf. Section 5.8.3.1); for a detailed description see [97]. The ATM cells are mapped into the 530 payload bytes.

In contrast to the 34 Mbit/s cell mapping, at 45 Mbit/s (using the multiframe format of ITU-T Recommendation G.704 [87]) the physical layer convergence protocol (PLCP) mapping is employed. PLCP has been adopted from the DQDB-slot mapping.

ATM user–network interfaces at the bit rates of 1.5/2 Mbit/s and 34/45 Mbit/s have not yet been included in ITU-T Recommendation I.432 [120]. However, it is already possible to implement them in compliance with above cell mappings.

5.4.3   'Private' ATM Interfaces

The ATM Forum has specified a **100 Mbit/s multimode fibre ATM interface** based on the FDDI physical layer. This interface is meant to be used as a private UNI which connects customer premises equipment, such as computers, bridges, routers and workstations, to a port on an ATM switch. According to the ATM Forum 'The private UNI does not need the OAM complexity or link distance provided by telecom lines' [10]. Details concerning the physical medium, bit timing and line coding are described in [10].

There is no frame with this interface, and not even a continuous stream of cells. Unless cells are actively being sent, the line contains idle codes. Cells can occur any time the line is idle. Each cell is preceded with the start-of-cell code (1 byte). (This byte, together with the 53 octets of a cell, must be contiguous on the line.)

HEC-generation/verification complies with ITU-T Recommendation I.432 [120].

The ATM interface with a bit rate of about 52 Mbit/s can use lower-cost in-house cabling (unshielded twisted pair) and bridge a distance of about 100 m. A subset of the SONET framing [6] is employed.

5.5   ATM Layer

ITU-T Recommendation I.150 [102] includes the functional characteristics of the ATM layer; its specification is given in ITU-T Recommendation I.361 [110].

5.5.1   Cell Structure

The cell is the basic element of the ATM layer. As mentioned in Section 5.1.5.1, the term 'cell' is also used at the physical layer. A cell consists of a 5 octet header and a 48 octet information field. Its structure is shown in Figure 5.22.

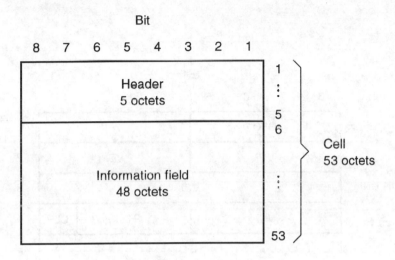

Figure 5.22: *Cell structure*

The following numbering conventions are defined in ITU T Recommendation I.361 [110]:

- Octets are sent in increasing order starting with octet 1. Therefore, the cell header will be sent first, followed by the information field.

- Bits within an octet are sent in decreasing order starting with bit 8.

- For all fields, the first bit sent is the most significant bit (MSB).

5.5.2 Cell Header

The cell header at the B-ISDN UNI differs from that at the B-ISDN network–node interface (NNI) in the use of bits 5–8 of octet 1. The B-ISDN NNI is the interface between network nodes (cf. Section 8.3). At the B-ISDN NNI these bits are part of the VPI, whereas at the B-ISDN UNI they constitute an independent unit, the GFC. Figure 5.23 depicts the cell header used at the B-ISDN UNI and the B-ISDN NNI.

The different fields defined within the cell header have no meaning for physical layer cells. Their significance is restricted to ATM cells.

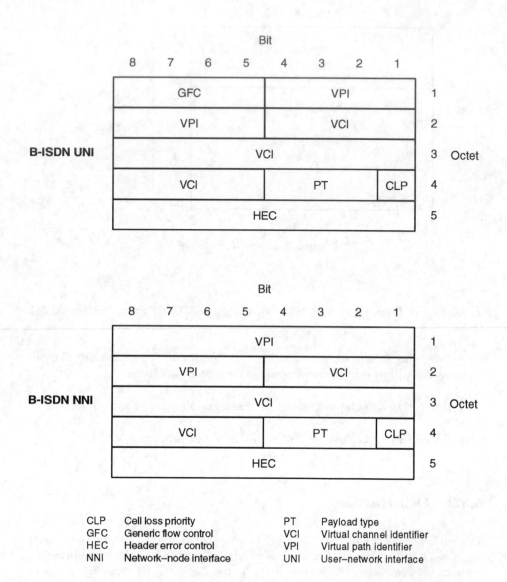

Figure 5.23: *Cell header at the B-ISDN UNI and the B-ISDN NNI*

5.5.2.1 Pre-assigned Cell Header Values

In order to differentiate cells for the use of the ATM layer from those cells only used at the physical layer as well as to identify unassigned cells, pre-assigned cell header values are used. These values are shown in Table 5.6. As shown in the table, physical layer cells and unassigned cells are characterized by an all-0 pattern of the header bits 5–28. All other values of the cell header can be used by assigned cells.

Table 5.6: *Pre-assigned cell header values at the UNI*

Type	Octet 1	Octet 2	Octet 3	Octet 4	Octet 5
Reserved for use of the physical layer	pppp0000	00000000	00000000	0000ppp1	HEC valid code
Unassigned cell	gggg0000	00000000	00000000	0000xxx0	HEC valid code
Meta-signalling	ggggyyyy	yyyy0000	00000000	00010a00	HEC valid code
General broadcast signalling	ggggyyyy	yyyy0000	00000000	00100aa0	HEC valid code
Point-to-point signalling	ggggyyyy	yyyy0000	00000000	01010aa0	HEC valid code
F4 segment OAM flow	ggggzzzz	zzzz0000	00000000	00110a0a	HEC valid code
F4 end-to-end OAM flow	ggggzzzz	zzzz0000	00000000	01000a0a	HEC valid code
Resource management	ggggzzzz	zzzzvvvv	vvvvvvvv	vvvv110a	HEC valid code
Reserved for future functions	ggggzzzz	zzzzvvvv	vvvvvvvv	vvvv111a	HEC valid code

  VCI values from decimal 8 to 15 are reserved for future use
a indicates the bit is available for use by the appropriate ATM layer function
g indicates the bit is available for use by the GFC protocol
p indicates the bit is available for use by the physical layer
v indicates any VCI value other than 0
x indicates the bit is a 'don't care' bit
y any VPI value. For VPI = 0 the specified VCI value is reserved for user signalling
   with the local exchange.
z any VPI value

The differentiation between physical layer cells and unassigned cells is based on the use of the least significant bit (LSB) of octet 4 of the cell header. This bit is thus not used for cell loss priority indication as in the case of assigned cells.

Several types of physical layer cells have already been defined by pre-assigned header values, as shown in Tables 5.2 and 5.3 (see pages 78 and 79). The use of these cells has been demonstrated in Sections 5.3.1.3 and 5.3.1.4. Other cell header values are pre-assigned for signalling, OAM, resource management and future functions (cf. Table 5.6).

5.5.2.2   Generic Flow Control

The **generic flow control** (GFC) field consists of 4 bits. Its default value is 0000 as long as the GFC function is not used. GFC information is carried either in **assigned** or **unassigned** cells [107].

The functional description of the GFC is included in ITU-T Recommendation I.150 [102]. The GFC mechanism helps to control the traffic flow from ATM connections at the B-ISDN UNI. It is used to alleviate short-term overload conditions which may occur in the customer network (cf. Sections 4.7 and 5.2.5).

The GFC mechanism supports both point-to-point and point-to-multipoint configurations. In configurations where each terminal is connected to the B-NT2 via its own line, GFC can be used to reduce the cell flow of each terminal. Because the GFC has no relation with the rest of the cell header, individual control of VPCs, VCCs and terminals which are connected to a common medium is impossible. In shared medium configurations, GFC is used globally for media access control.

The following requirements have to be met by the GFC protocol:

- The GFC protocol must be capable of ensuring that all terminals can access their assured capacities. This will be necessary for all constant bit rate (CBR) terminals as well as those variable bit rate (VBR) terminals which have an element of guaranteed capacity.

- The remaining spare capacity should be shared fairly among all VBR terminals contending for it. However, what does *fair* mean? Two proposals exist for the definition of fair:
  - Each VBR terminal contending for additional bandwidth gets the same amount of the spare capacity.
  - The spare capacity is distributed among the VBR terminals in such a way that each terminal gets the same percentage of the additionally requested bit rate.

- The GFC protocol should also support different delay and delay variation (jitter) requirements. For example, this can be met by introducing different priority levels.

- Direct terminal-to-terminal communication (without involving the B-NT2) should be possible in shared medium configurations. This requires a symmetrical implementation of the GFC procedure.

- The GFC protocol should be insensitive to the traffic mix (for example, number of active CBR and VBR sources, bit rate mix) as well as system parameters like the number of terminals and distance between terminals.

- Sufficient robustness is required in the case of lost, errored or misinserted GFC information.

GFC is provided at the B ISDN UNI, that is, the GFC field is present at the interfaces at the S_B, T_B and SSB reference points. (Here the notation SSB – see Figure 5.24 – is used for shared medium configurations in order to distinguish between different locations of the terminal interface: S_B denotes the reference point between B-NT2 and the first terminal, SSB the reference points between terminals.) GFC provides flow control for the information generated locally by terminals within the customer premises. This traffic may flow to and from the terminal across the interfaces at S_B and SSB. GFC does not control the traffic flow coming from the network.

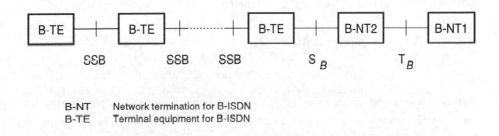

| B-NT | Network termination for B-ISDN |
| B-TE | Terminal equipment for B-ISDN |

Figure 5.24: *Scope of application of GFC*

An ATM network does not provide the sort of flow control which is implemented in packet networks and it has no facilities for storing cells over a longer period of time. Thus there is no need for GFC inside an ATM network. GFC only controls terminals connected to a customer network.

The exact GFC procedure is not yet defined, although several proposals have been made [55]. Some of the proposed GFC procedures are based on a distributed queueing algorithm which is well known from the DQDB network [69]. Modifications were necessary to support CBR traffic and different customer network topologies. Other proposals use a modified Orwell protocol [43] for controlling the cell flow of the terminals.

In order to determine the 'best' protocol, values of some system and traffic parameters (for example, number of active terminals, distances between terminals, service mix, bit rate mix) have been defined which will be the base for a performance evaluation. However, the decision cannot be made only on the results.

Other features like expense of implementation and reliability also have to be taken into account.

Up to now only the **uncontrolled mode** is specified, so no GFC procedure is supported. To differentiate between uncontrolled and **controlled** operation the following applies: any equipment which receives ten or more non-zero GFC fields within 30 000 cell times should consider the other ATM entity to be executing the 'controlled transmission' set of procedures [110].

5.5.2.3   Virtual Path Identifier

The **virtual path identifier** (VPI) field at the B-ISDN UNI consists of 8 bits and is used for routeing. The VPI at the NNI comprises the first 12 bits of the cell header, thus providing enhanced routing capabilities. Pre-assigned VPI values are used for some special purposes. As mentioned in Section 5.5.2.1, all bits of the VPI field are set to zero in an unassigned cell. Table 5.6 shows the currently predefined VPI/VCI values. Other uses of pre-assigned VPIs/VCIs are not excluded.

5.5.2.4   Virtual Channel Identifier

Together with the VPI field, the virtual channel identifier (VCI) field constitutes the routing field of a cell. A field of 16 bits is used for the VCI at the B-ISDN UNI as well as the NNI. It also has some pre-assigned values. The VCI value for unassigned cells is shown in Section 5.5.2.1. With this assignment in mind it is evident that the VCI value of zero is not available for user VC identification. Other pre-assigned VPI/VCI values can be found in Table 5.6, which is still open for further amendments.

5.5.2.5   Payload Type

Three header bits are used for the **payload type** (PT) identification. Table 5.7 describes the payload type identifier (PTI) coding:

The payload of user information cells contains user information as well as service adaptation functions. In network information cells, the payload is used to carry information the network needs for its operation and maintenance. One example is the F5 information flow (see Section 4.6.2) which supports OAM of VCCs. Here the PTI is used to distinguish between user cells and F5 cells pertaining to the same VCC. The **ATM-layer-user-to-ATM-layer-user** (AUU) indication will be used by AAL type 5 (see Section 5.6.5).

The **congestion indication** (CI) bit within the PTI of user cells may be modified by any network element that is congested to inform the end-user about its state.

The exact use of **resource management** cells is currently not defined.

Table 5.7: *PTI values*

PTI	Interpretation
000	User data cell, congestion not experienced, ATM-layer-user-to-ATM-layer-user indication = 0
001	User data cell, congestion not experienced, ATM-layer-user-to-ATM-layer-user indication = 1
010	User data cell, congestion experienced, ATM-layer-user-to-ATM-layer-user indication = 0
011	User data cell, congestion experienced, ATM-layer-user-to-ATM-layer-user indication = 1
100	OAM F5 segment associated cell
101	OAM F5 end-to-end associated cell
110	Resource management cell
111	Reserved for future functions

5.5.2.6 Cell Loss Priority

The **cell loss priority** (CLP) field consists of one bit which is used explicitly to indicate the cell loss priority. If the value of the CLP bit is '1' the cell is subject to discard, depending on the network conditions. However, the agreed quality of service (QOS) parameters will not be violated. In the other case (CLP = '0'), the cell has high priority and therefore sufficient network resources have to be allocated to it. The CLP bit may be set by the user or the service provider. Cells belonging to a CBR connection always have high priorities. Many VBR services require a guaranteed minimum capacity as well as a peak capacity. Some of these services may take advantage of the CLP bit to distinguish between cells of high and low loss sensitivity.

When a VBR connection is established, the rate of higher priority cells is determined. However, it can be renegotiated during the connection phase. Cells of higher priority which exceed the agreed parameters are subject to the normal UPC/NPC.

5.5.2.7 Header Error Control

This field is part of the cell header but it is not used by the ATM layer. It contains the **header error control** (HEC) sequence which is processed by the physical layer. The HEC mechanism is specified in ITU-T Recommendation I.432 [120]. A description of the mechanism is given in Section 5.3.1.5.

5.5.3   ATM Layer Connections

An ATM layer connection is the concatenation of ATM layer links in order to provide an end-to-end transfer capability to access points.

The VPI is used to distinguish different VP links which are multiplexed at the ATM layer into the same physical layer connection at an interface in one direction. Different VC links within a VPC are identified by their individual VCIs.

Two VCs belonging to different VPs at the same interface may have identical VCI values. Consequently both the VCI and VPI are necessary to correctly identify a VC.

A VPI is changed at points where a VP link is terminated (for example, cross-connect, concentrator and switch), while the VCI is changed at points where VC links are terminated. In this way, VCI values are preserved within a VPC.

5.5.3.1   Active Connections at the B-ISDN UNI

At the B-ISDN UNI, 24 bits are available for routing. However, the actual number of bits used is negotiated between the user and the network (for example, on subscription basis). The lower requirements of the user or the network determine the number of active routing bits. The following rules have been agreed by ITU-T [110] for the determination of the position of active routing bits within the VPI/VCI field:

- used bits of the VPI field and the VCI field will be contiguous;

- bit allocation will always begin with the LSB of its appropriate field;

- unallocated bits of the routing field, that is, bits not used by either the user or the network, will be set to zero.

5.5.3.2   Virtual Channel Connections

The virtual channel connection (VCC) is defined in ITU-T Recommendation I.113 [99] as follows (cf. Section 4.2.1):

> 'A concatenation of virtual channel links that extends between
> two points where the adaptation layer is accessed.'

One of four methods can be used to establish a VCC at the B-ISDN UNI:

1. Semi-permanent or permanent VCCs are established at subscription time. No signalling procedure is necessary.

2. A VCC is established/released by using a meta-signalling procedure. This approach is applied for establishing a signalling VC only (see Section 4.3.3).

3. Establishment/release of a switched end-to-end VCC can be done by a user-to-network signalling procedure.

4. If a VPC already exists between two B-ISDN UNIs, a VCC within this VPC can be established/released by employing a user-to-user signalling procedure.

Cell sequence integrity is preserved within a VCC. Traffic parameters are individually negotiated between the user and the network at VCC establishment. These parameters can be renegotiated during the connection phase. All cells originating from the user are monitored by the network to ensure that the agreed parameters are not violated. This mechanism is called usage parameter control (details can be found in Section 4.5.1.3).

The QOS for the connection is negotiated between the user and the network when the VCC is established.

The VCI can be determined by the network or the user, or by negotiation between network and user, otherwise a standardized value will be used. In general the value of the VCI field is independent of the service provided over that VC. However, to simplify terminal interchangeability and initialization, the same VCI value will be used at all B-ISDN UNIs for some fundamental functions, such as meta-signalling.

5.5.3.3   Virtual Path Connections

The definition of the virtual path connection (VPC) is given in ITU-T Recommendation I.113 [99] (cf. Section 4.2.1):

> 'A concatenation of virtual path links that extends between the point where the virtual channel identifier values are assigned and the point where those values are translated or removed.'

One of the following methods can be used to establish/release a VPC between VPC endpoints:

1. A VPC is established/released on a subscription basis and therefore no signalling procedure is necessary.

2. VPC establishment/release may be controlled by the customer. Network management procedures are used for this purpose.

3. A VPC can also be established/released by the network using network management procedures.

Cell sequence integrity within a VPC is preserved for each VCC carried and for the VPC as a whole. During VPC establishment, the traffic parameters for the VPC are negotiated between the user and the network. If necessary, these parameters can subsequently be renegotiated. Changing these traffic parameters can

improve traffic performance [65]. All input cells from the user to the network are
monitored to supervise the agreed traffic parameters.

At VPC establishment, the QOS is selected from the range of QOS classes supported by the network. A VPC can carry VCCs requiring different QOS classes.
Therefore, the QOS of the VPC must meet the most demanding QOS of the VCCs
carried.

Some VCIs within a VPC may be reserved for, say, network OAM (for example,
to implement the F4 flow, see Section 4.6.2) and will not be available to the user.

5.6   ATM Adaptation Layer

The AAL functions have already been described in Section 5.1.5.4. The AAL provides for the mapping of higher layer PDUs into the information field of cells and
the reassembly of these PDUs. Other AAL functions support different applications. The detailed specification of the AAL (see also ITU-T Recommendation
I.363 [112]) is presented in the following.

Several AAL protocol types are defined. Each type consists of a specific SAR
sublayer and CS. This classification fits the AAL service classes described in
Section 5.1.5.4 (for example, CBR services of class A will use AAL type 1). However, no strict relationship between the AAL service classes and the AAL protocol
types is requested. Other combinations of the described SAR and CS protocols
or other SAR and/or CS protocols may also be used to support specific services.
The definitions and relationships between PDU, SDU and PCI are described in
Section 5.1.2.

5.6.1   AAL Type 0

Although 'AAL type 0' is not an officially used term it can be considered important, being an AAL with empty SAR and CS. This means that no AAL functionality is required and that the content of the cell information field is directly and
transparently transferred to the higher layer. However, a detailed description of
such a service is not yet available in ITU-T standards.

5.6.2   AAL Type 1

Normally, **CBR services** (class A) use AAL type 1 because it receives/delivers
SDUs with a constant bit rate from/to the layer above. **Timing information** is
also transferred between source and destination. If necessary, information about
the **data structure** can be conveyed too. Indication of lost or errored information
is sent to the higher layer if these failures cannot be recovered within the AAL.

The functions performed by the AAL are as follows:

- segmentation and reassembly of user information
- handling of cell delay variation
- handling of cell payload assembly delay
- handling of lost and misinserted cells
- source clock frequency recovery at the receiver
- recovery of the source data structure at the receiver
- monitoring of AAL-PCI for bit errors as well as handling those errors
- monitoring of the user information field for bit errors and possible corrective actions.

In the case of **circuit emulation**, monitoring of the end-to-end QOS is necessary. This will be located at the CS. For this purpose, a cyclic redundancy check (CRC) may be calculated for the information carried in one or more cells. The result is transferred to the receiver within the information field of a cell or in a special OAM cell.

Circuit emulation is believed to be an important feature of B-ISDN as it allows existing circuit-based signals (e.g. 1.5 Mbit/s or 2 Mbit/s) to be transported, meeting the requirements on delay, jitter, bit error rate etc., for such signals. The user will not even be aware of the transfer mechanism involved.

5.6.2.1 Segmentation and Reassembly Sublayer

The SAR-PDU consists of 48 octets. The first octet includes the PCI; all other octets are available for the SAR-PDU payload. The PCI is subdivided into a 4 bit **sequence number** (SN) and a 4 bit **sequence number protection** (SNP) field. The SN consists of a **convergence sublayer indication** (CSI) bit and a 3 bit **sequence count** field. The SNP field contains a 3 bit CRC which protects the SN field and a even parity bit which has to be calculated over the resulting 7 bit code word. Figure 5.25 shows the SAR-PDU format of AAL type 1.

The sequence count value of the SN makes it possible to detect the loss or misinsertion of cells. For systems with high cell loss ratios this method is not very robust since the 3 bit sequence count field is relatively short. The CSI bit can be used to transfer timing information and/or information about the data structure.

The SNP provides error detection and correction capabilities. The following two-step approach will be used which allows the correction of all single-bit errors and the detection of multiple-bit errors:

1. The SN is protected by the polynomial $G(x) = x^3 + x + 1$.
2. The resulting 7 bit code word is protected by an even parity check.

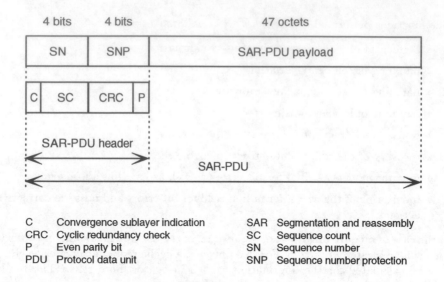

Figure 5.25: *SAR-PDU format for AAL type 1*

5.6.2.2   Convergence Sublayer

The functions of the CS depend strongly on the service to be supported. Some of these functions are listed in the following. If required a clock may be derived from the terminal interface. Examples on how these functions can be performed are also given:

- Handling of **cell delay variation**. A buffer is used to support this function. Buffer underflow or overflow may lead to the insertion of dummy bits or the dropping of excessive bits, respectively.

- Further handling of lost and misinserted cells, such as the insertion of dummy information or discarding of gained cells.

- **Source clock frequency recovery** using the synchronous residual time stamp method (SRTS). A residual time stamp (RTS) is used to measure and convey information about the frequency difference between a common reference clock derived from the network clock and a service clock. The 4 bit RTS is transferred by the CSI bit in successive SAR-PDU headers with an odd number of the sequence count field (SN = 1, 3, 5, 7). For details of this method see [112].

- Transfer of **structure information** between source and destination, for example, to support 8 kHz-based frame formats in circuit-mode services. Two modes of operation are possible, called **non-P** and **P** format. For the

P format an additional pointer field (1 octet) is provided in the SAR-PDU payload. This pointer indicates the start of a structured block. For P format operations the CSI value in SAR-PDU headers with an even SN (that is, SN = 0, 2, 4, 6) is set to 1. For details of this method see [112].

- **Forward error correction** (FEC) may be used to ensure high quality for some video and audio applications. This may be combined with bit interleaving to give more secure protection against errors. One example of an FEC for unidirectional video services uses a Reed–Solomon code; it is described in [112]. This method increases the overhead by 3.1% and the introduced delay is 128 cell cycles.

5.6.3   AAL Type 2

AAL type 2 is proposed for **VBR services** with a timing relation between source and destination (class B, for example, VBR audio or video). This type is not well defined yet and only the services and functions described below can be anticipated. It might also be possible that AAL type 1 is enhanced to provide AAL type 2 functions.

AAL type 2 provides services to the adjacent higher layer. They include the following features:

- SDUs originating from a variable bit rate source are exchanged between the AAL and the higher layer.

- Timing information is transferred between source and destination.

- If needed, the higher layer can be informed about errors (loss and misinsertion of cells) which cannot be corrected by the AAL.

So far the following functions have been defined which may be performed by the AAL to enhance the service provided by the ATM layer:

- segmentation and reassembly of user information

- handling of cell delay variation

- handling of lost or misinserted cells

- recovery of the source clock at the receiver

- monitoring of the AAL-PCI for bit errors and handling of these errors

- monitoring of the user information field for bit errors and possible corrective actions.

5.6.4   AAL Type 3/4

The name of this AAL reflects its development: as the service classes were specified, separate AALs were allocated for class C and class D services, namely AAL type 3 and AAL type 4. In the meantime both types have merged, thereby supporting both service classes.

Figure 5.26 shows the general structure of this AAL; the CS is split into a **common part** (CPCS) and a **service-specific part**. The service-specific convergence sublayer (SSCS) is application dependent and may be null; it is not discussed in this chapter.

Data applications like CBDS and SMDS (see Section 5.7.2.4) make use of AAL type 3/4.

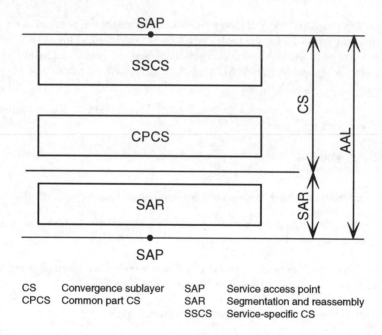

CS	Convergence sublayer	SAP	Service access point
CPCS	Common part CS	SAR	Segmentation and reassembly
		SSCS	Service-specific CS

Figure 5.26: *AAL type 3/4*

Two modes of service are defined for AAL type 3/4. The **message mode** service can be used for framed data transfer (for example, high-level data link control frame), and the **streaming mode** service is suitable for the transfer of low-speed data with low delay requirements. The application of these modes to a particular service depends on the service requirements.

The message mode service transports a single AAL-SDU in one, or (optionally) more than one, CS-PDU, which may build one or more SAR-PDUs. Figure 5.27 shows the operation of this mode.

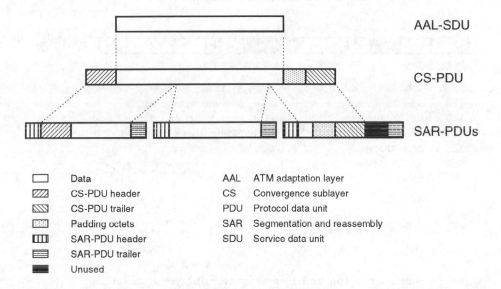

Figure 5.27: *Message mode service*

In the streaming mode, one or more fixed-size AAL-SDUs are transported in one CS-PDU. The AAL-SDU may be as small as 1 octet and is always delivered as one unit, because only this unit will be recognized by the application (one SAR-SDU contains at most one AAL-SDU). Figure 5.28 illustrates the operation of the streaming mode service.

Two peer-to-peer operation procedures are offered by both service modes:

- **Assured operation**: The assured operation retransmits missing or errored AAL-SDUs, therefore flow control is provided as a mandatory feature. This operation mode may be restricted to point-to-point connections at the ATM layer.

- **Non-assured operation**: In this mode, lost or errored AAL-SDUs are not corrected by retransmission. The delivery of corrupted AAL-SDUs to the user may be provided as an optional feature. In principle, flow control can be applied to point-to-point ATM layer connections. No flow control will be provided for point-to-multipoint ATM layer connections.

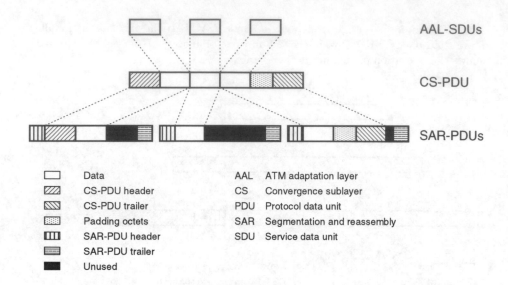

Figure 5.28: *Streaming mode service*

5.6.4.1   Segementation and Reassembly Sublayer

In general CS-PDUs are of variable length. When accepting such a PDU, the SAR sublayer generates SAR-PDUs containing up to 44 octets of CS-PDU data. The CS-PDU is preserved by the SAR sublayer. This requires a **segment type** (ST) indication and a SAR payload fill indication. The ST indication identifies a SAR-PDU as being **beginning of message** (BOM), **continuation of message** (COM), **end of message** (EOM) or **single-segment message** (SSM). The payload fill indication represents the number of octets of a CS-PDU contained in the SAR-PDU payload. In the case of message mode service, the SAR-PDU payload of all BOMs and COMs contains exactly 44 octets, whereas the payload of EOMs and SSMs is of variable length. In streaming mode, the SAR-PDU payload of all segments depends on the AAL-SDUs.

Error detection is the second function of the SAR sublayer. This function includes detecting bit errors in the SAR-PDU as well as detecting lost or misinserted SAR-PDUs. An indication is sent to the CS if one of these errors occurs.

The third function of the SAR sublayer is the concurrent multiplexing/demultiplexing of CS-PDUs from multiple AAL connections over a single ATM layer connection.

To support all these functions, 4 octets are used (2 for the SAR-PDU header and 2 for the SAR-PDU trailer). Therefore, of the 48 octets of the SAR-PDU only 44 remain for the payload. Figure 5.29 illustrates the SAR-PDU format. The coding of this PDU conforms to the conventions and rules described in Section 5.5.1.

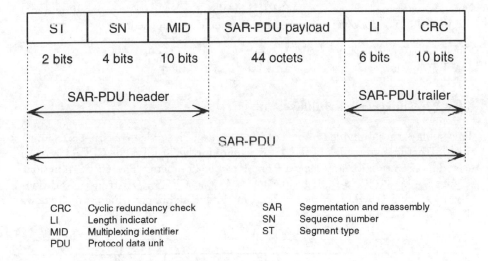

ST	SN	MID	SAR-PDU payload	LI	CRC
2 bits	4 bits	10 bits	44 octets	6 bits	10 bits

SAR-PDU header

SAR-PDU trailer

SAR-PDU

CRC	Cyclic redundancy check	SAR	Segmentation and reassembly
LI	Length indicator	SN	Sequence number
MID	Multiplexing identifier	ST	Segment type
PDU	Protocol data unit		

Figure 5.29: *SAR-PDU format for AAL type 3/4*

The segment type consists of 2 bits which are used to identify a BOM, COM, EOM or SSM.

Four bits are available for the sequence number field. The SN of a SAR-PDU is incremented by '1' relative to the SN of the previous SAR-PDU belonging to the same AAL connection (numbering modulo 16).

The remaining 10 bits of the SAR-PDU header form the **multiplexing identifier** (MID) field. SAR-PDUs with an identical MID value belong to a particular CS-PDU. The MID field assists in the interleaving of ATM-SDUs from different CS-PDUs and reassembly of these CS-PDUs. If multiple AAL connections use the same ATM layer connection, these AAL connections must have identical QOS characteristics. Multiplexing/demultiplexing is done on an end-to-end basis. The ATM layer connection which is used by different AAL connections is administered as a single entity.

The SAR-PDU field (44 octets) is filled with CS-PDU data (left justified). If this field is not fully filled the remaining unused bits are coded as zero.

The **length indicator** (LI) field consists of 6 bits and contains the number of octets, binary coded, from the CS-PDU which are included in the SAR-PDU payload field (with a maximum of 44 octets). An LI value of 63 is associated with an ST indicating an EOM leads to an abortion of partially transmitted CS-SDUs at the receiver.

The CRC field (10 bits) is filled with the result obtained from a CRC calculation which is performed across the SAR-PDU header, the SAR-PDU payload field and the LI field. The following generating polynomial is proposed:

$$G(x) = x^{10} + x^9 + x^5 + x^4 + x + 1$$

The LSB of the result is right-justified in the CRC field.

5.6.4.2   Convergence Sublayer

This sublayer is subdivided into a common part and a service-specific part. Functions, structure and coding of the SSCS require further study. The CPCS transfers user data frames with any length from 1 to 65535 octets. The CPCS functions require a 4 octet CPCS-PDU header and a 4 octet CPCS-PDU trailer. Additionally, a padding (PAD) field is provided for 32 bit alignment. Figure 5.30 shows the CPCS-PDU format.

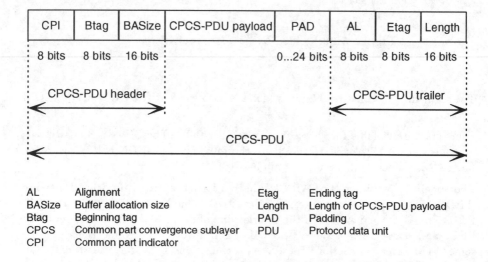

AL	Alignment	Etag	Ending tag
BASize	Buffer allocation size	Length	Length of CPCS-PDU payload
Btag	Beginning tag	PAD	Padding
CPCS	Common part convergence sublayer	PDU	Protocol data unit
CPI	Common part indicator		

Figure 5.30: *CPCS-PDU format for AAL type 3/4*

The common part indicator (CPI) field is used to interpret the remaining fields in the CPCS-PDU header and trailer. Currently it is set to all zeros and the resulting interpretation of the other fields is described in the following (other settings might be used to identify AAL layer management messages and are for further study).

The beginning tag (Btag) and ending tag (Etag) fields allow the proper association of CPCS-PDU header and trailer. The same numerical value is set into both fields. The BASize fields indicates to the receiving peer entity the maximum buffering requirements to receive the CPCS-SDU. The PAD field ensures that the CPCS-PDU payload is an integer multiple of 4 octets. It may be 0 to 3 octets long and does not convey any information. Similarly, the alignment (AL) field is used for 32 bit alignment of the CPCS-PDU trailer. The length field is used to encode the length of the CPCS-PDU payload field. It is also used by the receiver to detect the loss or gain of information.

5.6.5 AAL Type 5

AAL type 5 will be applied to variable bit rate sources without a timing relation between source and destination. It provides services similar to AAL type 3/4 and will mainly be used for data applications. The reason for defining this additional AAL type was its reduced overhead ('simple and efficient AAL'). Its message mode service, streaming mode service and assured/non-assured operation are identical to those defined in Section 5.6.4 for AAL type 3/4. However, one essential difference is that AAL type 5 does not support a multiplexing function, so there is no MID field. AAL type 5 will be used for signalling and frame relay over ATM. It is anticipated that it will also be used for future data applications.

AAL type 5 is subdivided into an SAR and CS, so the structure is the same as in Figure 5.26. The CS is further subdivided into a CPCS and an SSCS. This SSCS is application dependent and may be null. If needed, one possible function of the SSCS might be the multiplexing of different AAL connections (as known from the AAL 3/4 using the MID field). Another example of an SSCS can be found in Section 5.7.3.

5.6.5.1 Segmentation and Reassembly Sublayer

The SAR sublayer accepts SDUs which are an integer multiple of 48 octets from the CPCS. No additional overhead, that is, no more fields, are added to the received SDUs at the SAR sublayer. Only segmentation and, in the reverse direction, reassambling functions are performed. For the recognition of the beginning and end of a SAR-PDU, AAL type 5 makes use of the AUU parameter. This parameter is part of the PT field in the ATM header (cf. Section 5.5.2.5). An AUU parameter value of '1' indicates the end of a SAR-SDU, while a value of '0' indicates the beginning or continuation of a SAR-SDU. Thus a ST field (as provided in AAL type 3/4) is not used. The fact that this AAL type makes use of information conveyed in the ATM cell header can be considered as 'level mixing'. This means that the operations of AAL type 5 are no longer completely independent of the underlying ATM layer, which is an obvious infringement of the PRM specified for

ATM (cf. Section 5.1). Nevertheless, it was adopted because of its simplicity and efficiency.

5.6.5.2   Convergence Sublayer

The CPCS provides for the transfer of user data frames with any length from 1 to 65 535 octets. Additionally, 1 octet of user-to-user information is transparently transferred with each CPCS-PDU. A CRC-32 is used to detect bit errors. The CPCS-PDU format of AAL type 5 is shown in Figure 5.31.

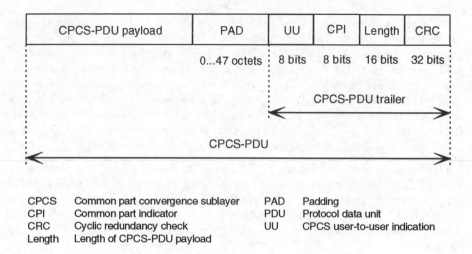

CPCS	Common part convergence sublayer	PAD	Padding
CPI	Common part indicator	PDU	Protocol data unit
CRC	Cyclic redundancy check	UU	CPCS user-to-user indication
Length	Length of CPCS-PDU payload		

Figure 5.31: *CPCS-PDU format for AAL type 5*

The functions of the CPCS require an 8 octet CPCS-PDU trailer. In addition, a PAD field provides for a 48 octet alignment of the CPCS-PDU.

The CPCS user-to-user indication field is used for the transparent transfer of CPCS user-to-user information. Functions of the CPI fields may be similar to those described for AAL type 3/4. For the time being it is merely used to align the CPCS-PDU trailer to 64 bits. The length field is used to encode the length of the CPCS-PDU payload field. It is also used by the receiver to detect the loss or gain of information. Setting the length field to zero leads to partially transmitted CPCS-SDUs being aborted. The CRC-32 is used to detect bit errors in the CPCS-PDU.

5.7 Higher Layers and Interworking of the User Plane

In the previous sections the lower layers (physical layer, ATM layer and AAL) of the B-ISDN PRM were described. Some aspects of higher layer protocols will be presented in this section. Control plane issues (signalling) will be dealt with in Chapter 6.

5.7.1 General

The higher layers of the user plane comprise all the service-specific protocols which are necessary for end-to-end communication. The higher layer protocols should be independent of the protocols used by the underlying layers.

In principle, existing higher layer protocols may be suitable. For some applications the existing higher layer protocols can be simplified because functions of higher layers are already performed by the ATM layer or the AAL. In other cases it may be necessary to extend existing protocols. In the long run, new optimized protocols may be developed to make the most efficient use of ATM-based networks.

5.7.2 Connectionless Service in B-ISDN

Besides **connection-oriented** (CO) communication, B-ISDN also supports **connectionless** (CL) communication. The provision of CL services in the B-ISDN may be important because one of the first applications in B-ISDN will be the interconnection of LANs/MANs which at present use predominantly CL protocols. As only the CO technique exists at the B-ISDN ATM layer, the CL services have to be realized on top of ATM. ITU-T Recommendation I.211 [103] describes two mechanisms for supporting CL services in the B-ISDN. ITU-T Recommendation I.327 [108] specifies the concept of CL capabilities within the B-ISDN functional architecture.

5.7.2.1 Connection-Oriented and Connectionless Communication

Many applications, like constant bit rate services or the X.25 data service [150], are best handled by CO communications. A connection has to be established before information transfer can start. This can be either a physical or a virtual connection. A separate procedure is necessary for establishing a connection. During this phase the path for the succeeding information transfer will be determined and the necessary resources will be reserved.

However, applications like mail services and other data services are characterized by sporadic behaviour and a small amount of data. For reasons of time and expense, no connection is established. Instead, user information is delivered in a message which includes all the necessary addressing and routing information. Each message is handled separately and therefore message sequence integrity cannot be guaranteed. There is also no guarantee of delivery and no acknowledgement of delivery within that layer.

5.7.2.2   Indirect Provision of Connectionless Service

In the first approach the CL service is provided *indirectly* via the B-ISDN CO service (see Figure 5.32). Transparent ATM layer connections are used between the B-ISDN interfaces. These connections may be either permanent, reserved or on demand. The CL protocols are transparent for the B-ISDN because all CL services and AAL functions are implemented outside the B-ISDN. CL services are independent of the protocols within B-ISDN. Support for CL services based on this approach is always possible.

The full intermeshing of the B-ISDN interfaces requires a lot of ATM layer connections. The use of permanent and reserved connections results in an inefficient deployment of these connections, whereas switched connections (establishment at the start of the CL service session) lead to increased signalling traffic for call/connection control as well as long call/connection set-up times. One of the characteristic features of the CL services used in LANs or MANs is the short

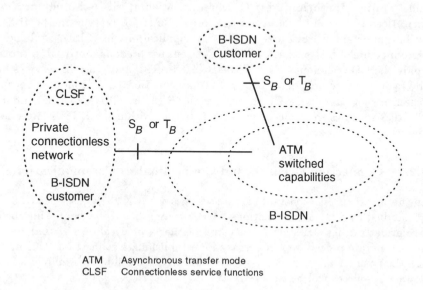

ATM   Asynchronous transfer mode
CLSF   Connectionless service functions

Figure 5.32: *Indirect provision of connectionless service*

transfer delay. In order to retain this feature, the connection set-up time should also be very short in B-ISDN.

The indirect provision of CL services is only applicable in the case of a few CL service users which are attached to B-ISDN. This approach can be considered as an interim solution.

5.7.2.3 Direct Provision of Connectionless Service

The second approach *directly* supports the CL service via the B-ISDN (see Figure 5.33). Connectionless service functions (CLSFs) may be located within or outside the B-ISDN; they terminate the CL protocols and route cells to their destination according to the routing information included in the cells.

The CL service is again on top of ATM. This requires an ATM connection between each user and the CLSFs which are implemented in the CL server. Such a connec-

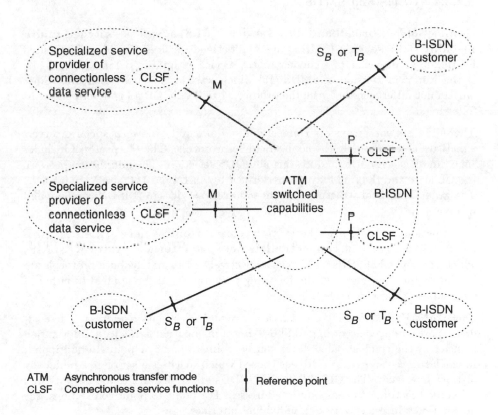

Figure 5.33: *Direct provision of connectionless service*

tion will be either pre-configured, semi-permanent or switched. Semi-permanent connections can be VPCs or VCCs, whereas switched connections will only be realized by VCCs. In the case of semi-permanent VPCs, all VCCs within the VPC could be used by CL services.

In the case of switched connections it may happen that a message cannot be delivered from the destination CLSF to the destination user because no connection exists. The destination CLSF will then reject the message.

The indirect provision of CL services for n users requires $n \times (n-1)/2$ connections for full intermeshing. In a system with direct provision of CL services and only one CL server, n connections are required for n users. The number of CL servers depends on the size of the B-ISDN and the volume of CL traffic to be handled. CLSFs can be implemented in a specific service node or in a separate part of an ATM switching node.

5.7.2.4   CBDS and SMDS

Connectionless broadband data service (CBDS) as well as **switched multi-megabit data service** (SMDS) are well-defined services which are both used for the direct provision of a connectionless service within the B-ISDN. CBDS [42] is the European version of SMDS [15] which was developed by Bellcore. Since only minor differences between the protocols exist, only CBDS is described in the following.

The ATM network transfers connectionless data units between specific servers which are able to handle the connectionless protocols. The CL protocol includes such functions as routing, addressing and QOS selection. The adaptation between the CL layer and the ATM layer is performed by AAL type 3/4 (see Section 5.6.4). The general protocol structure for connectionless services in B-ISDN can be found in Figure 5.34.

A distinction has to be made between the **connectionless network access protocol** (CLNAP) and the **connectionless network interface protocol** (CLNIP) which are applied at UNIs and NNIs, respectively. Fortunately, both protocols are similar so the description in the following paragraphs can be applied to either of them unless otherwise stated.

Each CLNAP/CLNIP-PDU contains a source and a destination address. These addresses are modelled according to ITU-T Recommendation E.164 [81]. Information transfer at the connectionless layer can be point-to-point or point-to-multipoint. In the latter case a **group address** is used which specifies a set of geographically distinct interfaces. The CLNAP/CLNIP-PDUs are copied inside the network and delivered according to these group addresses. For point-to-point connections, the destination address specifies an individual interface.

The size of the user data fields carrying the CLNAP/CLNIP-SDUs is variable,

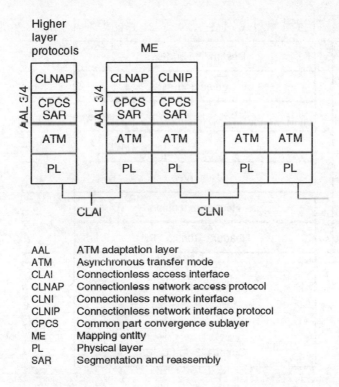

AAL	ATM adaptation layer
ATM	Asynchronous transfer mode
CLAI	Connectionless access interface
CLNAP	Connectionless network access protocol
CLNI	Connectionless network interface
CLNIP	Connectionless network interface protocol
CPCS	Common part convergence sublayer
ME	Mapping entity
PL	Physical layer
SAR	Segmentation and reassembly

Figure 5.34: *Protocol structure for connectionless service*

with an upper limit of 9188 octets for CLNAP-SDUs and 9236 octets for CLNIP-SDUs. The CLNAP-PDU has a maximum length of 9232 octets (maximum 9188 octets user data plus 40 octets CLNAP-PDU header plus 4 octets CRC). With the 4 octet alignment header, the CLNIP-SDU can be as long as 9236 octets. SDUs are transparently transferred through the connectionless layer in a 'best effort' manner, that is, lost or corrupted data units are not retransmitted. Figure 5.35 shows the structure of the CLNIP-PDU. The structure of the CLNAP-PDU is the same, with three exceptions:

1. The protocol identifier field, which is called the **higher layer protocol identifier** (HLPI) is transparently carried end-to-end by the network (except CLNAP-PDUs with HLPI values from 44 to 47, which are discarded).

2. The header extension post pad field does not exist, so up to 20 octets can be used for the header extension field.

3. The maximum length of the user data field is 9188 octets.

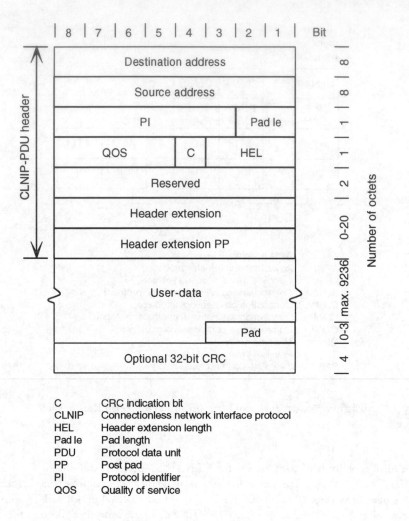

Figure 5.35: *Structure of the CLNIP-PDU*

The functions performed by AAL type 3/4 are identical to those for CLNAP and CLNIP. AAL type 3/4 provides a transparent and sequential transfer of CLNAP/CLNIP-PDUs between two layer entities in an unassured manner. This means that lost or corrupted data units are not retransmitted. More than one AAL 3/4 connection on a single ATM connection is possible by using different MID values (see Section 5.6.4). CLNAP/CLNIP-PDU sequence integrity is preserved for any individual AAL 3/4 connection. No SSCS functions are necessary; information is transferred either in message mode or in streaming mode:

- **Message mode**: In this mode the CL server collects all SAR-PDUs belonging to one CS-PDU and reconstructs this PDU (see Section 5.6.4). Then the routeing function is performed, after which the message is segmented again. Because of the reassembly function, this approach requires a large buffer capacity within each CL server. This may cause high transfer delays. The advantage of this method is the feasibility of detecting errored CS-PDUs and discarding them (unburden the network from worthless PDUs).

- **Streaming mode**: This approach takes advantage of the fact that as soon as a BOM has been received in the CL server the routing function can be performed because the BOM payload includes the destination address. The routing table will be updated with the correspondence of the incoming VPI/VCI/MID combination and the appropriate outgoing one. All COMs and the EOM belonging to a message are routed by a simple look-up in the routing table. After processing the EOM the corresponding registration in the routing table is deleted. When using this method, only a small buffer capacity per CL message is necessary in each CL server, enabling the transfer delay of a message to be kept low. This approach is similar to the CO technique of the ATM layer. A BOM is processed like a connection set-up message and the routing of the COMs and EOMs can be performed by the same mechanism used for cells.

The **mapping entity** (shown in Figure 5.34) is responsible for the proper encapsulation/decapsulation of CLNAP-PDUs into/from CLNIP-SDUs. After adding an alignment header to the CLNAP-PDU it is encapsulated into the CLNIP-PDU. The entire process, including the necessary AAL type 3/4 procedures, is shown in Figure 5.36. (The encapsulation technique need not be applied for NNIs within a single network operator's domain.)

Several 'access classes' are defined for CBDS. These classes constitute the maximum allowed rate with which a user can transfer information into the network. An access class enforcement mechanism is applied at the network entry point, limiting the actual transferred information rate. An access class is defined by three parameters [42]:

1. **Maximum information rate** (MIR): the maximum instantaneous value of the information rate during transmission of a burst.

2. **Sustained information rate** (SIR): the long term average of the information rate for bursty traffic.

3. **PDUs per time unit** (PPTU): the long-term average PDU rate for bursty traffic.

At the entry point to an ATM network the UPC function enforces the peak cell rate, which can easily be deduced from the MIR by using the following formula:

$$ATM \ peak \ cell \ rate = MIR \times (9188 + 44 + 8)/(9188 \times 44 \times 8)$$

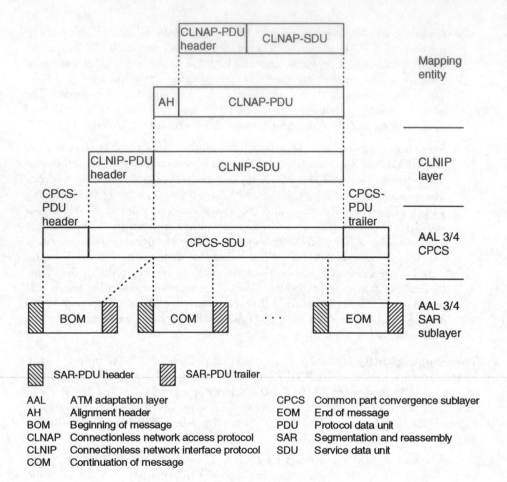

Figure 5.36: *CLNAP-PDU encapsulation*

How the UPC will enforce the SIR and PPTU is for further study. In DQDB networks these parameters are controlled by a mechanism called the 'credit manager' [69].

5.7.3   Frame Relay via B-ISDN

5.7.3.1   What is Frame Relay good for?

The need for fast and effective interconnection of LANs was the main incentive for the development of **frame relay** (FR). FR is based on the ISDN; compared with the available alternatives, such as leased-line services and X.25 [150] networks, it has some remarkable advantages:

1. high throughput

2. low delay (in contrast to X.25)

3. efficient use of resources (statistical multiplexing)

4. standards compliance.

FR is a **connection-oriented** communication technique. It allows statistical multiplexing of several connections, thus taking into account the bursty nature of typical LAN traffic.

Since modern digital networks can be operated at very low bit error rates, there is less need for stringent link-by-link error correcting mechanisms. Therefore, frame relay provides no error correction procedures inside the network. This leads to lower delays in comparison with, for instance, X.25 [150] networks because the processing of frames at network nodes can be limited to some very basic operations. However, frames with bit errors and invalid routing information can be detected and are discarded at FR network elements. The endpoints of a connection are responsible for detecting lost frames and have to initiate retransmission when required. This has to be done by higher layer protocols.

Frame relay is a **packet-based** technology and therefore similar to ATM. FR packets are called frames. The main difference between the technologies is the variable length of the frames in FR as compared with the fixed-sized cells in ATM. Although the transfer delay in FR is lower than in X.25, real-time services such as voice and video communications are restricted to small, geographically limited networks.

FR frames carry routing information, called the **data link connection identifier** (DLCI), which has only local (link-by-link) significance. A discard eligibility (DE) bit is defined which is similar to the CLP bit, and two bits are used for congestion notification. Frames are relayed according to the address information along a virtual connection. These virtual connections can be either permanent (established by subscription) or switched (established and released on demand via ISDN signalling procedures). Several virtual connections can share the same physical access line. The available transmission capacity can be used by each virtual connection up to the physical limits (bandwidth on demand). Bandwidth not being used by one virtual connection can be utilized by others (statistical multiplexing). For management purposes, special management frames are defined which can be recognized through a predefined DLCI value (similar to OAM cells). These management frames are used for the supervision of PVCs. They provide a means of determining the statuses of the physical and logical links between network and user equipment.

ITU-T Recommendation Q.922 [134] describes the core functions used to support the frame relaying bearer service:

- frame delineation and alignment
- frame multiplexing/demultiplexing using the address field
- inspection of the frame to ensure that it consists of an integral number of octets
- inspection of the frame to ensure that it is neither too long nor too short
- detection of (but not recovery from) transmission errors
- congestion control functions.

Frame relay operates at OSI layer 2. One great advantage is the possible use of existing hardware and software. Frames carry both FR routing information and user data. The payload is transparently transported, allowing the use of existing higher layer protocols. A set of standards exists describing the encapsulation of such protocols in FR frames.

Another advantage of FR is that it can convey information of variable size from 1 to 260 octets within a single frame (or more, if agreed at connection establishment), similar to the information generated by data systems (e.g. LANs). Future standards may specify the maximum payload size up to approximately 8000 octets; this will be the upper margin because of the limited error detection capabilities of the **frame check sequence** (FCS). The default length of the frame header is 2 octets. However, 3 or 4 octet long DLCI fields are also possible.

Figure 5.37 shows the FR frame.

Two different bits in the FR frame header are available for traffic management: **forward explicit congestion notification** (FECN) and **backward explicit congestion notification** (BECN). Both bits can be set by network elements when they experience congestion. The FECN might be used by the receiver for throttling down the transmitter via higher layer protocols. With BECN the transmitting terminal can be informed directly that congestion has occurred. All these mechanisms require that terminals react accordingly, meaning that they reduce the traffic sent into the network. Since user frames are in danger of being discarded at congested network nodes, terminals are assumed to support some kind of reactive congestion control mechanism.

Four parameters are defined in ITU-T Recommendation I.233 [104] for the resource management of individual virtual connection:

1. **Committed information rate** (CIR): The information rate which the network is committed to transfer under normal conditions.

2. **Committed burst size** (Bc): The maximum committed amount of data a user may offer to the network during a time interval Tc.

3. **Excess burst size** (Be): The maximum allowed amount of data by which a user can exceed Bc during time interval Tc. This data (Be) is delivered in general with a lower probability than Bc.

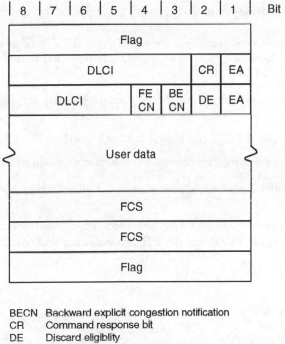

| 8 | 7 | 6 | 5 | 4 | 3 | 2 | 1 | Bit

| Flag |
| DLCI | CR | EA |
| DLCI | FE CN | BE CN | DE | EA |
| User data |
| FCS |
| FCS |
| Flag |

BECN   Backward explicit congestion notification
CR   Command response bit
DE   Discard eligiblity
DLCI   Data link connection identifier
EA   Address extension bit
FCS   Frame check sequence
FECN   Forward explicit congestion notification

Figure 5.37: *Frame format for frame relay*

4. **Committed rate measurement interval** (T_c). The time interval during which the user is allowed to send only the committed amount of data (Bc) and the excess amount of data (Be).

These parameters are defined by subscription or via signalling and may be enforced at the network's entry point. For excess frames (those belonging to Be), the DE bit might be set indicating that these frames should be discarded in preference to other frames, if necessary. As in B-ISDN, setting of the DE bit is called 'tagging'. Frames exceeding the agreed Be can be discarded.

A user can optimize each virtual connection for the traffic to be carried by choosing suitable values for CIR and Be. Additionally the user can set the DE bit according to the relative importance of the frame compared with others.

5.7.3.2   Frame Relay and B-ISDN

The high degree of commonality between FR and ATM facilitates interworking. Three scenarios have been identified for the support of FR by B-ISDN (ITU-T Recommendation I.555 [121]):

1. frame relay service function (FRSF) inside B-ISDN (cf. Figure 5.38, right part);

2. FRSF outside B-ISDN (cf. Figure 5.38, left part);

3. frame relay protocol support via ATM bearer capability (cf. Figure 5.39).

The FRSF handles frame relay protocols and routes frames according to their DLCI values.

The first two cases resemble the provision of connectionless services (see Section 5.7.2). In the third case the FR protocols are implemented in terminals

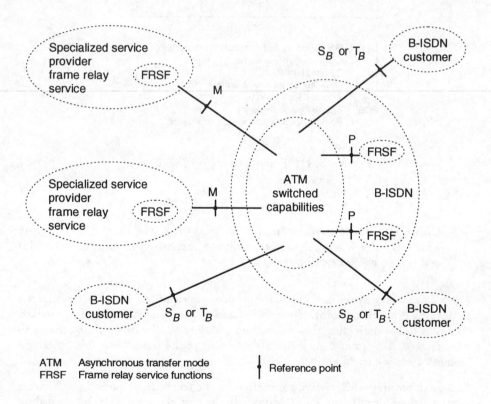

Figure 5.38: *Provision of frame relay outside and inside B-ISDN*

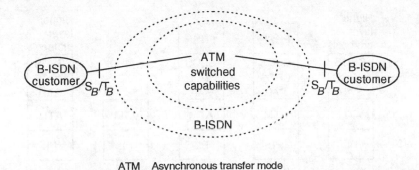

ATM   Asynchronous transfer mode

Figure 5.39: *Frame relay via ATM bearer capabilities*

connected via B-ISDN UNIs. The protocols are operated on top of the AAL and transparently conveyed through the B-ISDN network.

5.7.3.3   Frame Relay Interfaces

Two interfaces are defined: the frame relay B-ISDN **access interface** and the frame relay B-ISDN **network-to-network interface**. Both interfaces are nearly the same. Figure 5.40 shows the location of these interfaces and the associated FR protocol stack. For the adaptation of frame relay, AAL type 5 is used operating in message mode without the corrupted data delivery option (see Section 5.6.5). For the emulation of FR by and for interworking with B-ISDN, the **frame relaying service-specific convergence sublayer** (FR-SSCS) has been defined [121]. This sublayer preserves the FR-SSCS-SDU sequence integrity. Functions of the FR-SSCS are the same as the Q.922 [134] core functions.

The structure of the FR-SSCS-PDUs is the same as in Figure 5.37 apart from the flags and FCS. Interworking functions perform the Q.922 [134] core operations and remove flags and FCS from the original FR frame.

Two possibilities exist for carrying FR over B-ISDN:

1. Multiplexing at the FR-SSCS sublayer (also called many-to-one). Multiple FR-SSCS connections are carried on a single ATM connection. The DLCI allows unambiguous identification of the individual frame relay connection.

2. Multiplexing at the ATM layer (also called one-to-one). Each FR virtual connection is mapped on to a single ATM connection. The well known ATM multiplexing mechanisms using VCIs/VPIs are applied.

The mapping of DE to CLP and FECN/BECN to the congestion indication in the ATM cell header is explained in ITU-T Recommendation I.555 [121].

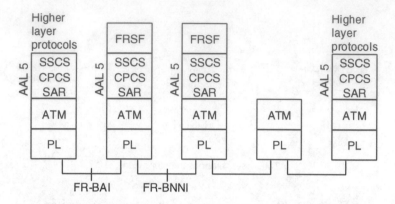

AAL   ATM adaptation layer
ATM   Asynchronous transfer mode
CPCS   Common part convergence sublayer
FR-BAI   Frame relay B-ISDN access interface
FR-BNNI   Frame relay B-ISDN network-to-network interface
FRSF   Frame relay service function
PL   Physical layer
SAR   Segmentation and reassembly
SSCS   Service-specific convergence sublayer

Figure 5.40: *The frame relay protocol stack*

Currently only peak cell rate allocation at the ATM layer can be used for traffic management. How the frame relay parameters CIR, Be, Bc and Tc can be adapted to ATM service parameters is for further study.

5.7.4   TCP/IP via B-ISDN

The **transmission control protocol** and **internet protocol** (TCP/IP) are defined in [70]. They constitute one of the most widely used protocol suites in the computer communication area. Since a very large number of different worksta-tions, hosts and even PCs are interconnected using TCP/IP, ATM-based networks must also be capable of carrying and supporting these protocols. During the in-troduction of ATM these protocols will be placed on top of ATM. At a later stage one can assume that the B-ISDN will offer a similar service. Services called 'best effort' or 'available bit rate' are currently being discussed by several standardiza-tion bodies. This service is supposed to replace the internet with higher transmis-sion speeds in an ATM-based environment. However, the detailed description of such a service is still pending.

IP is a connectionless technique designed for data applications. It can be run over various transmission systems like Ethernet, token ring and leased lines. The IP addresses are subdivided into a network identifier (ID) and a host ID. IP datagrams contain the source and destination addresses. Routing to the final destination is done via the **address resolution protocol** (ARP): an ARP request message is broadcast to all stations before data transmission starts. A station recognizing its own address within an ARP request sends back an ARP reply. Thus the source node gets the necessary information about the route to the desired destination.

IP packets are transferred in a best-effort manner. This means that no error correction capabilities and no information about successful delivery are provided. Only in the case of an unkown destination address can the **internet control message protocol** (ICMP) be used to inform the sender. ICMP messages are encapsulated and conveyed in IP packets.

IP data packets are transported in an unassured manner without any guarantee that they will arrive in the same order as sent out. Therefore, higher layer protocols, such as TCP, have to assure data integrity. TCP is a connection-oriented reliable transport protocol, whereas the **user datagram protocol** (UDP) is a connectionless unreliable transport protocol. On top of these protocols, applications like SNMP, file transfer protocol (FTP), simple mail transfer protocol (SMTP), and remote login (TELNET) can be found.

Although the layered approach of internet and ATM allows the reuse of higher layer protocols without changes, some problems have to be resolved at the boundary between IP and AAL. Some of these problems and possible solutions are:

1. **Encapsulation:** The transfer of IP datagrams requires encapsulation into ATM cells. Adaptation will be done via AAL type 5 (cf. Section 5.6.5). A general problem arises when several protocols, say TCP/IP and others, are used on top of ATM: an indication is needed about which higher layer protocol is being used. This indication can be provided by an IEEE 802.2 logical link control (LLC) [68] header, possibly followed by a subnetwork attachment point (SNAP) header. These headers are placed in front of the AAL type 5 PDUs. A second possibility is the use of different, dedicated virtual connections for each protocol. In this case a network element (bridge, router) recognizes the protocol encapsulated in the AAL through the VPI/VCI [72].

2. **Addressing**: A mapping function between the IP and ATM addresses is necessary. A simple look-up table might be possible in smaller networks but very difficult to maintain in large wide area networks. The same problem occurs when using ARP; in this case the ATM layer must provide multicast capabilities. However, for huge networks this is no longer a practical solution. A new technique called 'direct ARP' is currently being investigated and might offer a possible solution.

3. **Connection management**: Two possibilities exist for the interconnection of ATM users: permanent virtual connections or connections on demand

which are set up by means of signalling. During the introductory phase, permanent or semi-permanent connections, established via management communication, may be used. However, the use of on-demand connections can also be foreseen. This would then require signalling capabilities at routers.

4. **TCP aspects**: In principle it is possible to use the higher layer TCP without any changes. For protocols implementing flow control or acknowledgement mechanisms the *bandwidth* × *round trip delay* product has to be taken into account. For an ATM-based WAN this product might be high. Extensions of the TCP are available which can used on paths with large bandwidth delay product [71].

5. **Security**: The transfer of data through a public network results in higher security requirements compared with the (physically) limited extent of, for example, LANs, where normally all attached stations belong to the same domain. This issue has to be resolved before any end-user will send sensitive data through the public B-ISDN.

5.8   Operation and Maintenance of the B-ISDN UNI

This section covers OAM of the user–network interface and the customer access controlled by the network. The minimum functions required to maintain the physical layer and the ATM layer of the customer access, including the user–network interface, are described according to ITU-T Recommendation I.610 [123]. OAM of the layers above the ATM layer is not considered here.

First, the network configuration for OAM of the customer access is presented (Section 5.8.1). Then OAM functions of the physical layer and ATM layer and applications of the hierarchically structured OAM information flows – see Section 4.6.2 – are described (Section 5.8.2). In Section 5.8.3, implementation of these flows in the physical layer – flows F1, F2, F3 – and in the ATM layer – flows F4 and F5 – is discussed. The last section (Section 5.8.4) presents the interim local management interface (ILMI) as specified by the ATM Forum [10].

5.8.1   Network Configuration for OAM of the Customer Access

The general arrangement for maintenance of the customer access – based on the principles set out in ITU-T Recommendation I.601 [122] – is shown in Figure 5.41.

The customer installation in the figure comprises a maintenance entity that communicates with the customer access maintenance centre located in the B-ISDN.

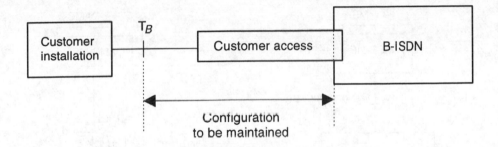

Figure 5.41: *Maintenance configuration of the customer access*

Comprehensive general maintenance services are also available in the network to support maintenance of the customer access.

B-ISDN will make use of functions provided by the TMN, the principles of which are described in ITU-T Recommendation M.3010 [126]. The architectural relation of the B-ISDN customer access with the TMN is shown in Figure 5.42.

The protocols used for maintenance are specified through Q interfaces. Results of network-element internal monitoring will be passed to the TMN via these Q interfaces.

5.8.2   OAM Functions and Information Flows

Figure 4.11 on page 44 shows the hierarchical level structure of the physical layer and ATM layer and the corresponding information flows. These levels and flows are summarized in Table 5.8.

Table 5.8: *OAM hierarchical levels and flows*

Level	Flow
Regenerator section	F1
Digital section	F2
Transmission path	F3
Virtual path	F4
Virtual channel	F5

Note that flows F1, F2 and F3 belong to the physical layer, and flows F4 and F5 to the ATM layer.

Two kinds of F4 and F5 flows can exist simultaneously on a VPC or VCC. One is an end-to-end flow used for end-to-end VPC/VCC operations communications.

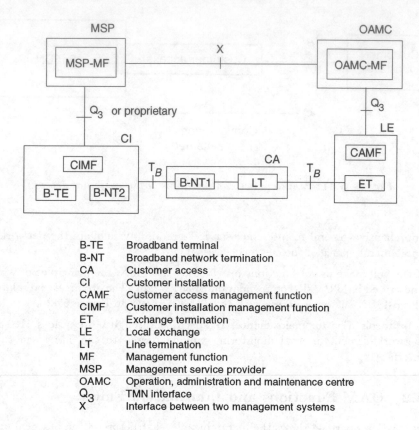

B-TE	Broadband terminal
B-NT	Broadband network termination
CA	Customer access
CI	Customer installation
CAMF	Customer access management function
CIMF	Customer installation management function
ET	Exchange termination
LE	Local exchange
LT	Line termination
MF	Management function
MSP	Management service provider
OAMC	Operation, administration and maintenance centre
Q_3	TMN interface
X	Interface between two management systems

Figure 5.42: *Example of TMN architecture for the customer access*

The other is a segment flow. A segment is a portion of a VPC or VCC which is under the control of a single network operator. Using these segment flows the network operator can monitor and operate the portions of VPCs/VCCs which are in its responsibility.

F4 and F5 flows, which are usually generated/terminated either at the endpoints of a VPC/VCC or at the connecting points terminating a VPC/VCC segment, may, optionally, also be monitored at intermediate points ('in-flight').

5.8.2.1   Physical Layer

Physical layer OAM functions are split into two categories:

1. OAM functions which are dedicated to the detection and indication of un-availability states and which require real-time failure information transfer

towards the affected endpoints for system protection. These functions are supported solely by the corresponding flows F1, F2 and F3.

2. OAM system management functions dedicated to performance monitoring and reporting, or for localization of failed equipment. These functions may be supported by the flows F1, F2 and F3 or by other means (for example, TMN via the Q interfaces; cf. Figure 5.42).

The functions described above are shown in Table 5.9 for the SDH-based interface and in Table 5.10 for the cell-based interface. The tables cover failures occurring on the B-NT2 to B-NT1 section (at reference point T_B) and on the transmission path beginning/terminating at B-NT2 (as illustrated in Figure 5.44 on page 130).

Table 5.9: *Physical layer operation and maintenance functions of the SDH-based interface*

Level	Function (category)	Failure detection
Regenerator section	Signal detection, frame alignment[1] Section error monitoring[2]	Loss of signal, loss of frame Degraded error performanace (optional)
Digital section	Section error monitoring[1] Section error monitoring and reporting[2]	Unacceptable error performance Degraded error performance
Transmission path	Cell rate decoupling[1] Cell delineation[1] Customer network status monitoring[1] AU-4 pointer operation[1] Path error monitoring and reporting[2]	Failure of insertion/ suppression of idle cells Loss of cell synchronization Customer network not available Loss of AU-4 pointer or path-AIS Degraded error performance

[1] category 1
[2] category 2

The 'customer network status monitoring' function shown in both tables on the transmission path level requires some explanation. The status of the customer network is continuously monitored and, in the event of a transmission failure, an **alarm indication signal** (AIS) is generated and delivered to its associated endpoint.

Table 5.10: *Physical layer operation and maintenance functions of the cell-based interface*

Level	Function (category)	Failure detection
Regenerator section	Signal detection, physical layer OAM cell recognition[1]	Loss of signal, loss of F1 cell recognition
	Section error monitoring[1]	Unacceptable error performanace
	Section error monitoring and reporting[2]	Degraded error performance
Transmission path	Cell rate decoupling[1]	Failure of insertion/ suppression of idle cells
	Physical layer OAM cell recognition[1]	Loss of F3 cell recognition
	Cell delineation[1]	Loss of cell synchronization
	Customer network status monitoring[1]	Customer network not available
	Path error monitoring and reporting[2]	Degraded error performance

  [1]   category 1
  [2]   category 2

AIS is a maintenance signal of the physical layer which indicates the detection and location of a transmission failure. AIS is applicable at both the section and path levels. The same holds for the **far end receive failure** (FERF) signal (see Table 5.12 on page 133). The two signals serve the following purposes [120]:

> 'AIS is used to alert the associated downstream termination point and connection point that an upstream failure has been detected and alarmed.
> FERF is used to alert the associated upstream termination point that a failure has been detected downstream.'

If a fault is detected at a section endpoint, the section FERF is sent in the backward direction. A path AIS is sent in the forward direction to inform the path endpoint B (see Figure 5.43) about the fault affecting the transmission path. This path endpoint will then notify the path endpoint at A using a (backward) path FERF. This concept is illustrated in Figure 5.43.

The AIS used for customer network status monitoring is an F3 path AIS. It protects and provides failure information on the transmission path between B-NT2 and the path termination.

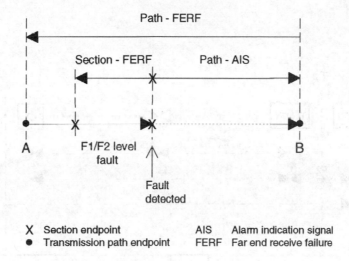

Figure 5.43: *Illustration of the AIS/FERF concept*

Figure 5.44 shows the span of the flows F1 to F3 relating to physical layer OAM for different access configurations.

The upper part of the figure shows a customer directly connected to the local exchange. The transmission path (and the related F3 flow) extends between B-NT2 and the exchange termination (ET). This path comprises the two sections between B-NT2 and B-NT1, and between B-NT1 and the line termination (LT). Each section is assigned an F2 flow. In the example given in the figure, the second section comprises two regenerator sections with corresponding F1 flows. In the configuration shown in the middle of the figure, the section starting at B-NT1 is terminated by an LT in front of an STM multiplexer. Another section begins after this STM multiplexer. (Possible division of these sections into regenerator sections is not shown.) In the last configuration (lower part of the figure) a customer is connected with a VP cross-connect which terminates the transmission paths.

5.8.2.2 ATM Layer

ATM layer OAM functions are monitoring of VP/VC availability and performance monitoring at the VP and VC levels (see Table 5.11).

The span of F4 and F5 flows is illustrated by the example in Figure 5.45. The VPC maintained by means of F4 here extends between B-NT2 and the ET, while the VCC extends between B-NT2 or a terminal and a termination point, which may be, for example, the B-NT2 of another customer.

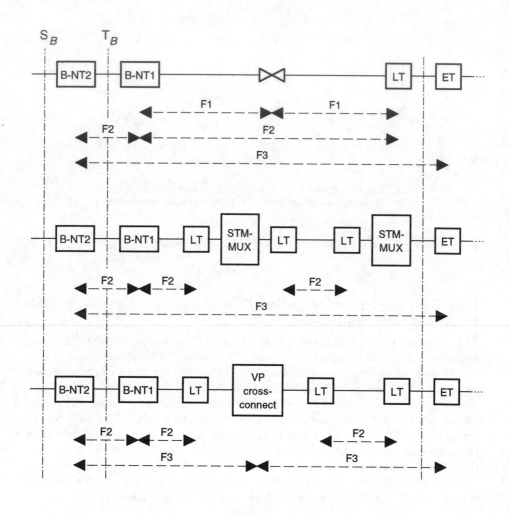

Figure 5.44: *Physical layer OAM flows*

Table 5.11: *OAM functions of the ATM layer*

Level	Functions	Defect/failure detection
Virtual path	Monitoring of path availability	Path not available
	Performance monitoring	Degraded performance
Virtual channel	Monitoring of channel availability	Channel not available
	Performance monitoring	Degraded performance

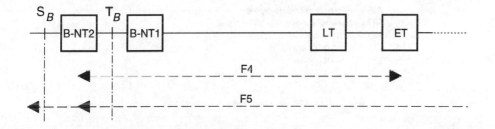

B-NT   Network termination for B-ISDN
ET   Exchange termination
LT   Line termination

Figure 5.45: *ATM layer OAM flows*

In the event of a fault the actions are similar to those at the physical layer. VP/VC-level alarms are sent to all affected active VPCs/VCCs from the connecting point of the VPC/VCC (for example, ATM switch) which detects the fault. VP-AIS/VC-AIS and VP-FERF/VC-FERF are used at the ATM layer in an analogous way to the physical layer alarms.

VP/VC alarms are generated following the detection of faults pertaining to the physical layer or the ATM layer. This is shown in Figure 5.46.

VP/VC-AIS and VP/VC-FERF are sent periodically during the failure condition with a frequency of 1 cell per second. The AIS/FERF status is declared after one AIS/FERF cell has been received. It is removed if no further AIS/FERF cell has

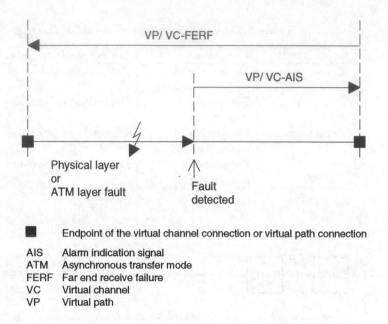

Figure 5.46: *VP/VC-alarms*

been received for 3 seconds or on receipt of one valid cell, that is, a user cell or continuity check cell.

To monitor VP/VC availability, continuity check cells may be sent downstream by a VPC/VCC endpoint when no user cell has been sent for a certain period of time (the value has not yet been fixed). If the endpoint of a VPC/VCC where continuity checking applies does not receive a cell within a certain time interval, it will send VP/VC-FERF to the far end.

VP/VC performance monitoring is based on monitoring blocks of N user cells. N may have the value 128, 256, 512 or 1024, with a tolerance of $\pm 50\%$ each. Specific performance monitoring/reporting cells are inserted and evaluated, respectively. Errored blocks, loss/misinsertion of cells, cell delay and so on can be detected or measured by means of VP/VC performance monitoring. Performance monitoring can be activated either during connection establishment or at any time after the connection has been established.

It should be noted that the above ATM layer OAM measures require the allocation of some extra bit rate to an ATM connection.

5.8.3   Implementation Issues

5.8.3.1   Physical Layer

Transmission overhead allocation and coding of the SDH physical layer functions, as defined in Table 5.9, are given in Table 5.12 (details of the SDH frame structure are presented in Section 5.3.1.1)

Table 5.12: *SDH overhead allocation at the B-ISDN UNI*

Byte	Function	Coding
STM-1 section overhead:		
A1	Frame alignment	11110110
A2	Frame alignment	00101000
B1	Regenerator section error monitoring[1]	BIP-8
B2	Section error monitoring	BIP-24 / BIP-96[2]
H1, H2	AU-4 pointer/path AIS	see [90]/all 1s
H3	Pointer action	see [90]
K2 (bits 6 - 8)	Section AIS/section FERF	111/110
Z2	Section error reporting (FEBE)	B2 error count
VC-4 path overhead:		
J1	Path ID/verification	see [90]
B3	Path error monitoring	BIP-8
C2	Path signal label	ATM cells = 00010011
G1 (bits 1 - 4)	Path error reporting (FEBE)	B3 error count
G1 (bit 5)	Path FERF	1

[1]   The use of B1 for regenerator section error monitoring across the B-ISDN UNI is application dependent and therefore optional.

[2]   BIP-24 for the 155 Mbit/s interface, BIP-96 for the 622 Mbit/s interface.

Transmission performance monitoring across the B-ISDN UNI in order to detect and report transmission errors is performed at section and path levels, as indicated in Section 5.8.2.1.

At the SDH section level, an incoming signal is monitored at the section termination point by means of the bit-interleaved parity 24 (BIP-24), which is inserted into the B2 field at the other section termination point.

The far end block error (FEBE) is used to monitor an outgoing signal. This error count, obtained by comparing the calculated BIP-24 and the B2 value of the incoming signal at the far end, is inserted in the Z2 field bits 18 to 24 and then sent back to the near end section termination point.

In a similar way, at SDH path level an incoming signal is monitored using BIP-8 of the B3 byte. An outgoing signal is monitored using the path FEBE of bits 1 to 4 of the G1 byte. This concept is illustrated in Figure 5.47 (only the case 'A sending towards B' is shown for simplicity).

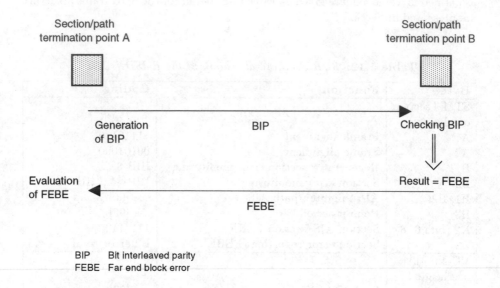

Figure 5.47: *Illustration of transmission performance monitoring*

SDH, as described in ITU-T Recommendations G.708 [89] and G.709 [90], provides additional OAM means that will not necessarily be used in the customer access network. One example is automatic protection switching across the B-ISDN UNI. In the event of failure of the transmission line, the system could automatically switch to a standby line to prevent longer out-of-order periods.

Allocation of the OAM functions (see Table 5.10) to the F1/F3 OAM cells is included in ITU-T Recommendation I.432 [120] for cell-based interfaces.

5.8.3.2   ATM Layer

ATM layer OAM flows F4 and F5 (cf. Table 5.11) are provided by cells dedicated to ATM layer OAM functions. This type of cell can be identified by specific values of the payload type identifier or VCI. The F4 cells use reserved VCI values while F5 cells use specific payload type identifiers (see Table 5.13). ATM layer OAM cells have a common information field format (see Figure 5.48).

Table 5.13: *OAM F4/F5 cell headers*

OAM flow	Span	Header
F4	end-to-end	VCI = 00000000 00000100
F4	segment	VCI = 00000000 00000011
F5	end-to-end	PTI = 101
F5	segment	PTI = 100

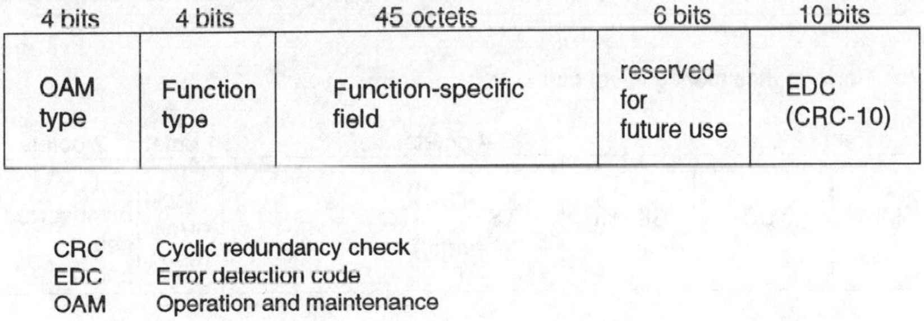

4 bits	4 bits	45 octets	6 bits	10 bits
OAM type	Function type	Function-specific field	reserved for future use	EDC (CRC-10)

CRC	Cyclic redundancy check
EDC	Error detection code
OAM	Operation and maintenance

Figure 5.48: *Information field of the ATM layer OAM cells*

The OAM type and function type codings are given in Table 5.14. Note that unused information field bits (incomplete octets) of the OAM cells are coded all zero while unused (complete) octets are coded 0110 1010.

Table 5.14: *OAM type/function codings*

OAM type	4 bit	Function type	4 bit
Fault management	0001	AIS	0000
		FERF	0001
		Continuity check	0100
Performance management	0010	Forward monitoring	0000
		Backward reporting	0001
		Monitoring & Reporting	0010
Activation/deactivation	1000	Performance monitoring	0000
		Continuity check	0001

The function-specific fields for different OAM cells are shown in Figure 5.49. For further details, refer to ITU-T Recommendation I.610 [123].

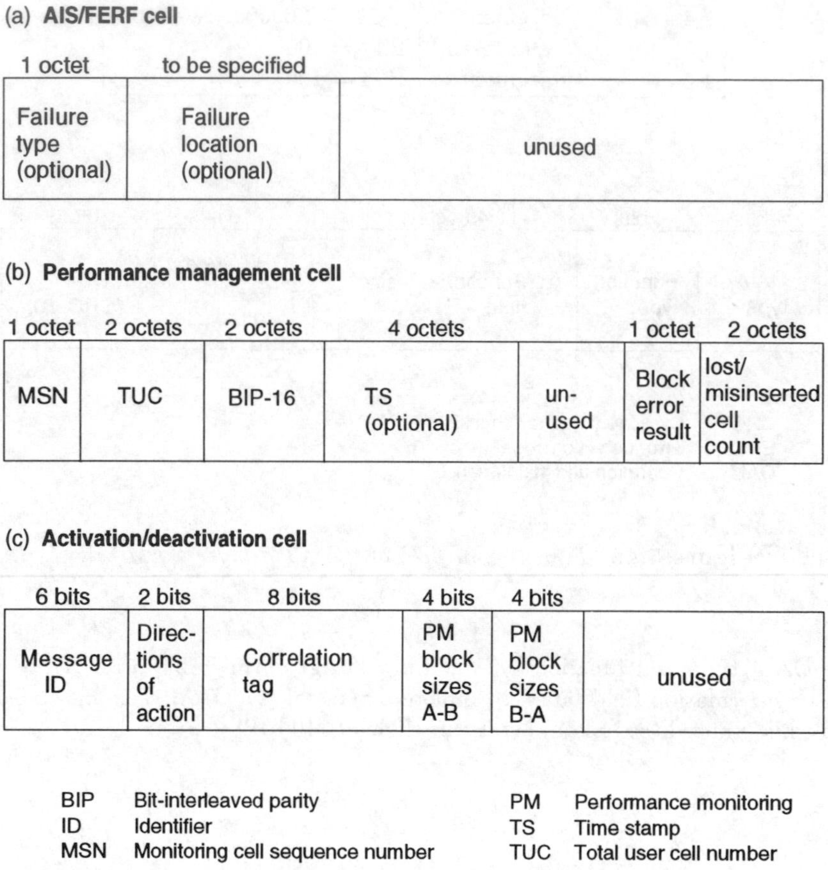

(a) **AIS/FERF cell**

1 octet	to be specified	
Failure type (optional)	Failure location (optional)	unused

(b) **Performance management cell**

1 octet	2 octets	2 octets	4 octets		1 octet	2 octets
MSN	TUC	BIP-16	TS (optional)	un-used	Block error result	lost/ misinserted cell count

(c) **Activation/deactivation cell**

6 bits	2 bits	8 bits	4 bits	4 bits	
Message ID	Direc-tions of action	Correlation tag	PM block sizes A-B	PM block sizes B-A	unused

BIP	Bit-interleaved parity		PM	Performance monitoring
ID	Identifier		TS	Time stamp
MSN	Monitoring cell sequence number		TUC	Total user cell number

Figure 5.49: *Function-specific fields of ATM layer OAM cells*

5.8.4   Interim Local Management Interface

5.8.4.1   Scope and Functionality

The interim local management interface (ILMI) has been specified in the ATM Forum's ATM UNI specification [10]:

'to provide any ATM user device with status and configuration information concerning the VP/VC connections available at its UNI. In addition, more global operations and network management information ... may also facilitate diagnostics procedures at the UNI'.

ILMI refers to the UNI, both the public and the private one (see Figure 5.50)

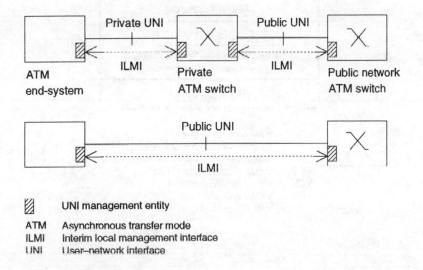

Figure 5.50: *Application scope of ILMI*

The term 'interim' is to indicate that it is a preliminary standard which may eventually be replaced with an ITU-T agreed standard offering more comprehensive functionality.

ILMI supports the bidirectional exchange of management information between UNI management entities (UMEs) which are located both at ATM end-systems and ATM switches (see Figure 5.50) and which terminate the ILMI protocol.

In terms of physical equipment, ILMI will be implemented in workstations and computers with ATM interfaces, in ATM switches, and in higher layer switches (for example, frame relay switches, LAN bridges/routers) that transfer their frames within ATM cells.

The ILMI functions pertain to the physical layer and the ATM layer of the UNI.

5.8.4.2   ILMI Protocol

ILMI employs the protocol stack shown in Figure 5.51.

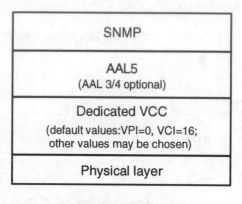

Figure 5.51: *ILMI protocol stack*

A dedicated, permanently available VCC is used for sending AAL-encapsulated SNMP messages between adjacent UMEs. SNMP [186] comprises four types of operation which are used to manipulate management information (see Table 5.15).

Table 5.15: *SNMP operations*

Operation	Function
Get	Retrieval of specific management information
Get-next	Step-by-step retrieval
Set	Altering management information
Trap	Reporting extraordinary events

SNMP messages of up to and including 484 octets are normally allowed. (The use of larger messages may be negotiated.) The throughput of SNMP traffic via the ILMI VCC should be no more than approximately 1% of the UNI load.

5.8.4.3 ILMI Services and Management Information Base

ILMI provides management information on the physical layer and ATM layer for monitoring and controlling ATM-based UNIs. This information will be accomodated by the management information base (MIB), which is structured into:

- physical layer
- ATM layer
- ATM layer statistics
- virtual path connections
- virtual channel connections.

Physical layer MIB information includes:

- interface address: 48 bit IEEE 802 [68], or 60 bit ITU-T E.164 [81] (public/private, individual or group address);
- transmission type: SONET 155.520 Mbit/s, 45 Mbit/s ...;
- media type: coaxial cable, single/multi-mode fibre or shielded/unshielded twisted pair;
- operational status: in-service, out-of-service, loop-back mode.

ATM layer MIB information comprises:

- maximum number of VPCs/VCCs
- VPI/VCI address width
- number of configured VPCs/VCCs
- UNI type (public/private ATM interface).

The ATM layer statistics part of the MIB contains:

- number of ATM cells received
- number of ATM cells dropped on the receiver side
- number of ATM cells transmitted.

Finally, the VPC/VCC-related MIB information provides information for each VPC/VCC on:

- VPI/VCI value
- shaping traffic descriptor
- policing traffic descriptor
- operational status
- quality-of-service category (deterministic/statistical/unspecified/other).

Chapter 6

Signalling

Basic aspects of B-ISDN signalling have already been described in Section 4.3. This chapter deals with details on signalling transfer and signalling applications.

Section 6.1 discusses the effects on signalling of the proposed phased approach for the introduction of B-ISDN. Section 6.2 gives an overview of the possible protocol architectures at the UNI and the NNI. The next two sections, Sections 6.3 and 6.4, deal with signalling transfer. The last two sections, Sections 6.5 and 6.6, describe some details of signalling applications.

6.1 Introduction Concept

The first set of 13 recommendations adopted by ITU-T in 1990 creates a frame work for the introduction of ATM-based networks, their subscriber equipment and applications. Only one of these recommendations includes some basic aspects of signalling [105].

On the one hand ATM-based networks should be available as early as possible, whereas on the other hand a variety of services (very simple as well as highly sophisticated) should be integrated in such a network. It is obvious that these two goals cannot be met in a single step. Therefore, a phased approach is required for the introduction of ATM-based networks supporting switched services.

ITU-T was aware of this fact and developed a timetable of B-ISDN network and service aspects. This concept comprises three steps which are called releases 1, 2 and 3. The main characteristic features influencing signalling are summarized in Table 6.1 [25].

In release 1, simple switched services with constant bit rates will be provided and interworking with the existing 64 kbit/s ISDN is foreseen. (Note that while variable bit rate services can be transported, a peak bit rate will be allocated.) Right from the beginning two signalling access configurations (see Section 6.2) can be used; one of them requires meta-signalling (see Section 6.3).

Table 6.1: *Timetable for B-ISDN signalling*

Release 1	Release 2	Release 3
Constant bit rate	Variable bit rate	
Connection-oriented service with end-to-end timing	Connection-oriented service	Multimedia and distributive service
	Quality of service indication by the user	Quality of service negotiation
Point-to-point connections (uni- and bidirectional, symmetric and asymmetric)	Point-to-multipoint connections	Broadcast connections
Single connection, simultaneous establishment	Multi-connection, delayed establishment	
	Use of cell loss priority	
Indication of peak bandwidth	Negotiation and renegotiation of bandwidth	
Peak rate allocation	Bandwidth allocation based on traffic characteristics	
Interworking with 64 kbit/s ISDN		
Point-to-point or point-to-multipoint signalling access		
Meta-signalling		
Limited set of supplementary services	Supplementary services	

More sophisticated services with variable bit rates (assuming that it is possible to take advantage of statistical multiplexing), point-to-multipoint connnections and multi-connections will be supported in release 2. With release 2, **call** and **connection control** will be separated, that is, connections can be set up and released during a call.

Finally, release 3 provides the full range of services, including multimedia and distributive services.

It is obvious that this timetable has a strong influence on the signalling application protocols which will be described in Sections 6.5 and 6.6. It is assumed that the influence of the timetable is not so strong on the signalling transfer protocols. Therefore, these protocols should be applicable for all releases (maybe with some small extensions and/or modifications).

The ATM Forum is focusing on the protocols which are necessary for UNI signalling. The specification delivered by this forum will be based on the specification of ITU-T. However, modifications and enhancements will be included. One of the main differences is that right from the beginning the ATM Forum will provide switched point-to-multipoint connections. Later on, the ATM Forum will also produce a specification for NNI signalling.

6.2   Protocol Architecture for Release 1

ITU-T differentiated between the following two signalling access configurations at the UNI [138]:

1. point-to-point signalling access configuration

2. point-to-multipoint signalling access configuration.

In the case of point-to-point signalling access configurations there is only one signalling endpoint on the user side. This may be a single terminal or an intelligent B-NT2 (for example, PBX) depending on the customer network configuration (see Section 4.7). Only a single permanently established point-to-point SVC is required for this signalling access configuration. This channel is used for call offering, call establishment and release.

Several signalling endpoints are located at the user side (for example, a point-to-multipoint terminal configuration) in point-to-multipoint signalling access configurations. In this case meta-signalling (see Section 6.3) is necessary to manage other signalling relations.

The protocol stacks related to these two signalling access configurations are shown on the left side of Figure 6.1.

At the NNI, either the existing STM-based common channel signalling system no. 7 (SS7) or an ATM-based network can be used to transport the signalling messages [138]. For both scenarios an appropriate application protocol is required which will be described in Section 6.5.2. The signalling protocol stacks associated with each option are depicted on the right side of Figure 6.1.

It is evident that the reuse of SS7 allows the rapid introduction of B-ISDN. However, a signalling transport network can also take advantage of the ATM technology, so in the future an ATM-based signalling transport network may be the preferred solution. In the case of ATM-based signalling transfer, the SVCs between two switches are managed by OAM protocols and therefore meta-signalling is not required at the NNI.

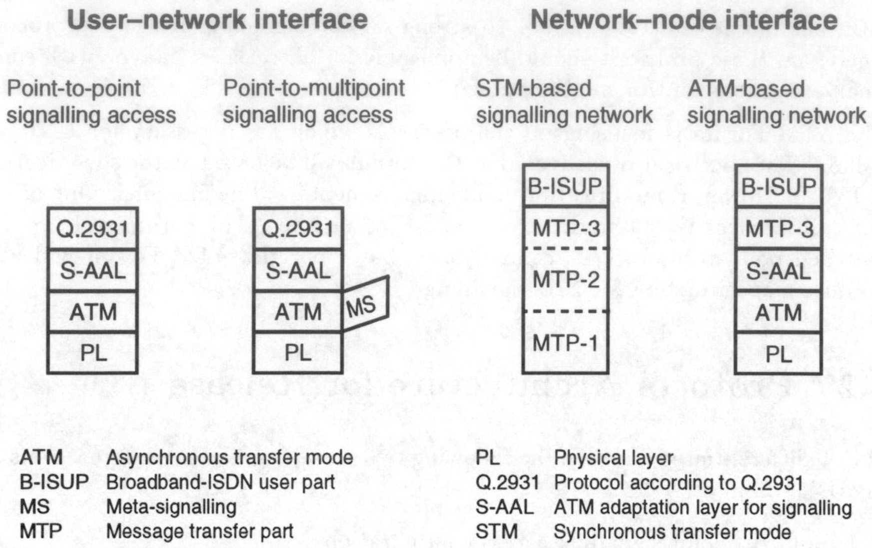

User–network interface   **Network–node interface**

Point-to-point   Point-to-multipoint   STM-based   ATM-based
signalling access   signalling access   signalling network signalling network

Q.2931		Q.2931			B-ISUP		B-ISUP
S-AAL		S-AAL			MTP-3		MTP-3
ATM		ATM	MS		MTP-2		S-AAL
PL		PL			MTP-1		ATM
							PL

ATM   Asynchronous transfer mode   PL   Physical layer
B-ISUP   Broadband-ISDN user part   Q.2931   Protocol according to Q.2931
MS   Meta-signalling   S-AAL   ATM adaptation layer for signalling
MTP   Message transfer part   STM   Synchronous transfer mode

Figure 6.1: *Protocol architecture for B-ISDN signalling*

6.3   Meta-Signalling

6.3.1   General

ITU-T Draft Recommendation Q.2120 [141] describes the meta-signalling protocol which is used for establishing, maintaining and removing user–network signalling connections at the UNI.

The meta-signalling protocol only operates over the MSVC. Currently it is the only protocol which uses that channel. The MSVC is defined by VCI = 1 in every VP (cf. Table 5.6 on page 91) and its default peak cell rate is 42 cells/s. In principle, the meta-signalling protocol can operate on each active VP. However, it is sufficient to use it only in one VP between the user and a local exchange [64]. This reduces the implementation effort.

The meta-signalling protocol is part of the ATM layer. It is located within the layer management plane (see Section 5.1) and is under the control of plane management. Currently, the ATM Forum does not support meta-signalling because the forum only considers point-to-point signalling configurations.

6.3.2   Scope and Application

The meta-signalling protocol provides procedures for the:

- assignment and removal of point-to-point SVCs (PSVCs) and their associated BSVCs
- checking of the status of these two channel types.

With these procedures it is possible to:

- associate a signalling endpoint with a PSVC and a BSVC
- allocate the cell rate to SVCs
- resolve possible contention problems for SVCs.

The assignment, checking and removal procedures are independent of each other. The necessary relationship between them is performed via plane management.

Normally the meta-signalling protocol is used between the user and the network. However, two users which are connected via a VPC can also use this protocol for managing PSVCs and BSVCs. In that scenario the predefined VCI value for the MSVC should be used (cf. Table 5.6 on page 91).

As mentioned in Section 6.2, the meta-signalling protocol is only used in point-to-multipoint signalling access configurations. As a network option it can also be applied in a **dynamic** signalling access configuration. In this case the user can use meta-signalling to inform the network whether the signalling access configuration is point-to-point or point-to-multipoint.

6.3.3   Protocol Issues

In this section we will focus on the following details of the meta-signalling protocol:

- message formatting (see Section 6.3.3.1)
- procedures (see Section 6.3.3.2).

6.3.3.1   Message Formatting

The message format for meta-signalling messages is depicted in Figure 6.2. It is independent of the message type, i.e. each message consists of the same structure. Fields which are not used by a message are coded with a 'null' value.

The first field is called the **protocol discriminator** (PD). It identifies messages on the meta-signalling channel as meta-signalling messages or messages belonging to another protocol. Currently the meta-signalling protocol is the only protocol using the meta-signalling channel.

Bit	Octet
8 7 6 5 4 3 2 1	number
Protocol discriminator	1
Protocol version	2
Message type	3
Reference identifier	4 ... 5
Signalling virtual channel identifier A	6 ... 7
Signalling virtual channel identifier B	8 ... 9
Point-to-point cell rate	10
Cause	11
Service profile identifier	12 ... 22
Null-fill	23 ... 46
	47
Cyclic redundancy check	48

Figure 6.2: *Format of meta-signalling messages*

The **protocol version** (PV) field differentiates between the individual versions of the meta-signalling protocol and identifies the general message format being used. The format described in this section is valid for version 1.

The names of the messages are identified by the **message type** (MT) field. It is also used to determine the exact function and detailed format of each message.

The following six messages are used for the meta-signalling protocol (their application is described in Section 6.3.3.2):

1. ASSIGN REQUEST

2. ASSIGNED

3. DENIED

4. CHECK REQUEST

5. CHECK RESPONSE

6. REMOVED.

The **reference identifier** (RI) field is used to differentiate between a number of simultaneous assignment procedures. The value is randomly generated for each ASSIGN REQUEST message by the individual terminal. The associated answer is identified by the same value of the reference identifier.

The contents of **signalling virtual channel identifier A** and **B** (SVCI A and B) fields depend on the procedure in use. The contents may be:

- a point-to-point signalling virtual channel identifier (PSVCI)
- a broadcast signalling virtual channel identifier (BSVCI)
- a global signalling virtual channel identifier (GSVCI).

A PSVC is identified by the PSVCI. The PSVC conveys all point-to-point call and/or bearer control signalling (see Section 6.5.1) for a given signalling endpoint. The BSVCI indicates the VCI value of a BSVC. A BSVC is always unidirectional and used in the direction from the network to the user for call offering. This channel may be the *general* BSVC or the *selective* BSVC. The general BSVC is identified by VCI = 2 (cf. Table 5.6 on page 91), whereas the selective BSVC is identified by a VCI value defined during the assignment phase. The selective BSVC has a close relationship to the service profile identifier which will be described later on in this section. The GSVCI indicates all signalling channels except the meta-signalling channel itself. It is a unique identifier and identified by VCI = 1. It is used for a global check (this is only one example), that is, all active signalling endpoints have to deliver a CHECK RESPONSE message after receiving a CHECK REQUEST containing the GSVCI.

The **point-to-point SVC cell rate** (PCR) field indicates the requested/allocated cell rate for the point-to-point signalling virtual channel. Currently only peak cell rate allocation is used. Later on, when it is possible to take advantage of the statistical multiplexing, the coding of this field may be extended to cover this enhanced feature. The following values are defined: 42, 84, 168, 336, 672, 1344, 2688 cells/s. (Note: 42 cells/s are approximately 16 kbit/s and 2688 cells/s are approximately 1024 kbit/s.)

The **cause** (CAU) field provides the user with more detailed information; it indicates the reason for sending the message (for example, why the network has sent a DENIED message).

The **service profile identifier** (SPID) field is used by the user to request a basic or specific level of service. The SPID points to the service profile, which is a set of information maintained by the network to provide either the basic or any specific service to a signalling endpoint. When both the network and the user support the service profile concept, calls can be offered via the selective BSVC. In this case only a subset of all signalling endpoints located at the user side receive the offered call and therefore the call offering procedure has been simplified.

All bits of the **null-fill** field are coded with '0'.

The last field in the meta-signalling message is the CRC field, which is used to detect errors in meta-signalling messages. A generator polynomial is used which is the same as that for AAL type 3/4 (see Section 5.6.4).

All meta-signalling messages, their associated parameters and their directions of flow are shown in Table 6.2.

Table 6.2: *Meta-signalling messages and associated parameters*

	Messages					
	ASSIGN REQUEST	ASSIGNED	DENIED	CHECK REQUEST	CHECK RESPONSE	REMOVED
PD	M	M	M	M	M	M
PV	M	M	M	M	M	M
MT	M	M	M	M	M	M
RI	M	M	M	—	—	—
SVCI A	—[1]	M	—	M	M	M
SVCI B	—	M	—	—	M	—
PCR	M	M	—	—	—	—
CAU	—	M	M	—	—	M
SPID	M	M	—	—	M	—
CRC	M	M	M	M	M	M
Direction	U → N	N → U	N → U	N → U	U → N	U → N or N → U

[1]	normally coded with null value, see [141]
M	mandatory valid value must be present
—	coded with null value
N → U	network to user direction
U → N	user to network direction

6.3.3.2   Procedures

The following procedures are used for the meta-signalling protocol:

- assignment
- check
- removal.

The assignment procedure is invoked by the user side sending an ASSIGN REQUEST to the network asking for a PSVCI and BSVCI. The network will – depending on its condition – send either an ASSIGNED message indicating the PSVCI/BSVCI pair or it will send a DENIED message with the appropriate reason. This procedure is supervised by a timer at the user side to cope with loss of messages.

The check procedure is initiated by the network sending a CHECK REQUEST message and waiting for CHECK RESPONSE. The simplest check concerns only a single PSVCI/BSVCI pair, whereas the most general check concerns all signalling channels. This procedure is also supervised by a timer at the network side.

The removal procedure can be initiated either by the network side or by the user side. In contrast to the other two procedures, no handshake procedure is used. The initiating side sends only a REMOVED message followed, after a random interval, by a second REMOVED message. This mechanism is very simple and prevents errors occurring if one REMOVED message is lost.

At the user side each message is delayed for some random time before it is delivered to the network. This is done for all messages even if it is not always necessary. However, this simple mechanism prevents certain network overload conditions which might otherwise occur (for example, when the network starts a global check all terminals would answer almost simultaneously).

6.4   ATM Adaptation Layer for Signalling

A suitable signalling AAL (S-AAL) is required in order to adapt the signalling application protocols for the UNI and the NNI (see Section 6.5) to the services provided by the underlying ATM layer (cf. Section 5.5). The S-AAL is subdivided into the following two parts (see Figure 6.3):

- common part (CP)

- service specific part (SSP).

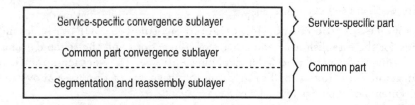

Figure 6.3: *ATM adaptation layer for signalling*

Section 6.4.1 discusses some aspects of the common part, while Section 6.4.2 deals with the service-specific part of the S-AAL.

6.4.1   Common Part

In principle both AAL type 3/4 (cf. Section 5.6.4) and AAL type 5 (see Section 5.6.5) are suitable for the CP. ITU-T decided to use AAL type 5 [112] because it is a simple protocol with only a small overhead.

AAL type 5 has a better performance (for example, higher throughput, lower mean transfer time) for long messages. However, in the case of small messages (1 to 3 cells) and a high cell loss probability, AAL type 3/4 has the better performance [185]. This is because if the last cell of an AAL-PDU is lost, the error cannot be detected immediately by AAL type 5. The error will be detected after receiving the adjacent PDU. However, the receiver cannot indicate which AAL-PDU has been errored and therefore discards both PDUs.

6.4.2   Service-Specific Part

ITU-T decided to use a common protocol for the UNI and the NNI, which is described in ITU-T Draft Recommendations Q.2100 [139], Q.2110 [140], Q.2130 [142] and Q.2140 [143], for the SSP. The commonality between UNI and NNI provides the following benefits:

- reduced complexity at network nodes
- short specification time
- flexibility in network operation and configuration
- efficient operation and maintenance of the network
- reduced operating and manufacturing costs.

It should be noted that full commonality is not possible because of the different protocols located above the S-AAL at the UNI and the NNI. To meet the different requirements of the protocols located above the S-AAL, the architecture shown in Figure 6.4 has been chosen.

The **service-specific connection-oriented protocol** (SSCOP) provides mechanisms for the establishment and release of connections and the reliable exchange of signalling information between signalling entities. The **service-specific co-ordination functions** (SSCFs) map the requirements of the layer above to the requirements of the next lower layer.

In the case of the SSCOP it would have been possible to use an existing data link layer protocol, such as the data link layer protocol for frame mode bearer services [134], with some modifications and enhancements [48]. Reuse of an existing protocol would have been the same approach as for the signalling application protocols for release 1, providing the same advantages (for example, short specification process). However, ITU-T decided to specify a new protocol for SSCOP, which has to be simple and efficient.

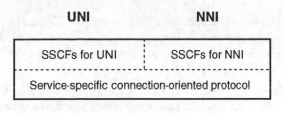

Figure 6.4: *Service-specific part of S-AAL*

The new SSCOP performs the following functions:

Sequence integrity: Preserves the order of the SSCOP-SDUs.

Error correction by retransmission: Missing SSCOP-SDUs are detected by the receiver using a sequencing mechanism. SSCOP then corrects the error by selective retransmission.

Flow control: The receiver controls the rate of messages which its associated peer transmitter sends by using a dynamic window mechanism.

Error reporting to layer management: The occurrence of errors is indicated to layer management.

Keep alive: Two peer entities will remain in connection even in the event of a prolonged absence of data transfer.

Local data retrieval: SDUs can be retrieved which have not yet been delivered or acknowledged (it is not agreed whether this function is part of SSCOP or SSCF).

Link management: This function establishes, releases and resets SSCOP connections.

Transfer of data: This function performs the transfer of messages between two peer-to-peer entities. SSCOP provides the **assured** and **unassured** data transfer mode.

PCI error detection: Errors within the PCI are detected.

Status reporting: The SSCOP transmitter and receiver can exchange status information using this function.

In order to achieve a high-speed protocol, the transmitter and receiver state machines are decoupled. This decoupling, the use of selective retransmission and the dynamic window mechanism for flow control, are the major feature changes compared with existing data link layer protocols. A more detailed list of protocol features, the messages used and the protocol operation are described in ITU-T Draft Recommendation Q.2110 [140].

As shown in Figure 6.4, two different SSCFs are needed, one for the UNI and another for the NNI. SSCFs [142] map the service primitives between SSCOP and the layer 3 protocol Q.2931 [148] at the UNI. At the NNI, the SSCFs [143] perform mapping of primitives between SSCOP and message transfer part level 3 (MTP-3) [129] and some local functions such as local retrieval.

6.5   Signalling Protocols for Release 1

As mentioned in Section 6.1, the proposed timetable strongly influences the signalling application protocols. Release 1 protocols have to be finalized in 1994. Because these protocols do not cover all the sophisticated features of B-ISDN, the best approach for meeting this deadline is the reuse of existing protocols with some modifications. The existing layer 3 protocol for 64 kbit/s ISDN according to ITU-T Recommendation Q.931 [135] will serve as a basis for the UNI, whereas the protocol at the NNI is based on the ISDN user part (ISUP) [130, 131, 132, 133].

The basic approach for the specification of these protocols is to reuse existing protocols, mechanisms and procedures as much as possible, and to keep the modifications as simple as possible. However, to ensure a smooth transition from release 1 implementations to release 2 and 3 solutions, measures will be taken in the release 1 protocols to prepare for the separation of call and bearer control. This extension of the basic approach guarantees compatibility and allows the reuse of release 1 protocols in further releases, thereby preserving investment.

In the following two sections (Sections 6.5.1 and 6.5.2) we will describe only those protocol issues which are related to the ATM-specific features of the UNI and NNI signalling protocols.

6.5.1   User–Network Interface Signalling

The layer 3 signalling protocol for B-ISDN is described in ITU-T Draft Recommendation Q.2931 [148]. It resides directly above the S-AAL (cf. Section 6.4). Q.2931 includes the specification of the signalling messages, information elements and communication procedures between signalling endpoints for the B-ISDN UNI.

Because Q.2931 is based on the existing layer 3 signalling specification for 64 kbit/s it provides the same set of functions for B-ISDN as are available for 64 kbit/s ISDN. However, Q.2931 is independent of the Q.931 protocol: this is achieved by the use of a new protocol discriminator for broadband signalling. The structure of Q.2931 directly corresponds to the well-known structure of Q.931. Most of the procedures of Q.931 have been transferred to Q.2931 with merely editorial modifications, in particular to the call establishment and release procedures.

There are two reasons why modifications were made to Q.931:

- adaptation to the new transfer mode ATM

- additional modifications which allow a smooth transition from release 1 signalling protocol to the release 2 and 3 protocols.

Adaptation to the new B-ISDN transmission system mainly refers to the description of the B-ISDN bearer services. A new broadband bearer capability has been developed which is used for the description of these services. In addition, the ATM cell rate describes the throughput of an ATM connection. For release 1 the value of the ATM cell rate is selectable, but only as a peak cell rate resulting in a constant throughput.

As described in Section 5.1.5.4, the user can select between different AAL classes and the associated protocols for his communication needs. A new information element was developed describing the attributes of the user plane AAL connection which are chosen by the user.

The old channel identifier of Q.931 became obsolete and was replaced by the new connection identifier information element. This information element consists of the virtual path connection identifier (VPCI) and the VCI already introduced in Section 5.5.2.4. The VPCI identifies a VPC, whereas a VPI only identifies a VP link. The use of the VPCI in the connection identifier information element is necessary because the user may be connected via a VP cross-connect network to the local exchange (see Figure 6.5). The VP network is controlled by network management and not by signalling. (A signalling endpoint only knows about its own VPI and not the VPI of the associated signalling endpoint.) Therefore, it became necessary to introduce the unique identifier VPCI between the user and the local exchange.

The modifications described above are the main ones. However, some parts of the messages and procedures also need to be modified slightly. Most of them remain the same as in Q.931. In addition to the existing procedures, the interworking between the Q.931 and Q.2931 protocols is specified in Q.2931.

Besides the modifications which result from the use of ATM for broadband communications, Q.2931 will also provide means to support a smooth transition between B-ISDN release 1 and planned future releases. In addition to some improvements and simplifications of the coding rules (see Table 6.3), the inclusion of compatibility instructors into messages and information elements of Q.2931 is discussed with regard to this objective.

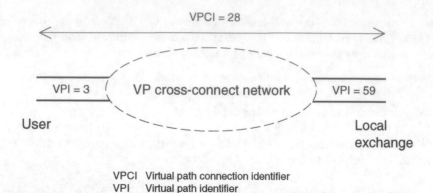

VPCI   Virtual path connection identifier
VPI   Virtual path identifier

Figure 6.5: *Example of the use of the virtual path connection identifier at the B-ISDN UNI*

Table 6.3: *Overview of major changes in ITU-T Recommendation Q.2931 compared to ITU-T Recommendation Q.931*

Protocol changes	
New/modified information elements	Broadband bearer capability
	ATM cell rate
	AAL parameter information element
	Connection identifier
New/modified coding rules	Indication of the message length
	Common variable format for information elements
	Free ordering of information elements within a signalling message except for the message header[1]
	Inclusion of compatibility information[1]
Modified procedures	Called-side compatibility checking
	VPCI/VCI allocation/selection

[1] currently being discussed

6.5.2   Network–Node Interface Signalling

The signalling application protocol for the NNI is described in ITU-T Draft Recommendations Q.2761 to Q.2764 [144, 145, 146, 147]. These recommendations are based on the description and definitions of the existing monolithic version for ISUP of 64 kbit/s ISDN [130, 131, 132, 133].

The signalling application protocol for the NNI is called broadband-ISUP (B-ISUP). To allow independence from existing protocols, it was agreed that the new protocol is a new ISUP. B-ISUP uses a new code point for the service information octet which differentiates it from the existing ISUP.

In order to meet the time schedule for B-ISUP the same approach is used as for the Q.2931 protocol. Modifications for B-ISDN can be categorized into two parts:

- modifications required to provide signalling for B-ISDN
- preparations to allow a smooth transition towards future releases.

6.5.2.1 Mandatory Modifications for B-ISDN

The most important modification with respect to the ISUP for 64 kbit/s is the substitution of the circuit identification code (CIC) and its functions. This also influenced the procedures that are related to the CIC. In ISUP the CIC identifies the:

- transmission channel (connection element)
- bearer control association
- call control association.

Transmission channel: The 12 bit value of the CIC is strictly related to a circuit, that is, a 64 kbit/s channel. In ATM, the transmission channel has to be identified by a new identifier relating to the VP and the VC. The VC is identified by the VCI, whereas the VPCI is required to identify the VP. The reasons why the VPI is not useful as a unique identifier at the UNI are also valid at the NNI. The VPCI is semi-permanent and consists of 16 bits. Both the VPCI and VCI are encoded in the connection element identifier (CEI) parameter. The CEI will be assigned and used bidirectionally, that is, the same value will be used for both directions.

Bearer control association: The dynamic behaviour of the CEI, which consists of 32 bits, is very disadvantageous for the identification of the logical bearer control association. Therefore, the control plane association is identified by a separate bearer control identifier (BCI). A transaction mechanism, (that is, using origination and destination BCI) will be used which is similar to the transaction capabilities application part (TCAP)

Call control association: In release 1 there is no distinction between call and connection. Therefore, identification of the call control association is implicitly provided by the BCI.

Bandwidth handling: In contrast to 64 kbit/s ISDN, the bandwidth of a connection has to be indicated explicitly. The new information transfer rate parameter will be used for this purpose. This parameter consists of the forward and backward peak cell rate.

OAM procedures: In ISUP, OAM procedures like *reset, blocking* and *testing* are strictly related to the CIC. Because CIC was removed, these procedures cannot be used for B-ISDN. It is very likely that these procedures will be separated from the bearer control procedures.

Bothway operation: Bothway operation of channels is applicable to VPs and VCs. In B-ISDN two types of dual seizure can be identified:

1. dual seizure of the CEI

2. dual seizure of cell rate, that is, simultaneous request for the last available cell rate in a VPC.

As the procedures for prevention and resolution of dual seizure in ISUP are not applicable, new ones have to be defined.

B-ISDN routing: Routing in ISUP is based on the indication of the required information transfer capability and signalling capability; both are single values. Routing in B-ISDN will become more complex because more information (cell rate, quality of service, broadband connection-oriented service subcategory, symmetry, etc.) has to be taken into account.

Parameter format: All B-ISUP parameters will have a common format: parameter name followed by a length indicator and the parameter content. This format is identical to the one used at the UNI.

Message format: Simplification of the parameter format (only one for all parameters), means that the message format will be simplified to include the routing label followed by the message type, a length indicator and the B-ISUP parameters. The fixed mandatory part and the variable mandatory part are no longer necessary. The ordering of parameters can be chosen arbitrarily. This format is also very similar to that used at the UNI.

Compatibility mechanism: To allow for forward compatibility, the ISUP mechanism will also be applied to B-ISUP. All messages and parameters will contain compatibility instructions for handling unknown (new) signalling information.

6.5.2.2   Protocol Evolution

In releases 2 and 3, call control and connection/bearer control will be separated. The application layer structure for OSI [137] will be applied to protocols. B-ISUP will mainly be used for bearer control. Therefore, reuse of the B-ISUP – with some modifications and enhancements – as a bearer control protocol in releases 2 and 3 should be possible (see Figure 6.6). Some provisions, for example on the syntax level, are required to allow for simple protocol enhancements and evolution. The use of modern description techniques like **abstract syntax notation no. 1** (ASN.1) [153], should be possible. Furthermore, harmonization between the UNI and NNI protocol elements will simplify interworking between them.

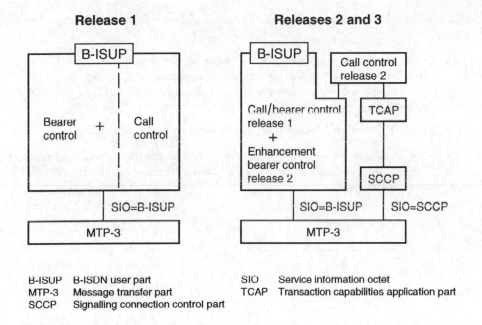

Figure 6.6: *Evolutionary path for B-ISDN NNI signalling protocol*

6.6 Requirements for Release 2 Signalling Protocols

In parallel with the specification of the signalling application protocols for release 1 of the UNI and NNI, ITU-T is already specifying the requirements for the release 2 signalling protocols. These specifications focus on the description of a functional model for release 2 signalling and on the description of the exchange of signalling information between the functional elements within this model.

This work will result in ITU-T Recommendation Q.73 [128]. In addition, a requirements document for release 2 signalling has been produced. These documents will be the basis for the detailed specification of release 2 protocols. ITU-T intends to finalize the work on detailed protocol specifications for release 2 in the second half of 1995.

One of the first results was an agreement that these specifications should be based on the separation of call control and bearer/connection control. Using this approach it will be possible to have calls with several connections (multi-connection calls), which is one of the powerful features required for the provision of multimedia

services. In addition, separation between call and bearer/connection control will
allow:

- Establishment and release of a call without any connection. Such a call
  might be useful for the negotiation of end-to-end service compatibility prior
  to reserving resources (look-ahead function), and is also useful for some supplementary services.

- Dynamic allocation/deallocation of connections to/from a call.

This basic structure of call and bearer/connection control separation allows
release 1 signalling protocols to be reused as bearer/connection control protocols
with only minor changes.

Chapter 7

ATM Switching

Two main tasks can be identified for an ATM switching or cross-connect node:

1. VPI/VCI translation

2. cell transport from its input to its dedicated output.

A switch fabric is necessary to establish a connection between an arbitrary pair of inputs and outputs within a switching node. In principle, a switch fabric can be implemented by a single switching element. Since such an element could not satisfy the requirements of a normal-size ATM switching node, larger switch fabrics are used built up from a number of switching elements.

The throughput of a switching node will be in the Gbit/s range and the cross-node delay and cell loss should both be kept very low. Therefore, central control cannot be used to switch cells. Only switch fabrics with highly parallel architectures can meet these stringent requirements.

7.1 Switching Elements

A **switching element** is the basic unit of a switch fabric. At the input port the routing information of an incoming cell is analysed and the cell is then directed to the correct output port. In general, a switching element consists of an inter-connection network, an input controller (IC) for each incoming line and an output controller (OC) for each outgoing line (see Figure 7.1). To prevent excessive cell loss in the case of internal collisions (two or more cells competing for the same output simultaneously), buffers have to be provided within the switching element.

Arriving cells will be synchronized to the internal clock by the IC. The OC transports cells which have been received from the interconnection network towards the destination. ICs and OCs are coupled by the interconnection network.

159

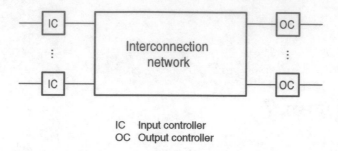

Figure 7.1: *General model of a switching element*

7.1.1 Matrix-Type Switching Elements

An internally non-blocking switching element can be constructed by using a rectangular matrix of crosspoints for the interconnection network (see Figure 7.2). It is always possible to connect any idle input/output pair. Whether or not a crosspoint connects an input to an output depends on the routing information of the cell as well as the occurrence of collisions.

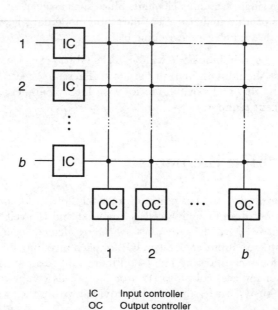

Figure 7.2: *Matrix-type switching element*

Various buffer locations are possible within this switching element [157, 182, 183]:

- at the input controllers
- at the output controllers
- at the crosspoints.

7.1.1.1 Input Buffers

The cell buffers are located at the input controller (see Figure 7.3). When using first-in first-out (FIFO) buffers, a collision occurs if two or more head-of-the-queue cells compete simultaneously for the same output. Then all but one of the cells are blocked. Cells following the blocked head of the queue cell are also blocked, even if they are destined for another, available output.

To overcome this disadvantage, FIFO buffers can be replaced by random access memory (RAM) [187]. If the first cell in the buffer is blocked, the next cell destined for an idle output will be selected for transmission. However, this operation mode requires more complex buffer control to find a cell destined for an idle output, and to guarantee the correct sequence of cells destined for the same output. The total buffer capacity will logically be subdivided in a load-dependent manner into single FIFOs (one FIFO for each output).

Further enhancements can be achieved if more than one cell can be transferred simultaneously from one buffer to different outputs. This requires a buffer with multiple outputs [163, 167] or a buffer with reduced access time.

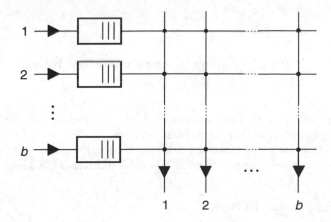

Figure 7.3: *Switching matrix with input buffers*

7.1.1.2   Output Buffers

Figure 7.4 shows a switching element consisting of a matrix with output buffers. Only if the matrix operates at the same speed as the incoming lines can collisions occur (several cells are hunting simultaneously for the same output). This drawback can be compensated by reducing the buffer access time and by speeding up of the switching matrix. These factors may lead to technological limitations on the size of the switching element.

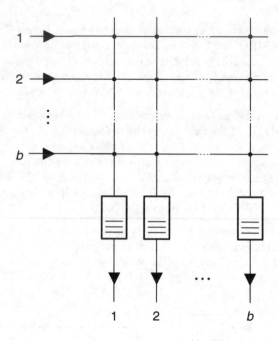

Figure 7.4: *Switching matrix with output buffers*

A switching element with output buffers will be non-blocking only if the speed-up factor of the matrix is b (that is, b cell simultaneously hunting for the same output can be switched) for a $b \times b$ switching element. In all other cases, additional buffers are necessary at the input to avoid cell loss caused internal blocking.

7.1.1.3   Crosspoint Buffers

The buffers can also be located at the individual crosspoints of the matrix (see Figure 7.5). This is called a **butterfly** switching element [26]. It prevents cells that are hunting for different outputs affecting one another. If there are packets in more than one buffer belonging to the same output, control logic has to choose which buffer will be served first.

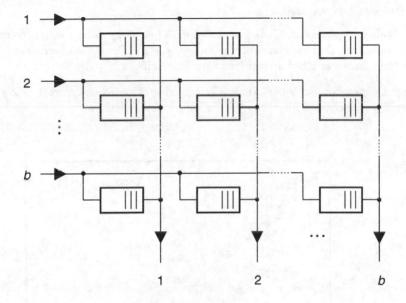

Figure 7.5: *Switching matrix with crosspoint buffers*

From the performance point of view, this buffer location strategy has the drawback that a small buffer is required at each crosspoint and no buffer sharing is possible. Therefore, it is not possible to achieve the same efficiency that a switching element with output buffers provides.

7.1.1.4   Arbitration Strategies

If several cells compete simultaneously for the same output, only one cell can be transferred and all other cells will be delayed. An arbitration strategy is required to determine the 'winning' cell. Objectives for such a mechanism can be fairness or minimization of cell loss, or minimization of cell delay variations. The following strategies can be applied [63, 183]:

1. **Random**: The line which will be served first is chosen at random from all lines competing for the same output. This strategy requires only a small amount of implementation overhead.

2. **Cyclic**: The buffers are served in a cyclic order. This approach also requires only a small overhead.

3. **State dependent**: The first cell from the longest queue will be served first. For this algorithm, the lengths of the buffers hunting for the same output have to be compared.

4. **Delay dependent**: This is a global FIFO strategy taking into account all the buffers that feed one output. However, it implies some overhead to store the relative order of arrival for competing cells.

A performance comparison of the different arbitration mechanisms is shown in Figure 7.6 (see also [183]).

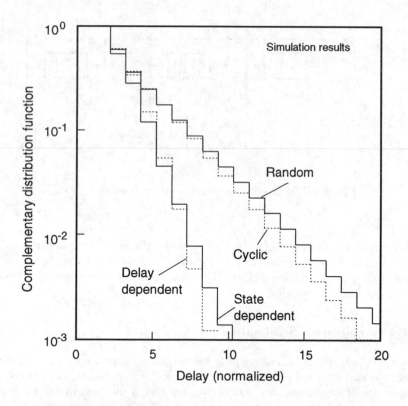

Figure 7.6: *Influence of different arbitration strategies on the delay*

The random strategy has the highest delay variations. An insignificant improvement can be achieved by using the cyclic strategy. The optimum strategy with respect to cell delay variation is the delay-dependent strategy. Minimum cell loss can be achieved by implementing the state-dependent algorithm. The performance with respect to the delay requirements of this strategy is slightly worse, but still acceptable.

7.1.2 Central Memory Switching Element

The principle of a central memory switching element is shown in Figure 7.7. All input and output controllers are directly attached to a common memory which can be written to by all input controllers and read by all output controllers.

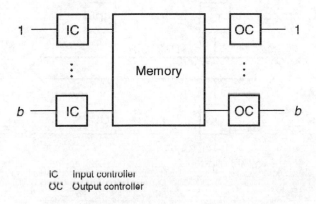

IC   Input controller
OC   Output controller

Figure 7.7: *Central memory switching element*

The first example of such a switching element was used in the PRELUDE experiment [30]. The common memory can be organized to provide logical input as well as logical output buffers. Research and Development of Advanced Communication in Europe (RACE) project 1012 'Broadband Local Network Technology' is using the *Sigma* switch [49], which is based on a common memory structure with logical output buffers. A possible realization of such a switching element is described in Section 7.2.3.1.

Since all the switching element buffers share one common memory, a significant reduction of the total memory requirements can be achieved in comparison with physically separated buffers. On the other hand, a high degree of internal parallelism is necessary to keep the frequency of memory access within a realizable range.

7.1.3   Bus-Type Switching Element

The interconnection network can be realized by a high-speed time-division multiplexing (TDM) bus (see Figure 7.8). Conflict-free transmission can only be guaranteed if the total capacity of the bus is at least the sum of the capacities of all input links [34]. Bit-parallel data transmission (e.g. 16 or 32 bit) on the bus system is required to achieve this high capacity.

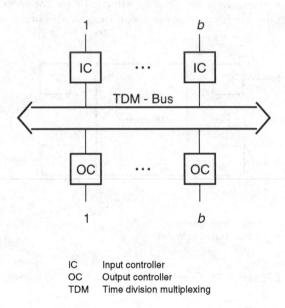

IC	Input controller	
OC	Output controller	
TDM	Time division multiplexing	

Figure 7.8: *Bus-type switching element*

Normally, a bus access algorithm is applied which allocates the bus to the individual input controllers at constant intervals. Each input controller is able to transfer its cell towards the destination before the arrival of the next cell is completed. No buffers are required at the input controller. However, several cells may arrive at the same output controller, whereas only one cell can leave the controller. Therefore, buffers are required at the output controller. This switching element has the same performance as the matrix-type switching element with output buffers.

7.1.4   Ring-Type Switching Element

The ring-type switching element is shown in Figure 7.9. All input and output
controllers are interconnected via a ring network, which should be operated in a
slotted fashion to minimize the overhead. In principle, a fixed time-slot allocation
scheme can be used but this requires a ring capacity which is the sum of the
capacities of all input links. If the ring capacity is less than the total input capacity,
a flexible allocation scheme is necessary, which results in an additional overhead.

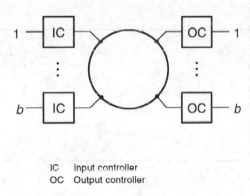

IC   Input controller
OC   Output controller

Figure 7.9: *Ring-type switching element*

The ring structure has the advantage over the bus structure in that a time-slot
can be used several times within one rotation. However, this requires that the
output controller empties a received time-slot. When using this destination release
mechanism, an effective utilization of more than 100% can be achieved. This
advantage has to be offset against the additional overhead for the destination
release mechanism and flexible time-slot allocation mechanism.

The ORWELL ring [2] is one approach to the implementation of a ring-type switching element. To meet the high throughput requirements, several rings are used in
parallel forming a so-called torus of rings.

7.1.5   Performance Aspects

Many publications offer performance comparisons of different buffering strategies
[157, 167, 176, 182, 183]. Figure 7.10 (see also [183]) shows the mean cell delay of
a 16 × 16 switching element with different buffer locations and buffer operation
modes.

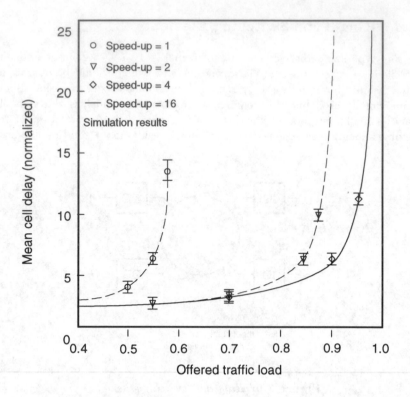

16 x 16 switching element with input and output buffers
Bernoulli arrival process

Figure 7.10: *Performance comparison of buffering strategies*

The results for the switching element with a simple FIFO input buffer correspond to the curve with speed-up factor 1. A speed-up factor i means that the buffer access time is reduced by the factor i, or i cells from one buffer can be transferred simultaneously. The maximum throughput of this element is limited to about 58 % of the total capacity [157]. A good performance improvement will be achieved using a speed-up factor of 2. The best results are obtained for switching elements with a speed-up factor of 16. In this case the behaviour is identical to a switching element with output buffers. However, the ideal throughput can almost be obtained even with a speed-up factor of 4 [183]. This may significantly simplify the implementation.

7.1.6 Technological Aspects

The performance results shown in Figure 7.10 are valid for infinite buffer sizes. However, only finite buffer sizes are possible. Table 7.1 presents the buffer sizes (in cells) for switching elements of different sizes and different buffer locations, assuming an average load of 85 % at each input and a permissible cell loss probability of 10^{-9} [107].

Table 7.1: *Buffer size requirements*

	Size	
Type	16 × 16	32 × 32
Central memory	113	199
Input buffer	320	640
Output buffer	896	1824

The central memory switching element requires the least memory capacity as a result of buffer sharing. The required memory capacity for a switching element with input buffers is low compared with the switching element with output buffers. This can be ascribed to the fact that in a switching element with input buffers only, one cell can be written into the buffer and several cells can be read from the buffer, whereas in the switching element with output buffers, several cells can simultaneously arrive but only one cell can leave.

In the following discussion it is assumed that a 16 × 16 or 32 × 32 switching element can be implemented in a single integrated circuit with complementary metal-oxide semiconductor (CMOS) or bipolar CMOS (BICMOS) technology. The chip area can be subdivided into the memory part and the random logic part (for example, serial-to-parallel converter). The memory area is smallest in the central switching element, whereas the required random logic area will be, without any doubt, larger than for the other two types.

Figure 7.11 shows the relationship between chip size and power dissipation for the three types of switching element (switching matrix with output buffer, switching matrix with input buffer and central memory switching element). It must be pointed out that specific implementation principles and a certain type of CMOS technology were used, which is why no scales are provided on the axes.

The power dissipation of CMOS memories is very small. On the other hand, high-speed random logic consumes a relatively high amount of power. This results in a non-linear relationship between chip size and power dissipation of the considered switching elements. From all these discussions it is evident that, as regards chip

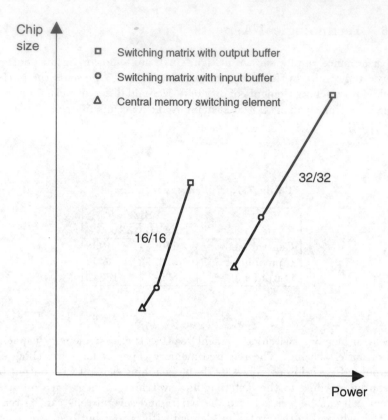

Figure 7.11: *Relationship between chip size and power dissipation*

size and power dissipation, the central memory switching element has clear advantages, while the switching element with output buffers is the least favourable one.

7.2   Switching Networks

This section deals with the general classification of switching networks. Existing and proposed ATM switch architectures of various manufacturers and research institutes will not be presented. A survey of various switches can be found in [3, 32, 166, 195].

Figure 7.12 gives an overview of the presented networks.

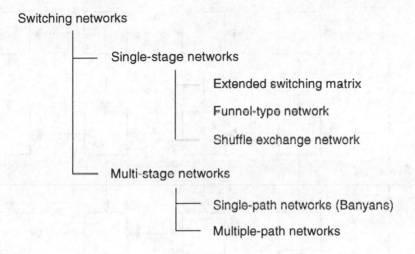

Figure 7.12: *Classification of switching networks*

7.2.1 Single-Stage Networks

A single-stage network is characterized by a single stage of switching elements which are connected to the inputs and outputs of a switching network.

7.2.1.1 Extended Switching Matrix

Figure 7.13 shows an example of an extended switching matrix which is formed from $b \times b$ switching elements. Basically, any desired size of switching network can be implemented with this approach.

To realize an extended switching matrix the switching elements described in Section 7.1 have to be extended by adding b inputs and b outputs. Input signals are relayed to the next column of the matrix via the additional outputs. The additional inputs are connected to the normal outputs of the switching element in the same column but in the row above.

The advantage of the extended switching element is the small cross-delay because cells will only be buffered once when crossing the network. It should be noted that the cross-delay is dependent upon the location of the input. The fact that the number of switching elements increases with the number of required inputs limits the size of an extended switching matrix. It is certainly possible to form a 64×64 or 128×128 single-stage network, but multi-stage networks will be preferred for larger systems.

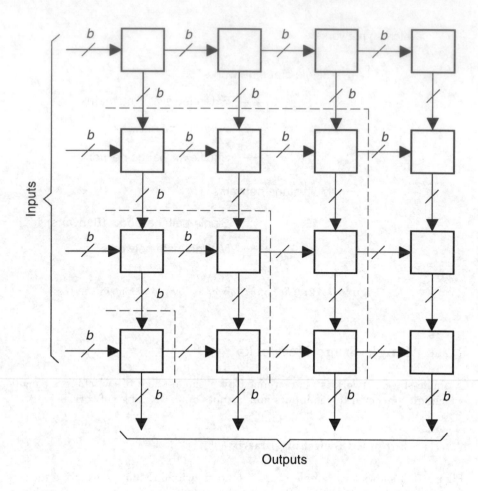

Figure 7.13: *Extended switching matrix*

7.2.1.2   Funnel-Type Network

In the $N \times N$ non-blocking switching network shown in Figure 7.14, switching elements are interconnected in a *funnel-like* structure [46]. All switching elements consist of $2b$ inputs and b outputs. Each funnel represents a $N \times b$ matrix, of which there are N/b in parallel. With current technology it is possible to realize 32×16 switching elements. A single-stage 128×128 switching network can be realized with these elements. The multi-stage approach will be the preferred solution for larger networks.

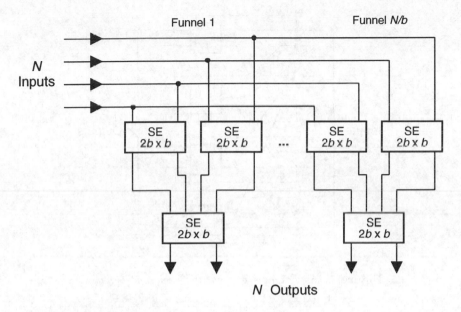

SE   Switching element

Figure 7.14: *Funnel-type network*

7.2.1.3 Shuffle Exchange Network

The **shuffle exchange** network [28] belongs to the class of single-stage networks. It is based on a perfect shuffle permutation which is connected to a stage of switching elements (see Figure 7.15). A feedback mechanism is necessary to reach an arbitrary output from a given input (this mechanism is depicted by dashed lines in Figure 7.15).

It is evident that a cell may pass through the network several times before reaching its proper destination. Therefore, this is also called a **recirculating** network. At the output of a switching element it has to be decided whether a cell can leave the network or has to be fed back to the input.

This type of network requires only a small number of switching elements but the performance is not very good. The cross-delay depends on the number of switching elements that have to be passed through.

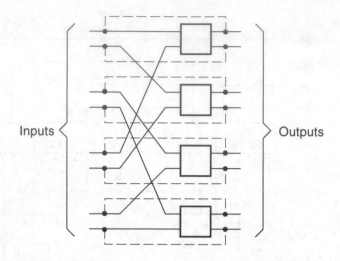

Figure 7.15: *Example of a shuffle exchange network*

7.2.2   Multi-Stage Networks

Multi-stage networks can be used to avoid the drawbacks of single-stage networks. They are built of several stages which are interconnected by a certain link pattern. According to the number of paths which are available for reaching a destination output from a given input, these networks can be subdivided into two groups called **single-path** and **multiple-path** networks.

7.2.2.1   Single-Path Networks

In single-path networks, there is only one path to the destination from a given input. These networks are also called **Banyan** networks [52]. Because only one path exists to the proper output, routing is very simple. Banyan networks have the disadvantage that internal blocking can occur. This results from the property that an internal link can be used simultaneously by different inputs. According to [63], Banyan networks can be classified into subgroups.

In **(L)-level** Banyan networks, only the switching elements of adjacent stages are interconnected. Each path through the network passes through exactly L stages. Furthermore, this class is subdivided into **regular** and **irregular Banyans**. Regular Banyans are constructed of identical switching elements, whereas irregular Banyans can use different types of switching element. The **generalized delta** network [37] belongs to the class of irregular Banyans.

Regular Banyans have the advantage that they can be implemented economically because they are constructed of identical switching elements. In the following, only **SW-Banyans**, which are a subclass of the regular Banyans, will be considered.

SW-Banyans can be constructed recursively from the basic switching element with F input links and S output links. The simplest SW-Banyan is a single switching element (called a (1)-level Banyan). An (L) level SW Banyan will be obtained by connecting several $(L-1)$-level SW-Banyans with an additional stage of $(F \times S)$ switching elements. These extra switching elements are connected in a regular manner to the SW-Banyans.

Delta networks [178] are a special implementation of SW-Banyans. L-level networks which are constructed of $(F \times S)$ switching elements have S^L outputs. Each output can be identified by a unique destination address, which is a number of base S with L digits. Each digit specifies the destination output of the switching element in a specific stage. This allows simple routing of cells through the delta network, which is called **self-routing**.

In **rectangular delta** networks the switching elements have the same number of inputs and outputs $(S = L)$. Consequently, the number of network inputs is equal to the number of network outputs. These networks are also called delta-S networks. Figure 7.16 shows a delta-2 network with four stages which has the topology of a **baseline** network [201]. The thick line indicates the path from input 5 to output 13 (binary destination address 1101).

Bidelta networks are a special class of delta networks. They remain delta networks even if the inputs are interpreted as outputs and vice versa. All bidelta networks are topologically equivalent and can be transformed into each other by renaming the switching elements and the links [37].

7.2.2.2 Multiple-Path Networks

In multiple-path networks, a multiplicity of alternative paths exist to the destination output from a given input. This property has the advantage that internal blocking can be reduced or even avoided.

In most multiple-path networks the internal path will be determined during the connection set-up phase. All cells on the connection will use the same internal path. If FIFOs are provided in the individual switching elements, cell sequence integrity can be guaranteed and no resequencing is necessary.

In this classification, multiple-path networks can be subdivided into **folded** and **unfolded** networks.

Figure 7.17 shows a three-stage folded network. In folded networks, all inputs and outputs are located at the same side of the switching network and the network's internal links are operated in a bidirectional manner (each link in Figure 7.17 represents the physical lines for both directions).

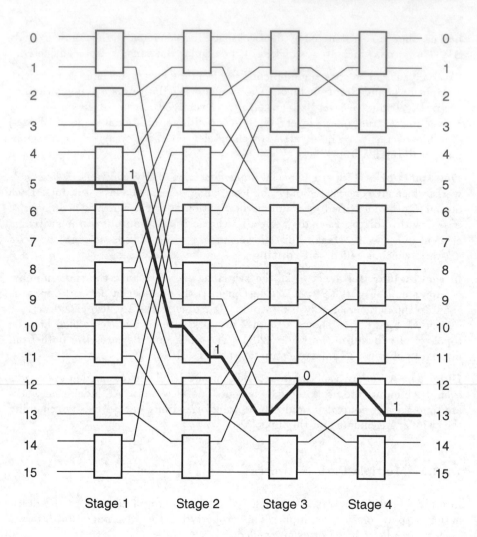

Figure 7.16: *Delta-2 network with four stages*

Folded networks have the advantage that short paths [167, 194] can be used. For example, if the input line and the output line are connected to the same switching element, cells can be reflected at the switching element and need not be passed to the last stage. The number of switching elements that the cells of a connection have to pass through depends on the location of the input and output lines.

The port capacity of a three-stage folded network built up from $b \times b$ switching elements is $(b/2)(b/2)b$. With today's technologies, switching elements of size

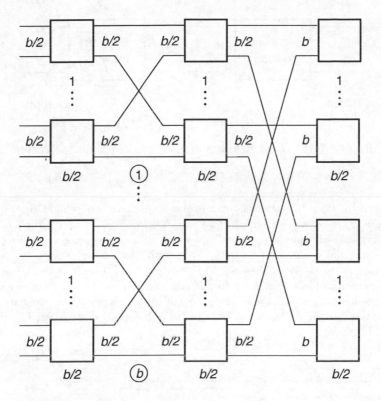

Figure 7.17: *Three-stage folded switching network*

16 × 16 and 32 × 32 can be realized, leading to three-stage networks with 1024 and 8192 ports, respectively.

In unfolded networks, the inputs are located on one side and the outputs on the opposite side of the network. Internal links are unidirectional and all cells have to pass through the same number of switching elements.

Multiple-path unfolded network structures will be based on single-path network structures. Again, the basis for these networks is $b \times b$ switching elements. For simplicity, only 2 × 2 switching elements are presented in the figures.

Turner [197] describes a switching network which consists of a buffered Banyan network and a preceding **distribution network** (see Figure 7.18). The distribution network has the purpose of distributing cells as evenly as possible over all inputs of the Banyan network. This approach can reduce internal blocking. However, the cell sequence integrity of a connection cannot be maintained and therefore an additional resequencing mechanism is required at the output.

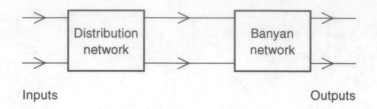

Inputs   Outputs

Figure 7.18: *Basic structure of a distribution/Banyan network*

Another realization of such networks is the combination of a **sorting network** [13] and a **trap network** in front of a Banyan network [62] (see Figure 7.19). The sorting network arranges arriving cells in a monotonous sequence depending on the network internal destination address. Cells with identical addresses are detected by the trap network and all but one of these cells are fed back to the input of the sorting network. Cells that have to pass through the sorting network again will be assigned a higher priority in order to maintain cell sequence integrity. Cells entering the Banyan network can be transported to their destination without any internal blocking.

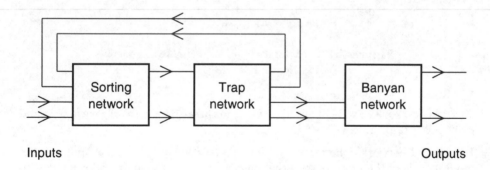

Inputs   Outputs

Figure 7.19: *Basic structure of a sorting/trap/Banyan network*

Multiple-path networks can also be realized by using several planes of Banyan networks in parallel (see Figure 7.20). This is called **vertical stacking** [164].

All cells belonging to the same connection will pass through the same plane. This will be determined during the connection set-up phase. An incoming cell will be switched to its appropriate plane by the distribution unit which is located at each input line. At the switch output, a statistical multiplexer collects cells from

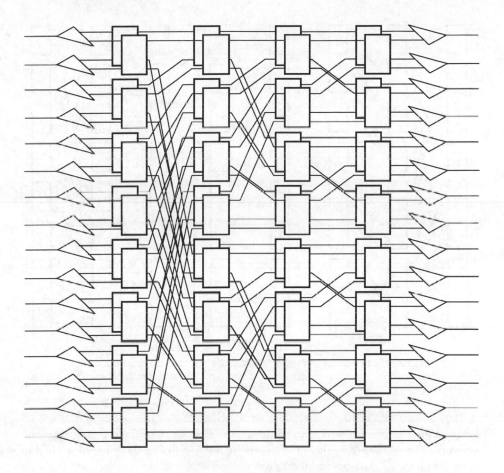

Figure 7.20: *Example of a parallel Banyan network*

all planes. In [194] it is shown that even with two planes in parallel a virtually non-blocking switching structure can be achieved.

Adding a number of stages to a given Banyan network is called **horizontal stacking** [164]. A **multi-path interconnection network** (MIN) [4] is realized by adding a baseline network with reversed topology to an existing baseline network (see Figure 7.21). The baseline network has already been presented in Figure 7.16.

Assuming $b \times b$ switching elements the $N \times N$ network has $2 \log_b N$ stages. In an $N \times N$ network, N internal paths are available to a given output from an arbitrary input. From a particular input the internal path can be selected arbitrarily until the output of the baseline network is reached. Then the way through the reversed baseline network is fixed.

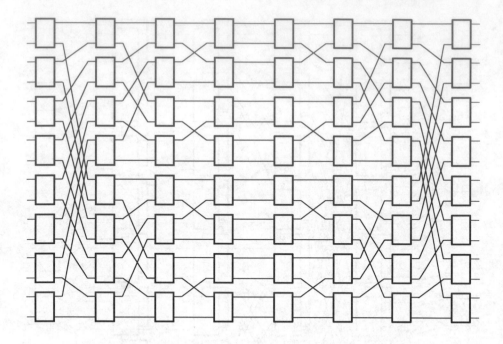

Figure 7.21: *Example of a multi-path interconnection network*

A Beneš network [17] is very similiar to a MIN. The difference is that the last stage of the baseline network coincides with the first stage of the reversed baseline network. Therefore, the number of stages is reduced by one compared with the MIN. Figure 7.22 shows a seven-stage Beneš network.

Again, assuming $b \times b$ switching elements, only N/b alternative paths are available to any output from any input. Each path is uniquely determined by the switching element passed in the centre stage.

7.2.3   Cell Header Processing in Switch Fabrics

The main tasks of ATM switching nodes are:

1. VPI/VCI translation

2. transport of cells from the input to the appropriate output.

In order to fulfil these tasks, two approaches can be applied [189]:

- **self-routing principle**
- **table-controlled principle**.

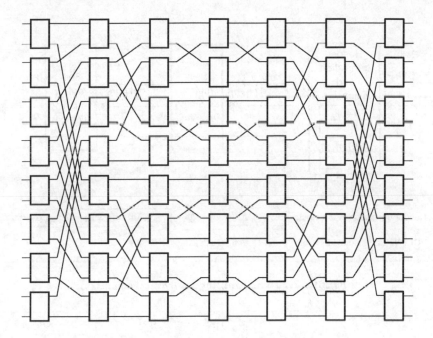

Figure 7.22: *Example of a seven-stage Beneš network*

7.2.3.1 Self-Routing Switching Elements

When using self-routing switching elements, VPI/VCI translation only has to be performed at the input of the switching network. After translation the cell is extended by a switching network internal header. This header precedes the cell header. Cell header extension requires an increased internal network speed.

In a network with k stages the internal header is subdivided into k subfields. Subfield i contains the destination output number of the switching element in stage i. Figure 7.23 shows the cell header processing in a switching network built up of self-routing switching elements.

Figure 7.24 depicts a generic realization of the self-routing switching element [45]. It contains a central memory (cf. Section 7.1.2) with logical output queues and is controlled by the routing information included in the internal cell header. In order to keep the buffer access speed within the range given by technological constraints, a wide parallel memory interface is used requiring serial-to-parallel conversion at the inlet and parallel-to-serial conversion at the outlet. The central control with address queues assigned to each outlet takes care of correct delivery of the cells.

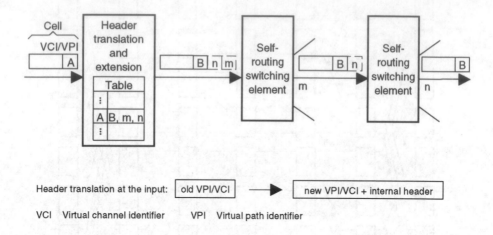

Figure 7.23: *Self-routing switching elements*

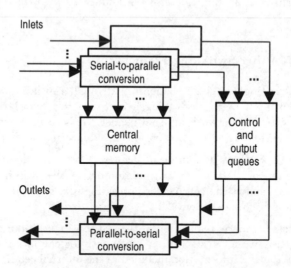

Figure 7.24: *Generic realization of the self-routing switching element with central memory*

7.2.3.2 Table-Controlled Switching Elements

When using the table-controlled principle, the VPI/VCI of the cell header will be translated into a new one in each switching element. Therefore, the cell length need not be altered. Figure 7.25 shows header processing in a switching network which consists of table-controlled switching elements.

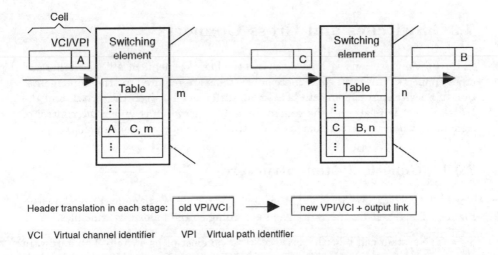

Figure 7.25: *Table-controlled switching elements*

The contents of the tables are updated during the connection set-up phase. Each table entry consists of the new VPI/VCI and the number of the appropriate output.

Extensive studies have been made to decide which principle is superior [189]. For large multi-stage switching networks the self-routing principle will be preferred because it is superior in terms of control complexity and failure behaviour. The need for a higher internal bit rate because of the cell extension is not critical.

7.2.4 Multicast Functionality

Some data services and distributive services are characterized by point-to-multipoint communication. This capability can be supported by an ATM switch fabric. For this purpose an ATM switching element must be able to transmit copies of an incoming cell to different outlets. In the case of the shared buffer switching element which minimizes the number of buffers, a cell is only deleted from the memory when all the necessary copies have been transmitted through the outlets.

In Section 7.2.3 it was shown that the self-routing switching element offers a lot of advantages. However, the principle shown in Figure 7.23 results in a low performance for multicast communication. Header translation is performed at the input of the switching network. All cell copies made within the switch fabric possess the same VPI/VCI value. This is an unnecessary restriction which can be overcome by marking 'multicast' cells and performing header translation for that type of cell at the output of the switching network.

7.3   Switches and Cross-Connects

In the previous sections we have discussed the basic elements of ATM switches and cross-connects. However, some more subsystems are required for the implementation of a switch/cross-connect. (The main difference between the switch and the cross-connect is related to the control function. A switch is under the control of signalling, whereas a cross-connect is controlled by network managment.)

7.3.1   Generic System Structure

The generic structure of an ATM system (switch or cross-connect) is shown in Figure 7.26 [46]. It has been designed according to the following principles:

- The system can be either used as cross-connect or as switch. The hardware can be identical, the software will be different. This architecture also provides the possibility to perform switch and cross-connect functions in the same node.

- The switching network employs the self-routeing principle because it is the most promising one (cf. Section 7.2.3).

- Connection-related information is stored in those peripheral units which are affected by the particular connection. This allows quick access to the per-connection information.

- The ATM switching network is non-blocking. It can easily be tested by sending node-internal test cells.

- A unique cell rate is used within the switching network/multiplexer. Adaptation of different cell rates used on subscriber/trunk lines is performed in the interface modules.

7.3.2   System Building Blocks

The generic switch/cross-connect depicted in Figure 7.26 consists of the following modules:

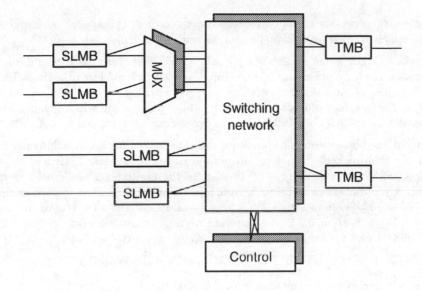

MUX   Multiplexer
SLMB   Subscriber line module broadband
TMB   Trunk module broadband

Figure 7.26: *Generic switch/cross-connect architecture*

- subscriber line module broadband (SLMB)
- trunk module broadband (TMB)
- multiplexer
- switching network
- system control.

A subscriber is connected to the switching network or multiplexer via an SLMB. In a first step the bit rate is 155.520 Mbit/s (or lower); later on 622.080 Mbit/s may also be supported. Connection to other switches and cross-connects is performed via the TMB. It supports existing plesiochronous systems as well as SDH transmission with bit rates up to 2.4 Gbit/s.

The multiplexer is used for local concentration of subscriber traffic within the switch.

The switching network connects the interface modules, the multiplexer and the control processor. It is also used for internal communication between the node subsystems.

The control processor is responsible for system control. It may also perform functions which are related to signalling or network management.

To achieve high system availability, the multiplexer, switching network and control processor are fully redundant. At the input an interface module (SLMB or TMB) sends copies of each cell to both multiplexer/switching network planes. At the output the interface modules decide from which plane a cell will be transmitted. More details on this node-internal redundancy concept are given in [45].

As mentioned in Section 7.3.1, a unique cell rate is used for the switching network and the multiplexer. Therefore, all peripheral units (SLMB, TMB and control processor) have the same type of interface to the multiplexer and switching network. A proprietary protocol with system internal cell formats is applied at these interfaces. The system internal cell format consists of the 53 octets of the standard cell (cf. Section 5.5.1), the internal routing information (cf. Section 7.2.3) and information for synchronization, housekeeping, control and test.

At the input of the node the SLMB/TMB perform the following functions:

- cell extraction, for instance from the SDH frame;

- rate adaptation to the node-internal speed;

- cell delineation and cell header error detection/correction according to the mechanisms described in Sections 5.3.1.5 and 5.3.1.6;

- VPI/VCI translation;

- generation of the new HEC value;

- usage parameter control;

- traffic measurement for billing, administration and traffic engineering;

- generation of the system internal cell format;

- transmission of cells to both switching planes.

At the ouput of the node the SLMB/TMB provide the following functions:

- selection of correct cells from the redundant switching plane;

- conversion of the internal cell format to the standardized format;

- adaptation of the cell rate to the outgoing transmission speed by insertion of idle cells;

- filling of cells in the transmission system (for example SDH frame).

Chapter 8

ATM Transmission Network

Sections 4.1 and 4.2.1 addressed general network aspects of the ATM-based B-ISDN. A main feature of an ATM network is the establishment of VCCs and VPCs as described in Section 4.2.1. Switching of ATM cells was discussed in Chapter 7. The present chapter discusses the transmission aspects of ATM networks. After a brief overview of network elements, like ATM multiplexers and cross-connects, transmission systems for ATM cell transport and network synchronization will be discussed. Emphasis will be put on possible local loop implementations.

8.1 Overview

8.1.1 Cell Transfer Functions

The transfer of cells through an ATM network is supported by the following functions:

- generation of cells (packetizer, or more precisely, ATM-izer, for example, in a B-ISDN terminal);

- transmission of cells;

- multiplexing/concentrating of cells;

- cross-connecting of cells;

- switching of cells.

Cell transmission will be addressed in Section 8.1.2, while the other functions will be discussed in this section.

187

8.1.1.1   Generation of Cells

A B-ISDN terminal will send all its information mapped into cells (besides transmission overhead in the SDH option, cf. Section 5.3.1.1), in which case no additional packetizing function is required in the ATM network.

Packetizers will be required, however, whenever interworking with non-ATM equipment has to be performed. An ATM packetizer either cuts STM channels into
pieces that fit the ATM cell format or adapts non-ATM packets to ATM cells.
This signal conversion is required at an B-NT2 (see Section 5.2.4) which provides
the user with both ATM and non-ATM interfaces or at any other place in the
network where the connection of non-ATM traffic is foreseen (for example, in an
ATM multiplexer or switch). The reverse procedure (depacketizing) has, of course,
to be performed when ATM traffic is converted to non-ATM traffic.

The use of ATM cell packetizers in a customer network is shown in Figure 8.1.
Figure 8.2 shows applications of ATM cell packetizers in the public network.

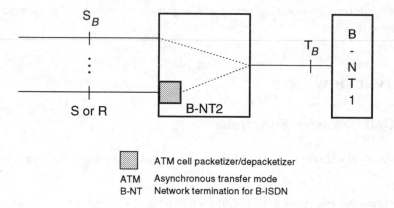

Figure 8.1: *The use of cell packetizers/depacketizers in the customer network*

The need to convert non-ATM signals to the ATM cell format will arise especially
during the introductory phase of ATM networks (see Chapter 9).

The problems caused by packetization delay for ATM speech connections will be
discussed in Section 10.1.

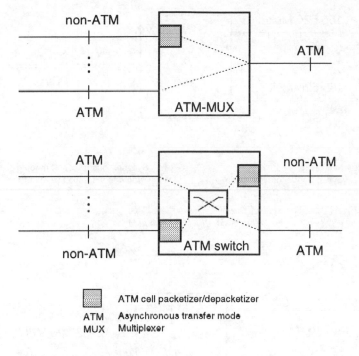

Figure 8.2: *The use of cell packetizers/depacketizers in the public network*

8.1.1.2 Multiplexing/Concentration of Cells

Figure 5.44 on page 130 showed the use of a STM multiplexer which multiplexes several signals originating from different B-ISDN customers onto a single access line. In this STM-type multiplexer, no (cell) concentration takes place, that is, idle cells are not removed as the STM multiplexer does not process the signal payload carrying ATM cells. A simple example is shown in Figure 8.3.

All incoming idle cells will be sorted out in an ATM multiplexer, thus concentrating the ATM traffic. The achievable degree of concentration depends on the traffic characteristics and the requested quality of service. Figure 8.4 shows an example of how an ATM multiplexer is deployed to enable customers share a common access line.

The ATM multiplexer unpacks arriving ATM cells from the transmission frame (the SDH STM-1 frame is shown in the figure), eliminates idle cells (and erroneous, uncorrectable ones) and multiplexes the valid cells into one STM-1 frame. In this example the ratio of the gross bit rates at both sides of the multiplexer is $1/m$. This can only work if m is a small number (up to 8) and the maximum sum bit

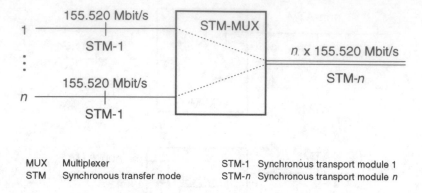

MUX   Multiplexer   STM-1   Synchronous transport module 1
STM   Synchronous transfer mode   STM-n   Synchronous transport module n

Figure 8.3: *STM multiplexer*

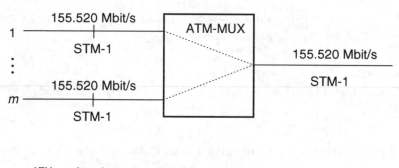

ATM   Asynchronous transfer mode
MUX   Multiplexer
STM-1   Synchronous transport module 1

Figure 8.4: *Example of an ATM multiplexer*

rate used at any time by any tributary is small compared with 155.520 Mbit/s, that is, it does not exceed, say, 20 to 30 Mbit/s.

8.1.1.3   Cross-Connecting of Cells

An ATM cross-connect, like a VP/VC switch, can flexibly map incoming VPs/VCs onto outgoing VPs/VCs and thus enable VPCs/VCCs to be established through the ATM network. The cross-connect also concentrates ATM traffic as it eliminates idle cells. (Morever, it performs necessary OAM functions at the physical layer and the ATM layer, as does the ATM multiplexer.)

A cross-connect can be used, for example, in the access network to separate customer traffic that is destined for the local switch from that to be transmitted on a fixed route through the network to a fixed endpoint (see Figure 8.5).

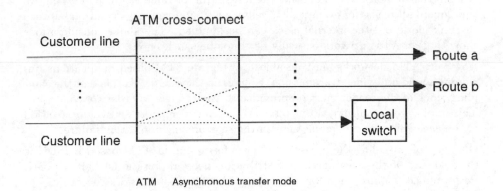

Figure 8.5: *ATM cross-connect*

While a VP/VC switch establishes and releases connections according to a signalling protocol (see Chapter 6), a cross-connect is controlled through management operations.

8.1.2 Transmission Systems

ATM cells can, in principle, be transported on many transmission systems. The only requirement is that bit sequence independence is guaranteed so that there are no restrictions on allowed cell information content.

ITU-T has defined two options for the user–network interface one based on SDH and the other on pure cell multiplexing (see Section 5.2.3). Other transmission systems may be used in the network. One example is the PDH as recommended in ITU-T Recommendation G.703 [86]. PDH provides gross bit rates of about 2, 34, 140 Mbit/s or 1.5 and 45 Mbit/s (these two branches of hierarchical levels are used, for example, in Europe and in North America, respectively). During the introductory phase of B-ISDN, some countries want to employ existing transmission systems like PDH to support ATM cell transport.

8.1.3   Network Synchronization

An ATM transport network needs bit timing and cell timing. At any entrance point to an ATM multiplexer or ATM switch, an individual synchronizer is provided which adapts the cell timing of the incoming signal to the internal timing. In principle, therefore, transmission links need not be synchronized with each other. Each synchronizer can adjust differing phases in units of a cell (idle cell stuffing/extraction). When limiting the maximum tolerable distance between two subsequent idle cells (for example, 256 cells), a certain frequency deviation between the link clock and the internal clock can be handled. The above considerations show that an ATM network basically need not be synchronous.

However, ATM networks must be able to integrate STM-based applications, including audio and video transmission, as long as they exist. To this end the sampling clock of the sender must be provided to the receiver in order to avoid slips. This implies requirements on the network in terms of support for synchronization of the access lines and tolerable slips in the case of synchronization failure.

One way of providing the necessary clock information in ATM-based B-ISDN is to make use of the existing clock distribution network for the 64 kbit/s ISDN. Performance requirements on the clock distribution network according to ITU-T Recommendations G.811 [92] and G.821-824 [93, 94, 95, 96] should then be considered as a basis for discussion on broadband networks and, if necessary, be redefined.

Derivation of the B-ISDN clock from the 64 kbit/s ISDN clock distribution network is shown in Figure 8.6.

The 64 kbit/s ISDN is structured into several hierarchical levels (four levels are indicated in the figure, as is the case in Germany). Each node receives its clock from the node of the higher level, the highest level node deriving its timing directly from the clock distribution network. In the event of failure, standby connections can be used to derive timing via alternative paths.

The simplest implementation for B-ISDN could be to derive the timing for each node from the corresponding 64 kbit/s ISDN node as shown in the figure (here, too, standby timing connections are provided to cover failure situations). Note that B-ISDN will most probably have fewer hierarchical levels than the 64 kbit/s ISDN. As clock accuracy decreases at the lower levels, it may become necessary to derive the clock for B-ISDN not from the corresponding 64 kbit/s ISDN level but from a higher one (or even directly from the clock distribution network).

8.1.3.1   Synchronization of Terminals

For a constant bit rate service the source sampling frequency f_s and the filling rate R_c of cells pertaining to this service are tightly correlated:

$R_c = f_s/48$

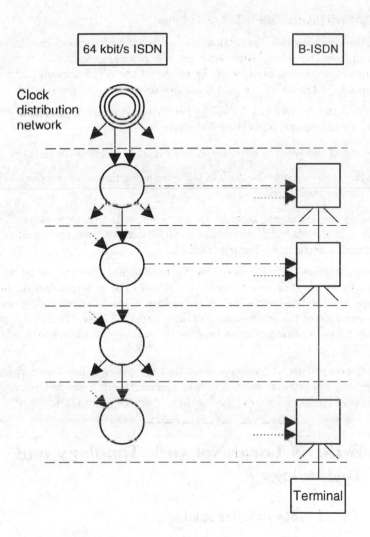

Figure 8.6: *Example of network synchronization for B-ISDN*

(The ATM cell information field has 48 bytes.)

Thus at the receiving side the original source sampling frequency can, in principle, be derived from the rate of those arriving cells belonging to the connection under consideration. However, because of the nature of the ATM network, arriving cells are subject to delay variations which are not so easy to compensate.

To overcome this problem, a STM-like mechanism can be adopted for ATM networks on an end-to-end basis provided that:

- timing of the sending side (terminal) is synchronized with network timing

- at the receiving side the clock of the sending terminal is reproduced by virtue of the network clock.

To this end the terminals have to be provided with the network clock via the access line. In the case of SDH the clock will be derived from the signal across the user–network interface (cf. Section 5.3.2.2).

In the synchronous B-ISDN shown in Figure 8.6, no slips can occur as long as network synchronization works correctly. Should the synchronization fail, local exchanges provide the access lines with a clock of sufficient accuracy to sustain orderly operation of the accesses for a defined period of time. Terminals connected to different local exchanges must be able to remove any slips which might then occur.

In a synchronous network, source signals that are not correlated with the network clock (for example, video sources in free-running mode) can be transmitted by means of positive justification (this method is described in [21]).

8.2 B-ISDN Local Network Topology and Technology

8.2.1 Local Network Structure

Conceptually the simplest realization of the B-ISDN local network is the star topology where there is one access line per customer. The remaining problem to be solved could then be to define the characteristics of the digital section extending between the T_B and V_B reference points (see Figure 8.7 (a)).

However, other structures are also being investigated as candidates for implementation in the B-ISDN local network. These include multiple star, ring, bus and tree configurations. Some examples are shown in Figure 8.7. Case (b) shows the multiple star configuration in which several customers' signals are multiplexed onto one access line. Optionally, there might be an additional cross-connect to provide different paths through the network. Its functionality may comprise:

(a) **Star configuration**

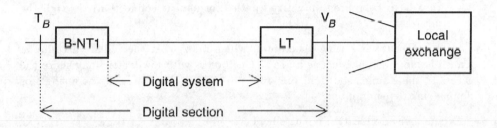

(b) **Multiple star configuration**

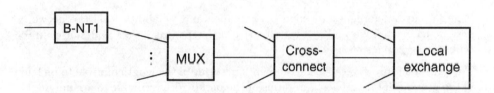

(c) **Ring configuration**

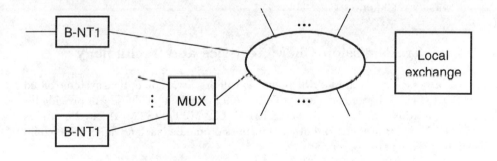

B-NT1   Network termination 1 for B-ISDN
LT   Line termination
MUX   Multiplexer

Figure 8.7: *Examples of local network structures*

- connection of customers with high traffic volumes directly to the local exchange

- separating traffic that is to be switched in the local exchange from traffic that is to be routed on a fixed path (permanent connection) through the network.

Configuration (c) is a ring structure in which many customers share a common transmission medium, such as a MAN. Customers with low traffic may share the access to the ring, as shown in the lower part of (c). The ring may be a single or double ring depending on:

- number and location of customers

- throughput requirements

- availability criteria

- cost aspects.

When a customer requests a high performance and reliability level the network may be connected via multiple interfaces to different ring access nodes or even to different exchanges.

The ring structure saves transmission lines in terms of the length of cable to be laid in the ground but is restricted in terms of the bandwidth available to an individual user and in terms of upgradability (the same holds for bus configurations). In a star or multiple star configuration it is easier to connect additional customers to the B-ISDN.

Tree configurations will be discussed later in connection with B-ISDN introduction scenarios (see Chapter 9).

8.2.2   Transmission Characteristics and Technology

In the access network most B-ISDN signals will be carried on optical systems based on SDH (ITU-T Recommendations G.707-709 [88, 89, 90]). These will provide bit rates of approximately 155 Mbit/s (STM-1), 622 Mbit/s (STM-4) and 2.5 Gbit/s (STM-16). PDH systems and other transmission media, such as radio links, could also be used where appropriate.

The use of single-mode fibres in accordance with ITU-T Recommendation G.652 [84] is favoured in the access network as they allow longer distances to be covered. Optical signals can be generated by laser diodes. The electronic parts will be based on CMOS technology for bit rates up to 155 Mbit/s and on bipolar technology for higher bit rates.

Two optical fibres (one for each direction of transmission) may be employed. Alternatively optical wavelength division multiplexing (WDM) on a single fibre can be used to separate both transmission directions by using different wavelengths (e.g. 1530 nm and 1300 nm).

The bit error probability of the optical transmission link should be less than 10^{-9}. An ATM switch will guarantee a cell loss probability of about 10^{-9} (see Section 7.1.6). Cell loss in an ATM switch is primarily caused by buffer overflow in the case of traffic congestion or the detection of uncorrectable errors in the cell header. If the transmission bit error probability is less than 10^{-9}, the latter effect is negligibly small as it requires the occurrence of specific multiple-bit errors in one cell header.

8.2.2.1 Maintenance Aspects of Optical Transmission

The following failures may occur in optical transmission systems:

- laser light emission failure
- laser sends continuous '1's
- receiver indicates continuous '0's or '1's.

In the event of such a failure the corresponding message will be delivered to a line maintenance entity (for example, located in the local exchange) which is responsible for setting the appropriate alarms. An urgent alarm will be generated if a unit is out of order or a warning issued if its performance is deteriorating.

8.3 Trunk Network Structure

A possible trunk network implementation is shown in Figure 8.8. (Realization of internodal signalling connections is not discussed in this chapter. Signalling may be established via the existing SS7 routes or, in the long term, over the ATM network itself.)

Figure 8.8 shows the following network elements:

- B-ISDN exchange
- ATM cross-connect
- STM multiplexer/cross-connect.

ATM cross-connects act like VP switches and can flexibly provide VP connections through the network (cf. Section 4.2). STM cross-connects may also be deployed to facilitate rearrangement of the physical paths, for example in the event of transmission failures (protection switching). Finally, STM multiplexers merge, for example, 155.520 Mbit/s STM-1 signals into the higher bit rate signals STM-4 or STM-16 of about 622 Mbit/s or 2.5 Gbit/s, respectively.

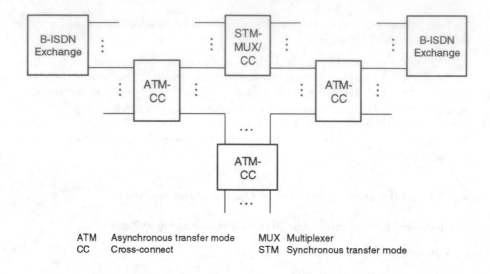

Figure 8.8: *Example of trunk network structure*

ATM cross-connects process each arriving cell. In line with its VCI/VPI value, a cell is routed in the direction defined by the associated VCC/VPC. Therefore, VCCs/VPCs with arbitrary bit rates can be established and switched through an ATM cross-connect. Establishment and release of VCCs/VPCs can, in principle, be initiated by the user or the network provider by means of ATM layer management procedures. The time required to establish or release VCCs/VPCs will be much shorter than is needed to meet the request for a reserved, permanent channel in today's networks, that is, VCC/VPC establishment can be performed within a couple of seconds.

Multiplexers and cross-connects can be used to decouple the logical point-to-point configuration of the ATM switching network from the actual topology of the fibre-based transmission network and to achieve:

- flexibility in the realization of hierarchically structured networks or networks with any other structure (e.g. meshed rings)

- easy provision of additional network capacity in the case of growing traffic

- a means for providing redundancy for ATM connections between exchanges.

Segregation of ATM traffic with low/medium bit rates per connection from ATM traffic with high bit rates in the trunk network may help to manage ATM traffic more efficiently.

Individual channels with the same destination can be grouped and carried on the same VP. Transit nodes of the ATM network act as VP switches with pre-established (redundant) VPC capabilities between the B-ISDN exchanges and need not handle VC switching. This facilitates the operation of transit nodes, especially in the case of many simultaneous low bit rate connections on a trunk line.

8.4   ATM Network Implementation Issues

ATM networks need a physical layer transmission capability. As long as ATM networks are rather thin overlay networks, it makes sense to use the existing PDH/SDH (SONET)-based transmission infrastructure, that is, to share the transmission network between STM and ATM traffic. (Cell-based transmission systems are not yet available; they only make sense when non-ATM traffic has decreased to a small quantity that can easily be adapted to ATM.) Figure 8.9 illustrates this principle.

With growing ATM traffic, dedicated ATM links (operating, for example, at STM-1, STM-4 or even STM-16 bit rates of 155 Mbit/s, 622 Mbit/s and 2.5 Gbit/s, respectively) can be installed to connect ATM nodes directly. (This is indicated in Figure 8.9 by the dashed line.)

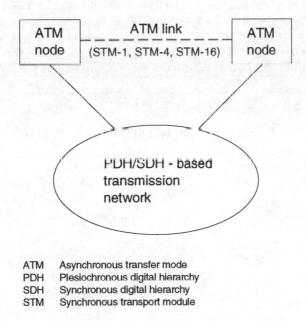

ATM	Asynchronous transfer mode
PDH	Plesiochronous digital hierarchy
SDH	Synchronous digital hierarchy
STM	Synchronous transport module

Figure 8.9: *ATM overlay network on top of PDH/SDH*

In the case of ATM on top of PDH/SDH, there is a strictly hierarchical relationship between the ATM network and the underlying transmission network: ATM is the client of the latter, the server network. If an ATM connection between two ATM nodes is to be established, the transmission network management will provide the necessary capacity, if possible (and monitor its performance). Should transmission fail, the physical layer is responsible for restoring a suitable link. However, if the ATM network cannot rely on the transmission network (perhaps because of a lack of supervision and restoration capabilities), it may provide redundant VPs so that in the event of any failure it can switch over from one VP to the other (VP protection switching).

When both the physical layer (PDH or SDH) and the ATM layer can provide protection switching, actions in both layers must be coordinated to avoid wasting resources or, even worse, the initiation of counteracting measures.

In an ATM network with dedicated ATM links, this problem seems to vanish as most, if not all, protection measures may be allocated to the ATM layer itself, that is, to the VP/VC level. More details on ATM network protection switching can be found in [56].

Another interesting question relating to ATM network implementation is the architectural concept for VP/VC handling. Although ITU-T allows cross-connection of both VPs and VCs (controlled by management) and signalling-controlled switching of VCs, for practical reasons (keep network management as simple as possible!) it may be better to restrict this functionality. It might be sensible to have a VP cross-connect network and, on top of it, a switched VC network. Leased line services would then be realized via the VP network and switched connections via the VC network. (The need for cross-connected VCs and switched VPs is still to be assessed.)

8.5   ATM Transmission Network Equipment

The ATM equipment required to perform the functions described in Section 7.3 has not yet been standardized by ITU-T in terms of functions, performance parameters and interfaces as is the case, for instance, for the standardized network equipment to be used in SDH transmission networks. Open issues relating to ATM equipment specification include:

- statistical multiplexing function
- multicast function
- OAM procedures: ATM-level protection switching
- ATM/physical layer relations
- performance requirements.

These problems affect all types of ATM equipment: multiplexer, switch and cross-connect. As to the equipment performance, the following values can be achieved with existing implementations:

cell loss probability $< 10^{-10}$
cell misinsertion probability $< 10^{-13}$
cell delay $< 100~\mu s$

Figure 8.10 outlines the possible use of different ATM equipment in an advanced ATM network.

The ATM multiplexer collects/distributes the ATM traffic (or ATM-ized STM traffic) for several users. The ATM add/drop multiplexer (ADM) inserts the upstream cell flow into an ATM access network ring and extracts the corresponding downstream cell flows from the ring. One or, for redundancy reasons, several

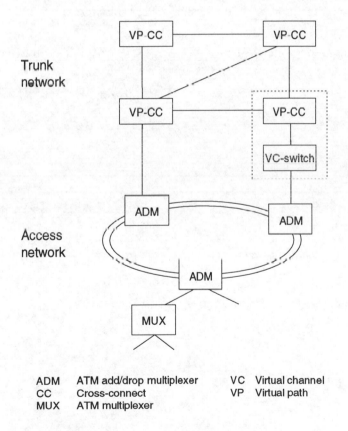

ADM	ATM add/drop multiplexer	VC	Virtual channel
CC	Cross-connect	VP	Virtual path
MUX	ATM multiplexer		

Figure 8.10: *Example arrangement of ATM network equipment*

ADMs are connected with the trunk network cross-connects, which are inter-meshed. (ATM cross-connects normally act at VP level, but VC cross-connection would also be possible.) The VC switch is operated as either a local exchange (terminating user-to-network signalling) or a transit exchange. The switching and cross-connecting functions may be integrated into a combined ATM cross-connect/switch, as indicated by the dashed box in Figure 8.10.

Chapter 9

Evolutionary Scenarios for B-ISDN

B-ISDN is based on:

- optical fibre transmission
- asynchronous transfer mode (i.e. a new switching and networking concept)
- new service categories (for example, multimedia services involving video)
- new network features like the intelligent network and telecommunications management network which, although not conceptually tied to B-ISDN, will most probably be implemented in any future network.

Consequently its implementation is a challenging task for both network providers and manufacturers. Its acceptance by potential customers requires a careful introduction strategy and evolution concept. As stated in [192]:

> 'Despite the convincing advantages of this universal broadband ISDN for all services, the high development and investment costs mean that it cannot in the short or medium term achieve wide coverage. The aim must therefore be to expand and add to the present-day telecommunication networks – of these primarily the network with most subscribers of all, the telephone network – in a market and demand-oriented manner with suitable technical concepts and in timed phases, thereby achieving a gradual transition to the ubiquitous, multi-subscriber network of the future. Any intended individual solutions or intermediate solutions must be designed such that they can later be incorporated with the least possible expense in the intelligent integrated broadband network.'

As today's telecommunication network structures differ from country to country and customers' needs also differ, there cannot be a single valid evolutionary path

towards B-ISDN all over the world. Thus all evolutionary scenarios are only examples which may shed some light on the development characteristics of networks
towards B-ISDN . They should not be taken as a straightforward implementation
plan for B-ISDN that would be viable in every country.

Introduction and evolution towards B-ISDN must, in any case, consider the strong
need to interwork with existing services and networks, including telephony,
64 kbit/s ISDN, data (packet) networks and TV distribution networks. Consequently the following sections look at interworking with, then the integration of,
such services and networks. In the opinion of most market experts the era of
broadband (public) networks will be ushered in with fast data services aimed at
business customers. To support existing customer networks (LANs etc.), which
are usually run with connectionless protocols, the future B-ISDN will have to
offer connectionless service capabilities (as discussed in Section 5.7.2) from the
beginning. This aspect will be described in Section 9.4.

A quite different introduction scenario foresees the provision of optical fibres to
the homes of residential customers (cf. Sections 9.1 to 9.3) who might primarily be
interested in entertainment programmes. Interactive services in addition to plain
telephony may gradually be offered according to the customers' wishes.

9.1   Fibre to the Customer

The demand for broadband services will develop only gradually, and

> 'it therefore seems advisable if the introduction of fibre optic
> technology for the subscriber access is not coupled firmly to
> new interactive broadband services. Instead, solutions are
> initially needed whereby optical fibres can be economically
> brought as close as possible to the subscriber, also for already
> existing services (television, telephony, data transfer)' [192].

Thus, the magic spell is **fibre to the office** or **fibre to the home**. A less
ambitious interim goal is **fibre to the curb** (cf. Figure 9.3). In the case of
business customers with large or rapidly expanding traffic volumes, it may already
pay for network providers to install individual optical fibre lines. Because of their
vast transmission capacities, they are deemed to be a future-proof investment. In
the case of residential customers the hope for quick returns is not so justified.
In this case, therefore, resource-sharing concepts have to be considered to allow
cost-effective introduction of broadband services.

9.1.1   Passive Optical Network

One of these cost-effective concepts is the passive optical network (PON) [44]. A
single fibre from the exchange feeds a number of customers via passive optical

branching (see Figure 9.1). This technique allows the fibre and laser in the local exchange to be shared between several customers. A TDM signal is broadcast from the exchange to all terminals on a single optical wavelength. The signal is detected by an optical receiver, then each customer's equipment demultiplexes only the channels intended for that destination.

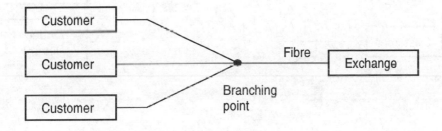

Figure 9.1: *Passive optical network technology*

In the return direction, data from each customer is inserted at a predetermined time to arrive at the exchange within an allocated time-slot.

This simple PON architecture admittedly has some drawbacks, such as:

- limited bandwidth for interactive services per customer
- multiplexing of upstream signals requires sophisticated measures
- privacy and security problems may arise
- restricted upgradability (how to overcome this problem will be discussed later on).

The PON concept can well support:

- unidirectional distribution services (TV and sound programmes)
- telephony and other 64 kbit/s ISDN services.

Different optical wavelengths $\lambda_1, \ldots, \lambda_n$ may be employed to separate services (and, possibly, transmission directions). For example, λ_1 for telephony, λ_2 for broadcast TV, λ_3 for video retrieval services, and so on, as illustrated in Figure 9.2. Note that different customers may wish to receive different service mixes.

In the long term it might be feasible, according to [44], to provide a separate wavelength to every customer with a specific mix of services multiplexed onto the wavelength as required by the customer. However, this concept can only work as long as the number of customers connected to one PON is not too large.

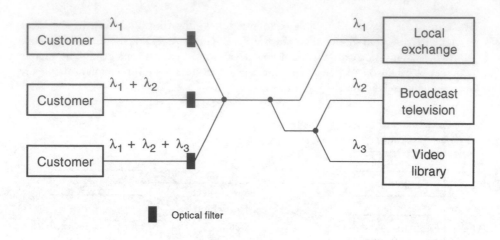

Figure 9.2: *Upgraded passive optical network*

Several modifications of the above concept are conceivable. Instead of, or in addition to, WDM (use of several λ_i) more than one fibre could be installed, perhaps one for TV distribution and the other for interactive services. Implementation of both service categories could thus be decoupled to a great extent.

Figure 9.3 shows an access configuration which deploys two fibres, one for TV distribution and the other for telephony or 64 kbit/s ISDN services (fibre to the curb). After conversion of the optical signals into electrical ones close to the customer's premises (at the curb), a bus-structured coaxial distribution system is used to deliver TV programmes to the customers, while a star structure is used to provide a customer with copper-based twisted pair telephony access.

In Figure 9.3 the opto-electrical conversion that is necessary to serve present electrical terminal interfaces is done only once for several customers, thereby saving on the cost.

To facilitate later evolution from a PON architecture to a full B-ISDN, it may be advantageous to install additional 'dark' fibres from the outset. These are fibres which are not immediately used but can support later point-to-point connection of individual customers to the local exchange (cf. [170]).

9.1.2 ATM on a Passive Optical Network

Section 9.1.1 introduced the PON concept which will support narrowband services and distribution services like TV. This section deals with a new version of a PON transmitting ATM traffic. Several strategies for ATM-PONs have already been

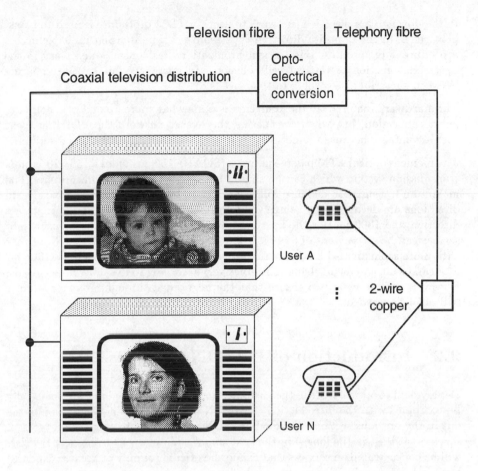

Figure 9.3: *Alternative fibre to the home architecture*

proposed [35, 39, 159]. An ATM-PON can either be used for upgrading existing PONs for broadband services or as a new and cost-efficient customer access network. An additional fibre or wavelength can be employed to broadcast cells to the customer and carry cells from individual customers to the node. The ATM-PON can be considered as a distributed flexible ATM multiplexer.

In an ATM-PON, several subscribers share a very large bandwidth (for example, 155.520 Mbit/s). The broadband communication requirements of a lot of subscribers can be simultaneously met by an ATM-PON because their required bit rates will predominantly be in the range of 10 to 30 Mbit/s [58]. (Only a few subscribers need the full capacity of 155.520 Mbit/s.)

In the downstream direction (network to user), a TDM procedure is used to transport cells. In the opposite direction (upstream), a time division multiple access procedure is required. A suitable synchronization mechanism is necessary in the upstream direction to prevent cell collision and guarantee fair capacity sharing between subscribers according to their needs.

The hardware required at the user side is somewhat more than for a point-to-point connection, but when considering the overall network the PON has clear cost advantages because the network equipment is shared by several subscribers.

The Siemens optical ATM passive network (SOAP) [159] provides a 155.520 Mbit/s transmission system which can be shared by a maximum of 32 subscribers. The maximum transmission distance will be around 10 km. Upstream and downstream directions are decoupled by using two wavelengths (1550 nm for the downstream direction and 1300 nm for the upstream direction). The data rate for each subscriber can be set in steps of 64 kbit/s up to a maximum of 45 Mbit/s. Note that with more sophisticated hardware the bit rate granularity can be smaller. The bit rate can be allocated and changed interactively according to the subscribers' needs. However, it is necessary to ensure that the negotiated throughput per customer will not be exceeded.

9.2 Introduction of B-ISDN Services

Deployment of optical fibre in the customer access network need not automatically be combined with the introduction of B-ISDN services in the network, as pointed out in the previous section. Although B-ISDN is conceived to support all types of services, at least in the long run, the customers' main interest in the new B-ISDN will be concentrated on services that cannot be offered (or only at greater expense) by existing networks.

B-ISDN will therefore initially coexist with other networks like public data networks, analogue telephone networks, 64 kbit/s ISDN, TV distribution networks and so on. The services offered by B-ISDN might be restricted to 'typical' broadband services, such as interactive services with bit rates above 1.5 Mbit/s or 2 Mbit/s. Access to other services, like 64 kbit/s ISDN bearer services, would still be provided by existing interfaces like the basic access [118].

Interworking facilities between B-ISDN and the other networks would have to be provided. For example, a customer using a dual function videotelephony/telephone set should be able to communicate with 64 kbit/s ISDN telephone users. This simple B-ISDN overlay model is shown in Figure 9.4.

Another step might be to introduce integrated access to different networks via a single, optical fibre-based B-ISDN interface on the network side of B-NT1. This configuration is depicted in Figure 9.5.

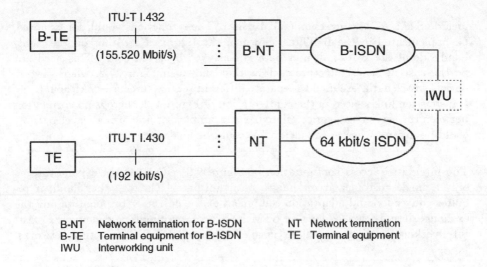

B-NT	Network termination for B-ISDN	NT	Network termination
B-TE	Terminal equipment for B-ISDN	TE	Terminal equipment
IWU	Interworking unit		

Figure 9.4: *Pure B-ISDN overlay network*

On the customer side, this configuration requires non-ATM interfaces to be adapted to the ATM format. This may comprise analogue/digital conversion in the case of analogue telephone interfaces or analogue TV interfaces, and will in any case

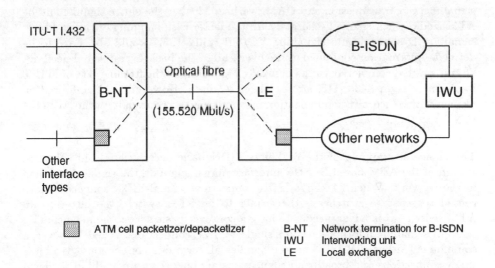

ATM cell packetizer/depacketizer

B-NT	Network termination for B-ISDN
IWU	Interworking unit
LE	Local exchange

Figure 9.5: *Integrated access configuration*

include STM/ATM conversion (ATM-izing). These functions could, for example, be implemented in the B-NT as shown in the figure. Note that on the right-hand side of the B-NT, all user data is conveyed by ATM cells. This need not be the case in an architecture such as that shown in Figure 9.2, where several optical wavelengths are used to separate different service categories. Although one transmission link is used in the configuration of Figure 9.2, there is no correlation between the service categories offered. For example, services using wavelength λ_1 could be digital, whereas broadcast TV could be analogue.

The integrated access configuration of Figure 9.5 reduces OAM expenditure as only a single customer access has to be maintained. On the other hand, it requires conversion and adaptation equipment at the customer termination and the exchange termination as long as STM interfaces, terminals and networks exist. Interworking functions are still necessary to connect B-ISDN with other networks.

Some specific problems arise with configurations like those of Figure 9.5. As signals from different networks may be multiplexed onto a single access line, OAM activities on this line must not interfere with connections that have been established by any network. Therefore, an entity is required to coordinate OAM activities on the customer's access.

The ATM-izing of non-ATM signals in the B-NT and in the corresponding unit in the network can be effected in different ways. Considering, for example, the basic access signal which comprises two 64 kbit/s B channels, a 16 kbit/s D channel for signalling and transmission and OAM overhead. Either the entire signal could be ATM-ized or each channel separately. In the latter case mapping of the 16 kbit/s signalling D channel onto signalling VC/VP connections would also have to be defined. Information contained in the overhead of the basic access signal need not be transmitted completely to the network. For example, the framing bits of ITU-T Recommendation I.430 [118] are no longer required. However, OAM information like activation/deactivation indication may still have to be exchanged between the B-NT and the network.

The choice of mapping of the 64 kbit/s ISDN basic access signal onto the cell stream of the ATM-based B-ISDN interface may depend on the signal processing in the network. When 64 kbit/s ISDN connections and B-ISDN connections are routed to separate switches – the former to an STM switch, the latter to an ATM switch – it is advantageous to have a compact basic access signal (including relevant signalling information) on a single VC/VP connection. When, however, a common ATM-based B-ISDN switch handles all incoming connections, 64 kbit/s ISDN connections and broadband connections are only separated behind the local exchange (that is, onto separate trunk networks), the use of individual VCCs for the B channels and the D channel information seems to be more suitable.

9.3   Integration of TV Distribution

TV programmes could be offered to the B-ISDN customer as switched or non-switched services (see Figure 9.6).

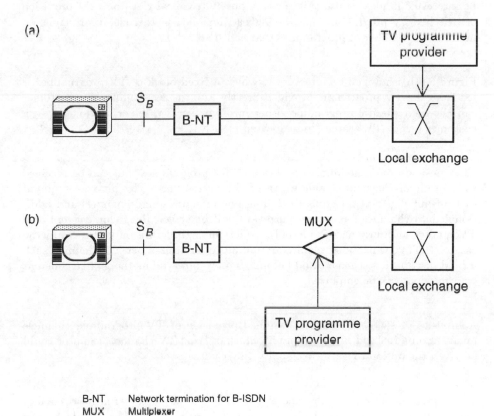

B-NT   Network termination for B-ISDN
MUX   Multiplexer
TV   Television

Figure 9.6: *Provision of TV programmes to the B-ISDN customer*

Figure 9.6(a) shows the full integration of TV distribution into B-ISDN. TV programmes are fed into the local exchange, which has sole responsibility for operation, administration and maintenance of the customer's access link. Programme selection is done via the usual B-ISDN signalling channels and procedures.

While this solution fully complies with the idea of an integrated broadband network, it may have market drawbacks. Switched TV programmes via optical fibres cannot compete in terms of cost with today's TV distribution to the customer via satellite or cable-based transmission systems. This fact may inhibit such a solution in some countries. Moreover, as the network provider knows what TV programmes are watched by customers, some critics are concerned about possible infringements of privacy by the unauthorized transfer of such information to people who might be interested in making use of it. From a purely technical viewpoint the provision of switched TV programmes has the highest flexibility as there is, in principle, no limit on the number of programmes that can be offered.

Figure 9.6(b) shows an architecture in which a fixed block of TV programmes is fed from the TV programme provider directly into the access link. The customer can choose a specific programme either in his or her TV set or, optionally, in a customer-owned TV switch (to be located in B-NT2).

This method limits the number of different TV programmes that can be received as a result of the limited bandwidth of the access line. The bit rate required to transmit digital TV signals (including one or more sound channels and additional data channels for control purposes) will be some Mbit/s for conventional TV quality and may be considerably higher for high definition pictures. In the case of HDTV, which may require around 30 to 50 Mbit/s per TV channel, such a rigid distribution scheme could fail unless more powerful methods, like coherent transmission, can be employed.

A mixture of switched and non-switched provision of TV programme channels might also be realized: in addition to a block of fixed TV channels the user could be given the option to select from a TV programme pool.

TV programme selection (unless merely performed in the customer network) makes some demands on the signalling procedures. The network must be able to handle numerous simultaneous signalling messages rapidly. Changing the TV channel must not take longer than the time that people are used to nowadays. Perhaps this is easier to achieve by (in-band) end-to-end-signalling between user and TV programme provider after the connection has been established. In this case, however, coordination between the customer equipment (TV sets and/or B-NT2), the local exchange and the TV programme providing unit is necessary to avoid conflicts and to make economic use of the available access line bandwidth. (When, for example, a customer switches on a TV set and selects a TV channel, a new connection normally has to be established unless the required TV channel is already provided to another TV set. If a new connection is to be established, the network must be checked (for example, in the local exchange) whether this can be done without interfering with existing connections on the customer's access line.)

9.4 Integration of LANs/MANs into B-ISDN

LANs (conventional and ATM-based) were introduced in Sections 4.7.5 and 4.7.6. The following section considers the step-by-step integration of the LAN/MAN world into ATM-based broadband networks.

9.4.1 Metropolitan Area Networks

The increasing demand for data communication beyond the local area has led to the introduction of MANs. These can be considered as an evolution of LANs, and their main application is the interconnection of existing LANs. The characteristic features of MANs are [20, 202]:

- coverage of areas of more than 50 km in diameter
- share a common medium
- distributed access control
- high transmission rates (100 Mbit/s or more)
- provision of isochronous, connection oriented and connectionless services
- evolution to B-ISDN in terms of capabilities and services.

MAN installations can be divided into *private* and *public* MANs [171]. A private MAN is owned or leased by a single customer and carries that customer's traffic. This simplifies billing as well as privacy and security functions.

However, many MANs are shared by a number of customers. From the point of view of the network operator, accurate billing and additional management functions are essential. Security and privacy are also serious issues because customers would not like to see their confidential data passing through the building of a competitor.

9.4.1.1 Fibre-Distributed Data Interface II

The fibre-distributed data interface II (FDDI-II) [5] can be used for MAN implementation. This is an enhanced version of FDDI [77] which is a ring system using an optical fibre for transmission with a data rate of 100 Mbit/s. Access to the ring is controlled by a modified token-passing protocol which is specially designed for high-speed transmission systems.

For reliability, two rings with opposite transmission directions are used, making the system capable of surviving a cable break or station failure. In the event of such a failure, only one ring will be used. The total length of both rings is limited to 200 km. Up to 1000 stations with a maximum distance between stations of 2 km can be attached to the ring.

FDDI supports only packet-switched traffic. In addition, FDDI-II is able to handle isochronous traffic, including voice or video.

9.4.1.2   Distributed Queue Dual Bus

The **distributed queue dual bus** (DQDB) (standardized for MAN/LAN applications) [69] is the result of the continued development of the **queue packet and synchronous circuit exchange** (QPSX) [174]. Isochronous, connection-oriented and connectionless services can be supported simultaneously.

The DQDB MAN consists of two unidirectional buses with opposite transmission directions to which multiple nodes are attached (see Figure 9.7). DQDB is independent of the underlying physical medium. This allows the use of existing PDH systems with transmission rates of, for example, 34, 45 and 140 Mbit/s [85], as well as SDH-based transmission systems according to [88, 89, 90] and possibly future systems with transmission rates in the Gbit/s range.

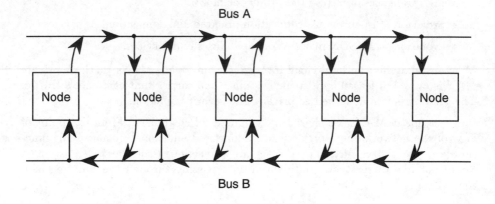

Figure 9.7: *Distributed queue dual bus network*

The dual buses can be looped or open ended. In the looped bus case the head and tail of each bus are collocated but not interconnected. Looping allows reconfiguration of the bus system in the event of bus failure. Head and tail will then be interconnected, while new head and tail points will be generated close to the location of the failure. Each node can act as head or tail. This self-healing mechanism makes the looped bus configuration the preferred choice.

All information in the DQDB network is transported within **slots**. A slot consists of a header with 5 octets and an information field with 48 octets – the same as in an ATM cell. The commonality of DQDB PDUs and B-ISDN PDUs simplifies the interconnection of these two networks.

A slot generator is located at the head of each bus. It creates empty slots and writes them on the bus. Isochronous services use **pre-arbitrated** slots. These slots are marked by the slot generator and have the appropriate VCI value inserted in the slot header.

All non-isochronous information is transported within **queue-arbitrated** slots. Pre-arbitrated and queue-arbitrated slots are distinguished by different values in the **slot type** field of the slot header. Queue-arbitrated slots are managed by the distributed queueing protocol (media access control). In contrast to the existing MAC procedures in a distributed queue system, each station buffers the actual number of slots waiting for access to the total network. With this in mind, a station which has a slot ready to send determines its own position in the distributed queue. Its own slot will be transported after satisfying the queued slots.

9.4.2 Interworking Units

For many years the need to interconnect individual computing systems and terminals has been increasing. Today, numerous networks coexist and increasing communication requirements demand that they be interconnected. IWUs are necessary to achieve this.

Two networks located close to each other can be coupled directly via an IWU. However, networks which are far from each other can only be interconnected via intermediate subnetworks.

In the following description it is assumed that different protocols are used at layer $(N - 1)$. The protocols of layer N and above are identical in the networks which will be interconnected. Networks can be coupled using various approaches [19, 193]:

1. Interconnection of the heterogeneous systems is achieved by protocol conversion at layer $(N\ 1)$. Often protocol transformation is difficult and not all functionalities can be retained after the conversion if the two networks do not provide the same functions.

2. In another approach, a common global protocol sublayer is placed on top of the different network protocols. This requires an additional adaptation sublayer between all layer $(N - 1)$ protocols and the common global protocol.

3. Coupling of two networks can also be performed at the first common layer. This approach avoids difficult protocol conversion but increases the transfer delay because the IWU has to process an additional layer.

The IWU is involved in important issues other than the selection of a protocol level at which different networks will be interconnected. **Naming, addressing** and **routing** are all necessary for the correct delivery of data to its appropriate destination. **Congestion control** has to be applied if the speeds of the networks are not matched. When different maximum packet sizes are defined for the two networks, the IWU has to perform **segmentation** and **reassembly** functions.

The following interconnection approaches are commonly used for today's networks:

- A **repeater** interconnects two networks at layer 1. Its main purpose is the enlargement of small networks.

- Interconnection at layer 2 is performed by **bridges**.

- A **router** interconnects two networks at layer 3.

- An IWU coupling networks at higher layers is called a **gateway**. Normally, only layer 4 gateways and application layer gateways (layer 7) are used.

9.4.3 Integration Scenarios

The first step in coupling LANs was to interconnect them via existing networks like the **circuit-switched public data network** (CSPDN), the **packet-switched public data network** (PSPDN) or the ISDN. LANs use transmission rates of up to 16 Mbit/s, whereas the transmission rates of the existing networks are very low (e.g. 64 kbit/s). Obviously this interworking strategy cannot provide good performance.

To achieve good LAN-like services across wide areas, LANs can be coupled via high-speed networks like MANs or ATM wide area networks. Several evolutionary steps are described below (cf. [27]).

9.4.3.1 Interconnection of ATM-based LANs

It is expected that ATM will first be introduced into the LAN world as a high-speed backbone network [173] which will interconnect several buildings forming a campus-wide LAN. Hubs will be located on the floors of each building. All the terminals, PCs, workstations and other data communication equipment will then be connected to these hubs (cf. Figure 4.15 on page 53).

As new (non-ATM) LANs often provide a physical point-to-point connection from terminal to hub (although still operating in a connectionless mode), one can anticipate that point-to-point configurations will dominate the ATM-LAN future. These configurations are known as **segmented LANs**. According to [173], advantages of a star-arrangement are: higher reliability, simpler management and easier expandability. Lower bit rates are sufficient for the individual terminal-to-hub connections, thus allowing cheaper interfaces. However, the interconnection of several hubs in the in one or more buildings requires more transmission capacity. Optical fibres and transmission rates of 155 Mbit/s (or even more) will be used.

These LANs can easily migrate to ATM, and this may happen in the near future. It is evident that the best approach for interconnecting ATM-LANs is the use of an ATM-based WAN. The use of a uniform technique throughout the system will simplify interworking. Processing will be cheaper and quicker. The user will benefit from better services and lower costs. One can conclude that the spread of ATM in corporate networks will force the deployment of ATM-based public networks. These public networks must be designed to accommodate the requirements imposed by the need for LAN–LAN interconnections.

Before this final stage is reached, several intermediate networking configurations will be used, as described in the following.

9.4.3.2 Interconnection of LANs via MANs

MANs have become a reality [202] and many conventional LANs are coupled via IWUs to MANs. Figure 9.8 shows this present application of MANs.

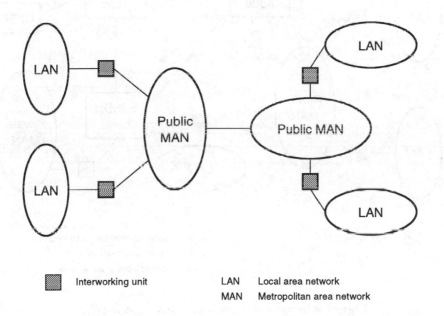

Interworking unit		LAN	Local area network
		MAN	Metropolitan area network

Figure 9.8: *Interconnection of LANs via MANs*

The MAN may be private or public. In both cases the increasing communication requirements lead to the interconnection of MANs via dedicated links (see Figure 9.8).

Initially MANs are being used mainly for connectionless services (LAN inter-connection), although in principle they can support isochronous and connection-oriented services.

9.4.3.3   Interconnection of MANs via ATM-WANs

The introduction of B-ISDN will be reinforced by the need for interconnecting MANs, as pointed out in the previous section. This approach allows access to wider areas with more flexibility, lower delay and higher throughput. Figure 9.9 depicts this evolutionary stage.

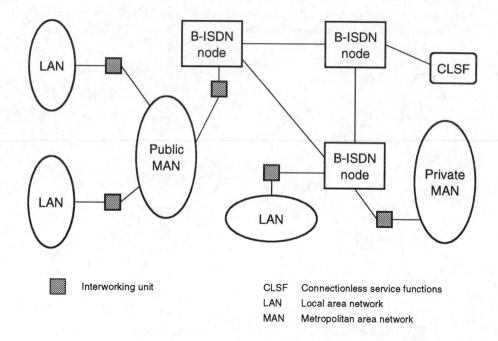

Figure 9.9: *Interconnection of MANs and B-ISDN*

LANs and private MANs can be directly coupled to an ATM-WAN. During this phase it is expected that more and more users will be attracted by the offered services and be encouraged to pass over the initial stage of the evolutionary path and immediately connect to the ATM network.

9.4.3.4   Coexistence of MANs and B-ISDN

Broadband terminals and new broadband CNs will be offered simultaneously with
the introduction of B-ISDN. These new CNs will, in many cases, have a star
structure. However, they can also deploy shared medium configurations like the
bus or ring structures which are widely used in existing LANs. Figure 9.10 shows
this intermediate stage when LANs, MANs, ATM-WANs and new CNs coexist.

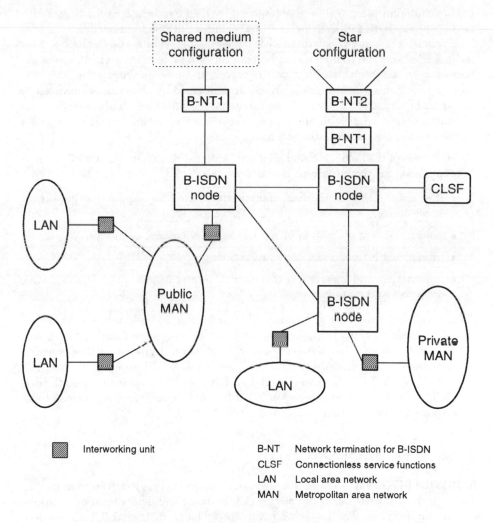

Figure 9.10: *Coexistence of MANs and B-ISDN*

9.5   ATM Trials and First Commercial Use

9.5.1   General Background

Many of today's communication requirements can be satisfied by the 64 kbit/s ISDN. However, a few genuine broadband applications already exist. In the in-house area, high-speed data communication has been facilitated by LANs, while in the public area, videoconferencing was introduced by using dedicated broadband circuit-switched networks.

Future communication will be characterized by high bandwidth utilization, multi-media applications and both point-to-point and multipoint connections . These facts require a new network with more intelligence, bandwidth and flexibility. New technologies and the complete standardization of new services and interfaces are necessary to achieve this objective. However, the obvious interest in new services, applications and systems is always accompanied by elements of uncertainty (acceptance, demand, technology, economy and organization). Laboratory implementations, field trials with pilot applications and test networks make it possible to overcome these uncertainties at an early stage.

Further goals of the field trials and pilot applications which have been implemented in preparation for the intelligent B-ISDN are [8]:

- the design of realistic communication scenarios for supporting important applications;

- requirements specification of commercial services and terminals;

- influencing international standardization;

- information and motivation of potential users, service providers, network operators and manufacturers.

All around the world, first-generation ATM switching nodes have been developed and field trials with pilot applications and test networks are running [8, 16, 30, 31, 51, 189]. Within the framework of RACE, several groups worked towards ATM demonstration models (for example, the B-ISDN UNI group [22]). Another project – RACE 1012 on 'Broadband Local Network Technology' – dealt with the definition of a second-generation ATM-based switching architecture and the development of an experimental switch model [49].

9.5.2   The BERKOM Trial

In 1986 the BERKOM (*Ber*liner *Kom*munikationssystem) project started in Berlin. The objective of this trial is the design, development and demonstration of applications for B-ISDN. The following items are included in the BERKOM project [179]:

- text and document processing in an office environment;

- high-quality printing and publishing;

- high-speed transfer of medical images (X-ray images, for example);

- applications in the field of computer-aided design (CAD) and computer-integrated manufacturing (CIM);

- distribution of HDTV programmes;

- access to information bases containing text, pictures and video;

- use of high-quality audio and video information in the residential area.

In autumn 1989, Siemens installed a pre-standard ATM switch as part of the BERKOM trial [51]. The switch fabric transfers cells (2 octet header and 30 octet information field) from 16 inlets to 16 outlets, all operating at 140 Mbit/s. The participants are located in Berlin and are attached to the ATM switching node via single-mode fibres.

Typical applications using this ATM switch are (see also Figure 9.11):

- interconnection of LANs;

- video communications at 64 kbit/s, 2 Mbit/s and 34 Mbit/s;

- joint editing over broadband links;

- interconnection of HICOM PBXs via ATM (private networking);

- access to 64 kbit/s ISDN via an EWSD exchange.

9.5.3   ATM Projects of Public Network Providers

At present the biggest push towards ATM can be observed in the field of in-house data communication and corporate networking. The reason is simply that ATM for the first time offers a unique, standard networking technique which both supports existing and upcoming data transmission protocols (X.25, frame relay, connectionless data services etc.), and promises to accomodate real-time service such as voice and/or video transmission or arbitrary combinations thereof (multi-media applications). In ATM the transport link capacity and the service bit rate are decoupled, so performance-limited shared-medium configurations (rings, bus systems) can be replaced with a star-configured topology with ATM switches/hubs where each user is entitled to establish a (switched) connection at the full interface bit rate to anyone on the customer network.

Public network operators also have good reasons for implementing ATM networks:

- create a common backbone network for data services;

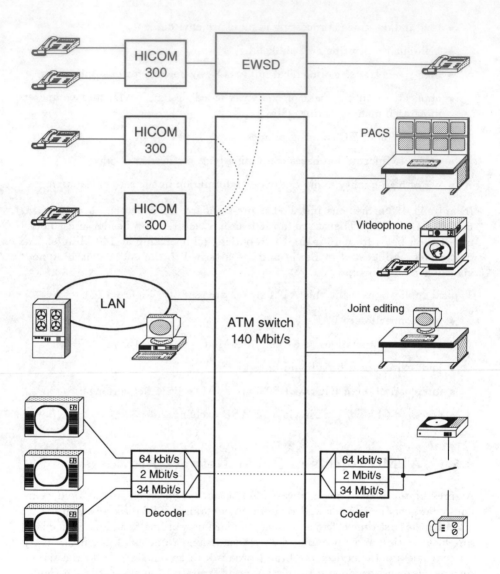

ATM   Asynchronous transfer mode
EWSD   Elektronisches Wählvermittlungssystem Digital
HICOM   High technology communication
LAN   Local area network
PACS   Picture archiving and communication system

Figure 9.11: *ATM applications of the BERKOM trial*

- be competitive against private networking (for example, offer ATM-based virtual private networks);

- test the acceptance of new services, especially multimedia sevices;

- use leading-edge technology.

Examples of the first public ATM network implementations are highlighted here. In North America all the major telecommunications network operators are running ATM trials with the intention of making commercial use of this installed basis as quickly as possible. The services mainly offered by these ATM networks are:

- ATM bearer service (cell relaying)

- frame relay

- SMDS

- circuit emulation (1.5/45 Mbit/s, for example)

- video applications.

In Europe the era of border-crossing ATM-based high-speed networking started in mid 1994. Many European network operators have committed themselves to this goal. The services to be offered to customers are the same as in North America. Also the ATM network infrastructure will be similar: both SDH-based transmission (where available) and PDH-based links (in Europe 34 Mbit/s and possibly 140 Mbit/s, in North America 45 Mbit/s) will be used. International VP nodes are foreseen, for example, in London, Paris, Cologne, Berlin, Madrid and Milan.

National network operators will also provide ATM infrastructure to their customers. In Germany, for instance, three ATM nodes in Berlin, Hamburg and Cologne, with remote ATM concentrators attached to each node, will give about 200 customers access to the ATM network. The network evolution plan foresees leased line services in 1994, switched ATM connections by mid 1995 and interworking with 64 kbit/s ISDN by the end of 1995, provided that the relevant international standards for signalling and interworking are available.

In Japan, Nippon Telegraph and Telephone Corporation (NTT) has drafted a most ambitious ATM network concept comprising ATM-based 2.5 Gbit/s add/drop rings in the local access area and an intermeshed VP trunk network. The cross-connected (leased line) VP network and the switched VC network will be clearly separated. Sophisticated OAM concepts (especially concerning VPC protection switching) have been introduced. A full public ATM network is expected by about the year 2015.

The above examples are far from exhaustive. To conclude this topic we would mention that ATM networks are also being field tested in Australia and the Pacific rim.

Chapter 10

Miscellaneous

10.1 Voice Delay and Echo Problems

In an ATM telephone connection, speech samples are collected until they fill the information field of a cell. As the information field consists of 48 octets, a delay of 48/8 kHz = 6 ms is encountered for 64 kbit/s telephony as a result of the packetization of speech. (If AAL type 1 – cf. Section 5.6.2 – is used for telephony, this delay can be slightly reduced to 47/8 kHz = 5.875 ms; as this is only a small effect it will be neglected here.) Depacketization of ATM speech also causes some delay. As individual ATM cells are subject to different transfer delays on their way through the network, this delay variation has to be smoothed out at the receiving side in order to generate the constant input required by the speech decoder. This procedure leads to an additional delay of approximately 1 ms.

The total delay may exceed the tolerable limit, especially when there are several transitions from STM to ATM, and vice versa, within one connection (for example, in the case of traversing three ATM islands the additional transfer delay resulting from packetization and depacketization would be 3 × [6 ms + 1 ms] = 21 ms).

The main problem is not the one-way delay itself but the delayed speaker echo received at the sending side. This arises primarily at the far end of the transmission line, specifically at the hybrid junction between four-wire and two-wire analogue circuits. The maximum one-way delay permissible for telephone connections is 400 ms according to ITU-T Recommendation G.114 [82]. This value has been chosen to take into account connections involving satellite links. A considerably lower one-way delay can be achieved for other connections, as is the case for ATM links.

However, echo received at the sending side will be perceived as disturbing by the speaker at a rather low value for the round-trip delay. As a rule of thumb, echo cancellation should be employed whenever a one-way delay of about 25 ms is exceeded.

225

Figure 10.1 (based on [82]) gives more information on the echo problem related to ATM speech connections. It is assumed that one ATM-based sub-network is inserted into an existing analogue or digital telephone network. This insertion causes additional delay and aggravates the echo problem. The use of ATM reduces the transmission length that can be covered without echo control measures. The curves drawn in Figure 10.1 directly show the effect of (non-processed) echo delay on the perception of human beings in terms of 'probability of encountering objectionable echo' (for example, 1% means that 1% of the speakers complain about the quality of their telephone connection). According to ITU-T Recommendation G.131 [83], no more than 1% objections to speech quality should be made in a network, although values up to 10% may be tolerated in exceptional cases.

The 1% limit of objections would confine the transmission length to about 300 km where one ATM area is inserted into an analogue environment, and to

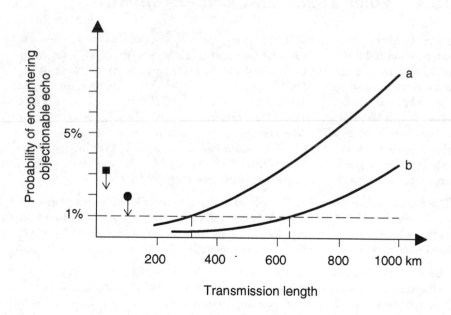

a   Insertion of ATM island into an analogue environment
b   Insertion of ATM island into a digital environment
■   Local connection
●   Inter-local connection
ATM   Asynchronous transfer mode

Figure 10.1: *Echo tolerance curves of telephone connections*

about 650 km where one ATM area is inserted into a digital environment, unless echo control is provided.

In Figure 10.1 the loss of the echo path was assumed to be 28 dB. The two isolated spots in the figure have been calculated for local connections (transmission length up to about 50 km) and inter-local connections (transmission length of about 100 km) with specified losses of 21 dB and 24 dB, respectively, according to current US standards (cf. [158]). As the low loss requirements in these cases may be reduced in future, the potential echo problems are expected to decrease. This is indicated in the figure by down-arrows.

To sum up:

- ATM introduces additional delay and thus increases echo problems on speech connections.

- The number of ATM/STM conversions should be kept to a minimum.

- Compared with today's telephone networks, more echo cancellation devices will have to be deployed with ATM. This could be avoided, if necessary, by using partly filled cells. For example, by filling only 24 octets of the 48 octet cell information field the packetization delay will be halved. The wastage of bandwidth may be tolerable, at least in the introductory stage of ATM networks. However, partly filling cells would require extra information to be exchanged indicating how much of a cell has been filled (either via signalling or an AAL-indicator). This might require additional standardization efforts. At least in the wide area network echo cancellation does not seem to be a major problem in the future in terms of cost and manageability.

10.2 Tariffing in B-ISDN

Tariffing of services in future ATM networks is a crucial factor that will strongly influence the acceptance of B-ISDN by customers. The following questions may be raised:

- How can tariffs for ATM networks be made cost-beneficial to operators' expenses (investments and operational costs)? What tariff components should be defined, and what parameters have to be measured for charging?

- How can a smooth transition from tariffing of services in existing networks to future ATM tariffs be achieved?

A brief overview of tariffing in existing networks is given before moving on to the topic of how to charge for ATM services.

10.2.1   Tariffing in Existing Networks

Two different charging categories are used at present:

- **Basic rate** (per month, for example) which is charged for network access irrespective of a customer's actual traffic load.

- **Traffic charges** which are determined by one or more of the following components:
    - charges for establishing/releasing connections
    - charging per connection time
    - charging per volume
    - flat rate.

For instance, in today's telephone networks calls are usually charged according to the connection time. Tariffs may vary during the day (higher charges at busy hours) and may depend on the distances to be covered. Volume-dependent tariffing is often chosen for data packet networks, that is, a charge is made for each packet delivered. In addition, small charges may be levied for establishing and maintaining a connection.

These two examples show that different networks may require different tariffing schemes to comply with the general requirements for cost-adequate charging and user acceptance (the latter often reflects the historical and social situation in a country and may outweigh the former).

10.2.2   Tariffing in ATM Networks

The ATM-based B-ISDN will supply both stream and packet-type applications. Charging in an ATM network is therefore a complex issue to resolve.

Although all information in an ATM network is transmitted in cells, simple (linear) volume-dependent tariffing, as used in conventional packet networks, may not be accepted. If a per-cell charge was introduced which led to phone call charges comparable to those of today, a broadband stream communication with a bit rate of, say, 10 Mbit/s would be so expensive that it would hardly be used.

Based on these considerations, ATM charging must meet the following requirements [57]:

- no change in charges for existing mass services like telephony, facsimile and data transmission;

- service-independent charging;

- flexibility with respect to the introduction of new services;

- transparency of tariffs;

- due consideration of peak bit rates (as these strongly affect network dimensioning and costs);

- fair charging for variable bit rate services;

- keep administrative efforts as low as possible (for example, avoid cell counting for telephone connections).

A proposal was made in [57] that tries to take into account all these requirements on ATM charging. It is based on:

- a basic rate

- traffic-dependent charges comprising two components:
    - charging for call establishment
    - charging according to the duration and bit rate of a call.

The basic rate reflects the cost of providing the customer access. When a customer wishes permanently to restrict access to a bit rate below the maximum (only 30 Mbit/s, say), and this actually reduces network access costs, the basic rate may be adjusted accordingly.

As the processing effort for setting up a connection is almost independent of the requested bit rate, call establishment may be charged at the same rate in all cases. However, the setting up of virtual connections implies the reservation of network resources. By raising different charges for call establishment in the case of prioritized, high quality of service or high bit rate connections, users could be dissuaded from reserving network resources that would not be needed.

The second component of the traffic-dependent charges – charging according to call duration and bit rate – takes into account the cost of using transmission systems in the network. This charge would normally increase with the bit rate in a non-linear way. The time unit for charging should be sufficiently low to ensure adequate charging for variable bit rate services. The peak bit rate during this short time unit could be used to determine the charge for such a connection.

A charging mechanism of this type would reflect the network efforts to support ATM connections better than a plain volume-dependent tariff (charging per cell).

Discussion within ITU-T on charging in ATM networks has yielded some general charging principles as outlined above, but no detailed charging procedures are yet available. The following ATM-specific items will have to be taken into account:

- existence of two cell loss priorities (see Section 5.5.2.6)

- usage parameter control capabilities (see Section 4.5.1.3)

- actual resource allocation in the network.

Chapter 11

Outlook

In this book, we have focused on B-ISDN and the techniques which will be used to meet short- and medium-term broadband communication needs. While MANs and B-ISDN are becoming a reality (field trials and commercial use have already started), people in research laboratories are already reflecting on the next stage. Thus the ATM-based B-ISDN – like any new concept – faces a two-fold problem concerning its implementation. First it has to be accepted by users and network providers in order to replace existing networks. Second, its full-scale realization may be jeopardized at some point in time by new, competing network concepts.

Such new ideas (some will be briefly discussed in the following), need not necessarily render the ATM-based B-ISDN superfluous. On the contrary, they will most probably be incorporated in the B-ISDN to make it an even more powerful telecommunication tool.

11.1 Universal ATM Network: Realistic Target?

The universal integrated ATM-based broadband network is easy to depict, as shown in Figure 11.1, but in reality it will most probably be a bit more complicated, as in Figure 11.2, for an indeterminate period of time (cf. [54]).

As ATM network implementation will not start from scratch but will have to take into account existing network services and customer needs, the transition to a universal ATM-based broadband network will take a long time. Perhaps the **universal ATM target network** will only be approached asymptotically with occasional deviations from the ideal line. Some telecommunication service providers may never be convinced to use ATM-based B-ISDN exclusively. At present, no one can know exactly.

In this book, some of the special technical problems of ATM-based transmission (for example, those relating to speech connections and TV distribution) have been addressed. However, economic factors or acceptance problems may prove more

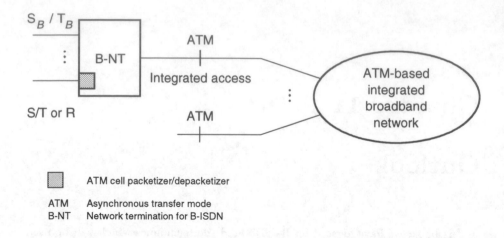

Figure 11.1: *Universal ATM network*

critical than technical considerations. We want to emphasize that we believe that ATM-based network implementations will become more and more important for the flexible provision of a variety of services, and that the above observations only apply to the envisaged long-term development towards an all-embracing ATM network. When moving forward in this direction, before entering a new evolutionary stage its technical impact should be evaluated and careful market and cost analyses should be undertaken to define the appropriate time scale for ATM network implementation.

Reference [50] mentions four decisive areas – according to the authors' opinion – for the acceptance of ATM. These are **quality of service, compatibility, charging** and **scaling**.

Quality of service requirements and their impact on ATM networking were discussed in Sections 4.4 and 4.5. It was pointed out there that refined models of the ATM traffic statistics have yet to be developed and that sophisticated traffic control and resource management techniques may have to be employed to build an efficient ATM network which can meet the quality of service demands of its customers.

Compatibility of ATM with existing or upcoming telecommunication networks is important. In [50] the fear is expressed that existing networks and services might have to be modified to cater for the introduction of ATM. An example is the possible need for more echo control devices as a result of the interconnection of ATM networks and non-ATM networks (as outlined in Section 10.1). Compatibility between ATM networks and DQDB MANs has already been achieved to a certain degree (cf. Section 9.4.1.2). This is deemed an important feature of ATM

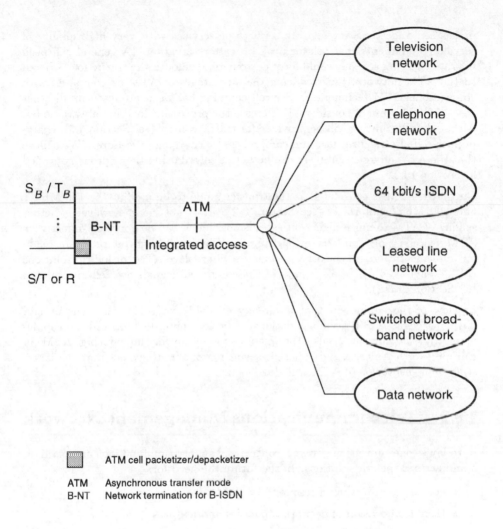

Figure 11.2: *Intermediate state public network architecture*

which facilitates its introduction. Another crucial point is the capability of ATM networks to emulate existing circuit-oriented transmission and to interwork with other networks. Circuit emulation is supported by AAL type 1 (see Section 5.6.2); interworking procedures are specified in Section 5.7.

Another important feature of ATM networks is charging (cf. Section 10.2). Usually, in packet networks, charges are on a per-packet basis or at a higher level, such as per call set-up. Charging for ATM network usage on a per-call basis only makes sense for constant bit rate services or services with very high quality of service requirements that ask for peak bit rate reservation. (A general call peak bit rate charging scheme would force customers to smooth the traffic load offered to the ATM network, thus reducing the advantages of ATM as compared with conventional STM techniques.) Per-cell charging has been proposed in all other cases [50]. This might considerably increase the processing load in network nodes. Although cell counting will be provided for traffic control (see Section 4.5), charging per cell also requires fast and comprehensive charging procedures. We believe that the ATM charging problem can be better solved using the approach outlined in Section 10.2.

Currently, ATM is considered as the transfer mode to be used at the 150 Mbit/s and 600 Mbit/s interfaces (see Section 5.2). It is not clear, however, whether scaling of ATM to much higher bit rates is possible or can be done cost-effectively. ATM switching of Gbit/s is an open issue. When such high bit rates are ready for implementation, maybe other techniques will replace ATM, or hybrid solutions will be envisaged where only parts of the compound signals are cell-multiplexed (cf. Section 11.5.2).

In view of the equipment that is already available for ATM, the concept laid down in several ITU-T recommendations (to be continuously improved and supplemented), the current trials, the plans announced for introducing ATM in Europe, North America and Japan, it seems reasonable to expect that the large-scale implementation of ATM will start soon.

11.2   Telecommunications Management Network

In today's communication systems, control and supervision functions are based on manufacturer-specific solutions. In the future the need for:

- economic utilization of resources
- flexible allocation of network capacities and features
- installation of virtual private networks

will require a computer-aided telecommunication management system [200]. This can no longer be a manufacturer-dependent solution. It will be tailored according to the principles for a telecommunications management network as laid down in ITU-T Recommendation M.3010 [126].

The TMN is an independent information processing system. It enables network operators (of public as well as virtual private networks) to supervise components of the telecommunication network via defined interfaces and protocols. Figure 11.3 shows the relationship between TMN and the telecommunication network.

Network management application functions supported by TMN include [192]:

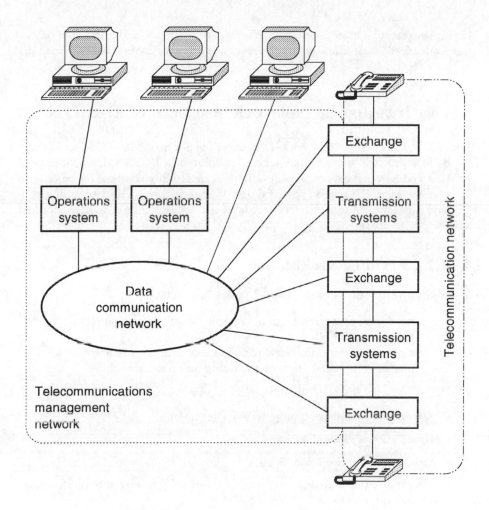

Figure 11.3: *Relationship between telecommunications management network and telecommunication network*

- performance management
- fault management
- configuration management
- accounting management
- security management.

The goal of defining a commonly accepted set of TMN objects, functions, procedures and information flow structures is an ambitious one, and a number of experts are striving hard to resolve this issue. Nevertheless, TMN seems to be in a more advanced stage than the other network features addressed in the remainder of this chapter.

11.3   Intelligent Network Aspects of B-ISDN

Like TMN, the intelligent network (IN) concept is not being developed specifically for B-ISDN but will most probably be incorporated in B-ISDN. INs will provide existing and new service components that can be flexibly combined according to the user's wishes. INs require powerful signalling procedures, effective service control and management of service-related data. ATM-based networks offer excellent support for IN features.

11.3.1   Architectural Model

The term **intelligent network** is used (according to [80])

> 'to describe an architectural concept for all telecommunication networks. IN aims to ease the introduction of supplementary services (universal personal telecommunication, freephone, etc.) based on more flexibility and new capabilities'.

The IN concept for the creation and provision of services is characterized by:

- extensive use of information processing techniques
- efficient use of network resources
- modularity of network functions
- integrated service creation and implementation by means of reusable standard network functions
- flexible allocation of network functions to physical entities
- portability of network functions among physical entities
- standardized communication between network functions via service independent interfaces
- service provider access to the process developing services by combining of network functions
- service subscriber control of subscriber-specific service attributes
- standardized management of service logic.

The functions required for IN and their division into functional entities are depicted in Figure 11.4.

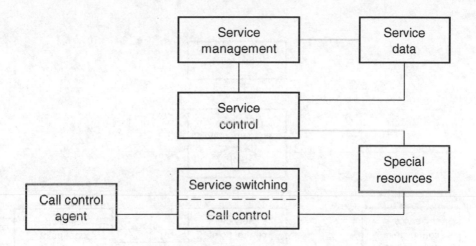

Figure 11.4: *Intelligent network functional entities*

The main principle is the distribution of service control between call control/service switching and service control. To illustrate this concept, Figure 11.5 gives an example of how these functions are mapped onto the physical entities of a telecommunication network. Call control/service switching is located in the exchanges which use trigger tables to determine whether they can complete a call themselves or if it has to be handled by the service control point. Exchanges communicate with the service control point via the signalling network (for example SS7, as shown in Figure 11.5). The special resource functions (located in this example in an intelligent peripheral) may provide protocol conversion, speech recognition, synthesized speech provision etc.

The service control point contains the IN service logic and handles service-related processing. It uses the service data function which provides access to all necessary service-related data and network data and also carries out consistency checks on data.

Finally, the service management function involves service management control, service provision control and service deployment control. Example service management control functions are: collection of service statistics, reporting of usage of non-existent freephone numbers and reporting of unauthorized access in a virtual private network. Service provision control handles operation and administration for service provisioning (creating new subscribers, modifying subscription records etc.). Service deployment control is invoked when a new service is introduced into the network. It deals with service logic allocation, signalling and routing definition, service data introduction, allocation of trigger capabilities, special service feature allocation and so on.

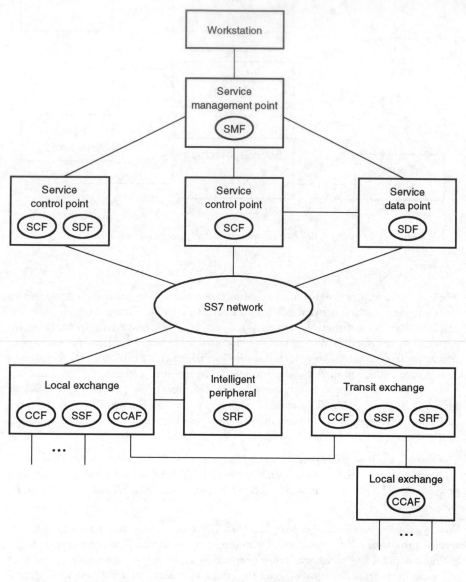

CCAF	Call control agent function	SMF	Service management function
CCF	Call control function	SRF	Special resources function
SCF	Service control function	SSF	Service switching function
SDF	Service data function	SS7	Common channel signalling system no. 7

Figure 11.5: *Example of functions mapping onto physical entities*

11.3.2   Overview of IN Services

IN services can be grouped into three categories according to the network capabilities that are required for their implementation [47]. Examples of IN services are described in Table 11.1.

Table 11.1: *Intelligent network services*

Category	Service	Description
B (called party) number services	Basic green number service (free phone)	Toll-free service paid for by called party. A special access code, e.g. 800, serves as trigger.
A + B (calling and called party) number services	Alternate billing service	Allows the user to bill the call to a number other than his or her own number.
	Enhanced emergency response service	Dialling of a special countrywide emergency number serves as a trigger. The service control point determines the appropriate emergency response control number for call completion.
	Virtual private network	Provides the functionality of a private or dedicated network using the shared facilities of the public network.
	Area wide centrex	Offers dynamic resource allocation and uniform numbering plan over geographically dispersed locations. The centrex service utilizes a public network local exchange to provide PBX-like features to a group of business customers. Area wide centrex interconnects multiple customer locations as if they were connected to a single switch.
Interactive services	Interactive green number service	Allows the user to select one of a set of offered alternatives associated with a single green number.
	Voice messaging	Requires a user dialogue for entering control commands, for example.
	Call completion	Comprises various features to assist the calling party in completing the call to the called party.

Another field of application for IN capabilities is **universal personal telecommunication** (UPT). It is described as follows [80]:

> 'Universal personal telecommunication is anticipated to bring network personal identification to reality by transparently replacing the static relationship between terminal identity and subscriber identity common in existing networks with a dynamic association and thus provide complete mobility across multiple networks.'

The aim of UPT is to provide user-to-user telecommunication services with:

- network-transparent user identification
- personal mobility
- charging and billing on the basis of subscriber identity instead of terminal identity.

Users who have subscribed to the UPT service should be able to establish and receive any type of call on the basis of a network-transparent universal personal telecommunication number (UPTN) across multiple networks at any user–network access.

The network capabilities required to support UPT are specified in ITU-T Recommendation I.373 [114].

IN services will have to be offered by any future public network, including B-ISDN:

> 'IN and ISDN enhance one another because they provide complementary capabilities with respect to network services, i.e. flexible service control on the one hand and powerful user-network access and network-internal signalling on the other hand' [47].

11.4   Gbit/s Local Area Networks

Currently LANs provide throughputs in the 100 Mbit/s range (e.g. FDDI [77]). However, there are communication requirements, like the interconnection of super-computers with high-resolution graphic terminals and the need for a high-speed backbone network, which demand networks operating in the Gbit/s range.

At these high speeds, only optical fibres are suitable for the physical medium. Point-to-point systems can already operate at Gbit/s. However, LANs are much more complicated.

Research on LANs in the Gbit/s range has already started. Many problems exist which have to be resolved in the future. Some of the open questions are:

- optical power limitation [60]

- electronic bottleneck [60]

- network topologies [1]

- medium access control [172]

- definition of protocols for high speed applications

- compatibility with ATM.

Interconnection of such very high-speed LANs would obviously require high-speed links operating at 600 Mbit/s or higher.

Several approaches are currently being considered for these very high-speed LANs which are also applicable to the metropolitan area:

- ATM-LANs: This type of LAN offers a total throughput of several Gbit/s using a small central ATM switch to which the terminals are connected in a star fashion. More details on ATM-LANs can be found in Section 4.7.6.

- Shared medium network (ring or bus) with a suitable MAC mechanism. Possible MAC protocols are DQDB [69] (cf. Section 9.4.1.2), ATM ring [156], HANGMAN [199] or cyclic reservation multiple access II (CRMA-II) [9]. This list of MAC protocols is not complete. Good overviews on basic topologies and fundamental algorithms for the shared medium access protocols are given in [165, 177]. Most of these LANs have MAC-PDUs the size of an ATM cell.

- Optical LANs using the WDM principle (cf. Section 11.5.2). The throughput of these LANs can be in the range of several tens of Gbit/s.

11.5 Optical Switching

11.5.1 General Aspects

Optical transmission and electronic switching are used for the B-ISDN as currently developed. For most of the services envisaged today, switched bit rates of several hundred Mbit/s seem to be more than sufficient. Only in the area of holographic imaging are Tbit/s (Tbit $= 10^6$ Mbit) rates being discussed.

Existing experimental switching systems use CMOS technology as well as emitter coupled logic techniques to realize systems that are capable of operating up to the Gbit/s range. In the future, speeds of up to a few Gbits/s will be achieved using gallium arsenide technology, but this seems to be the limit of electronic switching.

There are a number of reasons for considering optical switching networks [175]:

Historical perspective: Analogue transmission was followed by electro-mechanical switching. Then digital transmission was introduced which was followed by digital switching. Now optical transmission is used, and if history repeats itself, optical switching networks will be the next step.

Speed limitation: As already mentioned, the speed of electronic switching networks will be limited to the lower Gbit/s range (approximately 10 Gbit/s). Higher speeds require optical switching networks.

Cost reduction: In systems with optical transmission and electronic switching, optical/electrical and electrical/optical interfaces are necessary. These expensive units can be avoided by staying entirely in the optical range.

As a first step, optical switching matrices using space or wavelength division multiplexing systems can be introduced in optical cross-connects. Information will not then need to be converted from optical to electrical and vice versa in the individual nodes. Control of the switching matrices is only necessary when a connection is set up or released, and this can be performed by electronics. The optical cross-connect network can be used for a **universal transport network**, as shown in Section 11.5.2. This universal network is available to other networks as well as to end-users who need very high bit rate leased line services.

However, the B-ISDN uses asynchronous time division multiplexing and information is transported in cells. This requires the cell header to be processed in each switching element so that it can be forwarded to its proper destination output. Cell header processing requires extensive logic manipulations, and must at present be done electronically. Maybe in the future it will be possible to use optical computing and optical memories for cell header processing.

Other drawbacks of optical switching/cross-connecting, like optical losses, must be overcome. Furthermore, the regeneration and amplification inherent in digital electronic switching needs some counterpart in optical networks. Another very important point for the success of optical networking is the existence of an appropriate OAM concept.

Optical switching will only succeed in competing against electronic switching if it can be implemented economically or becomes absolutely necessary.

In conclusion, the large-scale implementation of optical switching will not take place in the near future and it may take several decades to replace today's electronic switching techniques. However, all-optical transport networks with space and wavelength division multiplexing may be introduced much more quickly (cf. Section 11.5.2).

11.5.2   Optical Networks

Currently, parallel to ATM networking there is a vision of all-optical networks within the private and public areas [14, 23, 61, 154, 188]. Some of these networks are already running in field trials, while others are still in the planning phase.

Passive optical networks using WDM technology are one of the most favoured solutions for the local/metropolitan area. Figure 11.6 shows two possible realizations of an optical star network based on the splitter/combiner approach [53]. All transmitted signals are broadcast to all receivers.

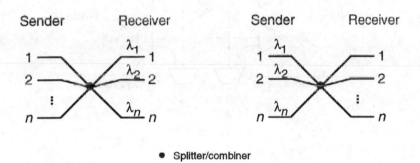

Figure 11.6: *Passive optical networks with splitter/combiner*

In both configurations the network consists of n nodes, which may be end-users or electronic nodes (depending on the application of the network). In the left-hand configuration a node has a fixed receiving wavelength. Thus, each node needs only one filter with a fixed wavelength in the receiving direction. However, in the opposite direction each node needs a tunable sender which allows the connection of an arbitrary pair of nodes by selecting the appropriate wavelength. A suitable access protocol is necessary to prevent several senders attempting to transmit to the same receiver simultaneously.

The transmitting wavelengths in the right-hand configuration are fixed. To prevent information loss, each node has to receive $(n-1)$ wavelengths simultaneously or a suitable access protocol is required. Multicast communication can be offered very easily in this way with different receivers receiving an optical signal simultaneously.

In the normal operation mode a node receives only one signal at a time. The fully meshed interconnection of all n nodes in such a passive optical network will require $n \times (n-1)$ wavelengths. Technological limitations (the number of wavelengths on one fibre) restrict this network to a small number of nodes. This drawback can be avoided by using a passive optical star network, as shown in Figure 11.7 [169].

This network is not based on the splitter/combiner concept. The star coupler consists of passive wavelength multiplexers/demultiplexers with the given specific

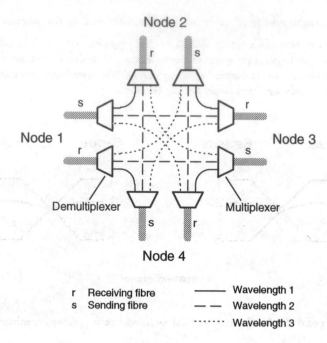

Node 2

Node 1   Node 3

Demultiplexer   Multiplexer

Node 4

r	Receiving fibre	—————	Wavelength 1
s	Sending fibre	— —	Wavelength 2
		··········	Wavelength 3

Figure 11.7: *Passive optical networks with multiplexer/demultiplexer*

interconnection. Only $(n-1)$ wavelengths are required for the full meshing of all n nodes. However, it should be noted that the sending and receiving directions are decoupled by using two fibres.

A bus topology can be used instead of the star topology. In terms of the number of required wavelengths and the necessary access protocols to the shared fibre it behaves like a star network. However, from the optical power budget point of view it has real drawbacks compared with a star network with splitter/combiner because it has a much higher attenuation.

In these systems it has been assumed that information is transmitted from the sender to receiver as light without being converted back to electrical form. The implementation effort required for these so-called **single hop** networks is very high. **Multihop** networks can be used to reduce the implementation complexity [23, 53, 60, 181]. In this case the destination node is not reached directly by the optical signal transmitted by the source. The signal emitted by the source first passes through an intermediate node which converts the optical signal back to an electrical one and analyses it. This node decides whether the signal is addressed to it or if it has to be transmitted to the next node. Figure 11.8 shows a passive optical star network and its associated logical topology for multihop communication. It should be noted that the physical network structure of a multihop network is not limited to the star topology.

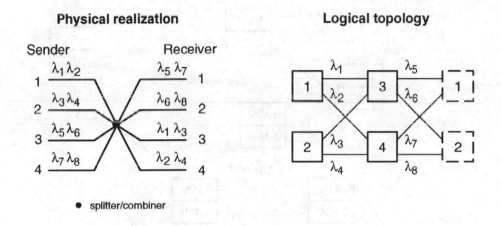

Figure 11.8: *Multihop network*

In the configuration shown in Figure 11.8 each node uses two wavelengths with fixed values in the receiving and transmitting directions. This reduces the implementation complexity for the individual nodes. In this example, node 1 has no direct optical link to node 2. Thus to send information to node 2, node 1 sends the information to node 3 using wavelength λ_1. Node 3 converts the signal to an electrical one and analyses it, then converts the signal back to an optical one using wavelength λ_6. This optical signal is then received by node 2.

Multihop networks have the following drawbacks:

- optical–electrical conversion is required in intermediate nodes

- additional delays are introduced by the intermediate nodes

- enlargement of a system (e.g. addition of a new node) requires a rearrangement of the existing connections.

In all the networks described above and later on, the electrical information may be SDH-frames, ATM-cells or have any other structure. The bit rate of the signal using wavelength λ_i may be different from the one which uses wavelength λ_j.

The star network should only be used in the access network because of its limitations in terms of transmission distance and number of nodes. Cross-connects (CCs) and ADM networks may be the preferred solutions for the core area of a

WAN [14, 29, 155]. Figure 11.9 depicts a possible scenario for an all-optical wide area transport network and its association with the electronic parts. It consists of a meshed cross-connect network and WDM rings [40, 66].

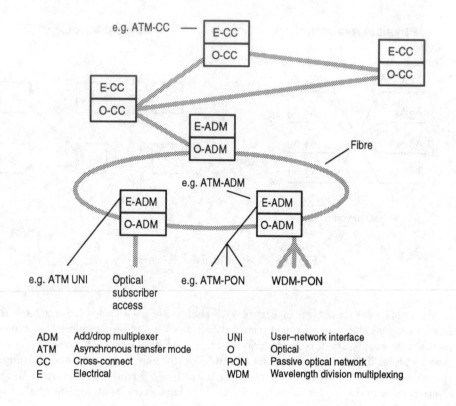

ADM	Add/drop multiplexer	UNI	User–network interface
ATM	Asynchronous transfer mode	O	Optical
CC	Cross-connect	PON	Passive optical network
E	Electrical	WDM	Wavelength division multiplexing

Figure 11.9: *All-optical transport network*

Such a CC/ADM network offers a lot of advantages to the network operators and users:

- nearly unlimited bit rates

- universal transport network carrying signals with different formats and bit rates

- flexibility based on the enhanced CC/ADM functionality and improved reliability as a result of using small nodes with an increased number of passive optical components and suitable protection mechanisms for the network and its systems

- future-proof system because new applications can be integrated very simply by using an unoccupied wavelength

- cost-effectiveness by avoiding unnecessary optical–electrical conversion and by reducing the efforts for electronic processing.

The generic architecture of a WDM-CC (or a WDM-ADM) is shown in Figure 11.10 (without the required node control). It consists of the following subsystems:

- Multiplexer/demultiplexer: The wavelengths used on the fibre are separated at the inlet of the CC so that they can be individually cross-connected. At the outlet, the multiplexer combines the different wavelengths onto the outgoing signal.

- Switching network: The space division multiplexing switching network performs the space switching of the individual wavelengths.

- Wavelength converter: This subsystem converts the wavelength λ_i at its inlet to the new wavelength λ_j for the outlet. Wavelength converter is a key function in WDM networks because without it the performance of the node would be very low. (A WDM-CC without wavelength conversion would be like a TDM node without time-slot interchange.)

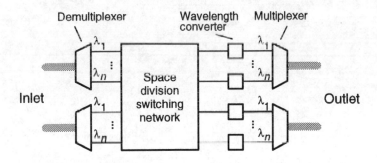

Figure 11.10: *WDM cross-connect*

WDM networks are still in an early phase. Although a lot of research into optical components has already been done, much work is still needed to improve the characteristic parameters of the components. In addition to the technological improvement of optical components, enhanced communication protocols and OAM protocols have to be developed to enable full advantage to be taken of all-optical networks.

Appendix A

B-ISDN/ATM Standardization

A.1 Overview of ITU-T Recommendations

A variety of standards have to be agreed worldwide in order that any two customers can indeed communicate with each other via B-ISDN. These standards are set by recognized standards bodies, amongst which the ITU-T (previously CCITT) plays an outstanding role in the context of B-ISDN as it produces standards (called **recommendations**) which are acknowledged worldwide.

Table A.1 (see pages 251 and 252) summarizes the current B-ISDN-related ITU-T I-series recommendations. The scope of application of these recommendations is illustrated by Figure A.1.

Open issues which will lead to future enhancement of the existing recommendations or to new supplementary recommendations are indicated in the following section.

A.2 Ongoing ITU-T Activities

As well as ongoing revision of the existing recommendations, ITU-T plans to issue several additional documents relating to B-ISDN/ATM. Some examples (of ITU-T Study Group 13) are given below.

I.31x	B-ISDN network requirements – Rel 2/3	(1995)
I.341	B-ISDN connection types	(1995)
I.35BA	B-ISDN availability performance	(1996)
I.581	Interworking requirements for B-ISDN	(1996)
I.sig.2	B-ISDN signalling requirements Rel 2	(1994)
I.sig.3	B-ISDN signalling requirements Rel 3	(1995)
G.atmta	ATM transport network architecture	(1994)
G.96x	Access digital section for B-ISDN	(1996)

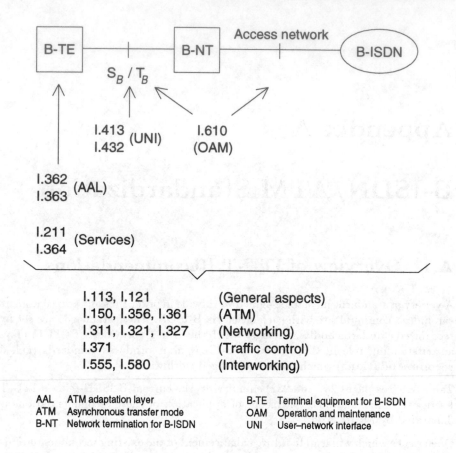

Figure A.1: *Application scope of B-ISDN I-series recommendations*

Other Study Groups will supplement the set of ATM recommendations by producing documents on services, signalling, interworking, OAM, ATM equipment (multiplexer, cross-connects, exchanges), tariffing etc.

Recommendations to be finalized by Study Group 11 (mainly signalling) are documented in Table A.2.

Table A.1: *ITU-T I series recommendations for B-ISDN*

Number: Title	Contents
I.113. Vocabulary of Terms for Broadband Aspects of ISDN	Definition of terms used for B-ISDN
I.121: Broadband Aspects of ISDN	Principles of B-ISDN

I.150:
B-ISDN ATM
Functional
Characteristics
	• Functions of the ATM layer (cell header):
	  − virtual channel connection
	  − virtual path connection
	  − payload type
	  − cell loss priority
	  − generic flow control

I.211: B-ISDN Service Aspects	• Classification and general description of B-ISDN services • Network aspects of multimedia services • Service timing, synchronization aspects • Connectionless data service aspects • Videocoding aspects

I.311:
B-ISDN General
Network Aspects
	• Networking techniques:
	  − VC and VP level
	  − VC and VP links/connections
	• Signalling principles:
	  − signalling requirements
	  − signalling VCs at the user access
	    meta signalling channel

I.321: B-ISDN Protocol Ref- erence Model and its Application	• Extension of I.320 • Overview of functions in layers and sublayers • Distinction between physical layer and ATM layer functions
I.327: B-ISDN Functional Architecture	• Enhancement of I.324 • Basic architecture model, network capabilities • Reference connection, connection elements • Connectionless service function, access via VCCs or VPCs
I.356: B-ISDN ATM Cell Layer Transfer Performance	• Performance model • Performance parameters • Performance measurement methods
I.361: B-ISDN ATM Layer Specification	• ATM cell structure: − 5 octet header + 48 octet information field • Coding of cell header

Table A.1: *ITU-T I series recommendations for B-ISDN (continued)*

Number: Title	Contents

I.362:
B-ISDN ATM Adaptation Layer Functional Description
	• Basic principles of the AAL:
	  – service dependent
	  – may be empty for some applications
	• Sublayering of the AAL:
	  – SAR and CS
	• 4 AAL service classes based on:
	  – timing relation source/sink
	  – constant/variable bit rate
	  – connection-oriented/connectionless mode

I.363:
B-ISDN ATM Adaptation Layer Specification
	• AAL protocol types defined with respect to:
	  – services
	  – SAR/CS functions
	  – SAR-PDU structure and coding

I.364: Support of Broadband Connectionless Data Service on B-ISDN	• Framework for service provision • Protocols (UNI/NNI)
I.371: Traffic Control and Congestion Control in B-ISDN	• Traffic descriptors and parameters • Functions and procedures for traffic control and congestion control
I.413: B-ISDN User–network Interface	• Reference configurations • Examples of physical configurations • Interfaces at T_B and S_B: 155.520 (622.080) Mbit/s
I.432: B-ISDN User–network Interface – Physical Layer Specification	• Electrical/optical parameters • Interface structure (e.g. SDH frame) • Header error control generation/verification • Cell delineation
I.555: Frame Relaying Bearer Service Interworking	• Interworking between frame relaying bearer service and B-ISDN
I.580: General Arrangements for Interworking between B-ISDN and 64 kbit/s based ISDN	• Interworking configurations • Interworking functional requirements
I.610: B-ISDN Operation and Maintenance Principles and Functions	• OAM principles: – hierarchical structure of OAM functions and information flows • OAM functions for B-ISDN UNI and access network • Implementation of OAM functions of the physical layer and ATM layer

Table A.2: *ITU-T Q series recommendations for B-ISDN*

Number	Title
Q.2010 (Q.141x)	General Introduction to Signalling in B-ISDN
Q.2100 (Q.SAAL.0)	B-ISDN Signalling ATM Adaptation Layer (SAAL) Overview Description
Q.2110 (Q.SAAL.1)	B-ISDN ATM Adaptation Layer – Service Specific Connection Oriented Protocol (SSCOP)
Q.2120 (Q.1420)	B-ISDN Meta-signalling Protocol
Q.2130 (Q.SAAL.2)	B-ISDN Signalling ATM Adaptation Layer – Service Specific Coordination Function for Support of Signalling at the User-to-Network Interface (SSCF at UNI)
Q.2140 (Q.SAAL.3)	B-ISDN Signalling ATM Adaptation Layer – Service Specific Coordination Function for Support of Signalling at the Network–Node Interface (SSCF at NNI)
Q.2500 (Q.50A)	B-ISDN Network Nodes, Introduction and Field of Application
Q.2510 (Q.51A)	B-ISDN Interfaces on B-ISDN Network Nodes
Q.2520 (Q.52A)	B-ISDN Exchange Node Functions
Q.2530 (Q.52B)	B-ISDN Network Node Connection Types
Q.2550 (Q.54B)	B-ISDN Network Node Performance Design Objectives
Q.2610 (BQ.850)	Use of Cause and Location in B-ISDN and B-ISUP
Q.2650 (BQ.699)	Interworking between B-ISUP and B-ISDN Access Signalling
Q.2660 (BQ.6XX)	Interworking between B-ISUP and N-ISUP
Q.2761 (BQ.761)	Functional Description of the B-ISDN User Part of Signalling System No. 7
Q.2762 (BQ.762)	General Function of Messages and Signals
Q.2763 (BQ.763)	Formats and Codes
Q.2764 (BQ.764)	Signalling Procedures
Q.2931 (Q.93B)	B-ISDN User–Network Interface Layer 3 Protocol

Old numbering scheme is denoted in brackets

A.3   Other Standards Bodies

A.3.1   ANSI and ETSI

The American National Standard Institute (ANSI) and the European Telecommunication Standard Institute (ETSI) define North American and European standards, respectively. Normally these regional standards are largely compatible with ITU-T standards.

Table A.3 gives a short overview of ANSI standards and ETSI documents relating to ATM.

Table A.3: *ANSI and ETSI standards relating to ATM*

Topic	ANSI	ETSI
UNI	T1.624-1993	pr ETS 300 299
		pr ETS 300 300
ATM layer	T1.627-1993	pr ETS 300 298-1
		pr ETS 300 298-2
Resource management/ traffic control		pr ETS 300 301
AAL	T1.629-1993	DE/NA - 52617 (AAL 1)
		DE/NA - 52618 (AAL 3/4)
	T1.630-1993	DE/NA - 52619 (AAL 5)
		DE/NA - 52 620
OAM		DE/NA - 52209
		DTR/NA - 52204
		DE/NA 52806
UNI signalling		DE/SPS - 5024 (Basic call)
		DE/SPS - 5034
		(Supplementary service)
Signalling AAL		DE/SPS - 5026 -1
		DE/SPS - 5026 - 2
Connectionless service		DTR/NA - 53203
		DE/NA - 53205
		DE/NA 53206
Frame relaying		DE/NA - 53204

A.3.2   ATM Forum

Although not an official standards body, the ATM Forum now has worldwide presence and strongly influences ATM development.

The ATM Forum has produced the following specifications:

- UNI specification (Version 3.0, Sept 1993).
- B-ISDN intercarrier interface (B-ICI) specification (Version 1.0, Aug 1993).

The ATM Forum covers private networking as well as interconnection with public networks. In many respects the ATM Forum is ahead of ITU-T or broadens the scope of ITU-T recommendations [11]:

- definition of a 51.84 Mbit/s UNI;
- private UNI specification(including models for administration, routing and addressing);
- B-ICI (defining interfaces and services across network boundaries);
- network management (definition of the basic management functions: exchange of fault information and provision of circuit set-up data);
- traffic management, including:
  - traffic parameter specification (peak cell rate, sustainable cell rate, maximum burst size)
  - leaky bucket conformance checking method
  - quality of service classes definition for the support of circuit emulation, packet video/voice, connection-oriented data, connectionless data, and unspecified;
- definition of an 'available bit rate' ATM service.

A.3.3   Bellcore

Table A.4: *Bellcore documents relevant to ATM*

SR-TSY-000857	Preliminary special report on broadband ISDN access
FA-NWT-001109	B-ISDN transport network framework generic criteria
TA-NWT-001110	Broadband ISDN switching system generic requirements
FA-NWT-001111	Broadband ISDN access signaling framework generic criteria for class II equipment
TA-NWT-001112	Broadband ISDN user to network interface and network node interface physical layer generic criteria
TA-NWT-001113	Asynchronous transfer mode (ATM) and ATM adaptation layer (AAL) protocols generic requirements
TA-NWT-001114	Generic requirements for operations interfaces using OSI tools: broadband ATM network operations
TA-TSV-001238	Generic requirements for SMDS on the 155.520 Mbps multi-services broadband ISDN inter-carrier interface (B-ICI)
TA-NWT-001248	Generic requirements for operations of broadband switching systems
TA-TSV-001408	General requirements for exchange PVC cell relay service
SR-TSY-001453	Vendor responses to Bellcore request for information (RFI 88-04) on broadband ISDN
SR-NWT-002071	B-ISDN industry forum
SR-NWT-002076	Report on the broadband ISDN protocols for providing SMDS and exchange access SMDS
SR-NWT-002480	Broadband switching system (BSS) technical analysis description

Appendix B

Abbreviations

AAL	ATM adaptation layer
ADM	Add/drop multiplexer
AIS	Alarm indication signal
AL	Alignment
ANSI	American National Standard Institute
ARP	Address resolution protocol
ASN.1	Abstract syntax notation no. 1
ATM	Asynchronous transfer mode
AU	Administrative unit
AUU	ATM layer user to ATM layer user
B-ICI	B-ISDN intercarrier interface
B-ISDN	Broadband integrated services digital network
B-ISUP	Broadband ISDN user part
B-NT	Network termination for B-ISDN
B-TA	Terminal adaptor for B-ISDN
B-TE	Terminal equipment for B-ISDN
Bc	Committed burst size
BCI	Bearer control identifier
Be	Excess burst size
BECN	Backward explicit congestion notification
BERKOM	Berliner Kommunikationssystem
BICMOS	Bipolar complementary metal-oxide semiconductor
BIP	Bit interleaved parity
BOM	Beginning of message
BSVC	Broadcast signalling virtual channel
BSVCI	Broadcast signalling virtual channel identifier
Btag	Beginning tag
C-i	Container i
CAD	Computer-aided design
CATV	Cable television

CAU	Cause
CBDS	Connectionless broadband data services
CBR	Constant bit rate
CC	Cross-connect
CCITT	Comité Consultatif International Télégraphique et Téléphonique
CEI	Connection element identifier
CI	Congestion indication
CIC	Circuit identification code
CIM	Computer-integrated manufacturing
CIR	Committed information rate
CL	Connectionless
CLNAP	Connectionless network access protocol
CLNIP	Connectionless network interface protocol
CLP	Cell loss priority
CLSF	Connectionless service function
CMI	Coded mark inversion
CMIP	Common management information protocol
CMIS	Common management information service
CMOS	Complementary metal-oxide semiconductor
CN	Customer network
CO	Connection oriented
COM	Continuation of message
CP	Common part
CPCS	Common part convergence sublayer
CPI	Common part indicator
CPN	Customer premises network
CRC	Cyclic redundancy check
CRMA	Cyclic reservation multiple access
CS	Convergence sublayer
CSI	Convergence sublayer indication
CSMA/CD	Carrier sense multiple access with collision detection
CSPDN	Circuit-switched public data network
DAN	Desk area network
DC	Direct current
DE	Discard eligibility
DLCI	Data link connection identifier
DMDD	Distributed multiplexing distributed demultiplexing
DQDB	Distributed queue dual bus
EOM	End of message
ET	Exchange termination
Etag	Ending tag
ETSI	European Telecommunication Standard Institute
EWSD	Elektronisches Wählvermittlungssystem Digital
FCS	Frame check sequence

FDDI	Fibre-distributed data interface
FEBE	Far end block error
FEC	Forward error correction
FECN	Forward explicit congestion notification
FERF	Far end receive failure
FIFO	First-in first-out
FR	Frame relay
FR-SSCS	Frame relaying service-specific convergence sublayer
FRSF	Frame relay service function
FTP	File transfer protocol
GFC	Generic flow control
GSVCI	Global signalling virtual channel identifier
HDSL	High-speed digital subscriber line
HDTV	High-definition television
HEC	Header error control
HICOM	High technology communication
HIPPI	High-performance parallel interface
HLPI	Higher layer protocol identifier
HSLAN	High-speed local area network
IC	Input controller
ICMP	Internet control message protocol
ID	Identifier
IEEE	Institute of Electrical and Electronic Engineers
ILMI	Interim local management interface
IN	Intelligent network
IP	Internet protocol
ISDN	Integrated services digital network
ISO	International Standard Organization
ISUP	ISDN user part
ITU	International Telecommunication Union
IWU	Interworking unit
LAN	Local area network
LI	Length indicator
LLC	Logical link control
LLS	LAN-like switching
LSB	Least significant bit
LT	Line termination
MAC	Media access control
MAN	Metropolitan area network
MIB	Management information base
MID	Multiplexing identifier
MIN	Multi-path interconnection network
MIR	Maximum information rate
MSB	Most significant bit

MSVC	Meta-signalling virtual channel
MT	Message type
MTP	Message transfer part
NNI	Network–node interface
NPC	Network parameter control
NRZ	Non-return-to-zero code
NTT	Nippon Telegraph and Telephone Corporation
NTSC	North American Television Standards Committee
OAM	Operation and maintenance
OC	Output controller
OSI	Open system interconnection
PAD	Padding
PAL	Phase alternating line
PBX	Private branch exchange
PC	Personal computer
PCI	Protocol control information
PCR	Point-to-point SVC cell rate
PD	Protocol discriminator
PDH	Plesiochronous digital hierarchy
PDU	Protocol data unit
PL	Physical layer
PLCP	Physical layer convergence protocol
PM	Physical medium
POH	Path overhead
PON	Passive optical network
PPTU	PDUs per time unit
PRM	Protocol reference model
PSPDN	Packet-switched public data network
PSVC	Point-to-point signalling virtual channel
PSVCI	Point-to-point signalling virtual channel identifier
PT	Payload type
PTI	Payload type identifier
PV	Protocol version
PVC	Permanent virtual connection
QOS	Quality of service
QPSX	Queued packet and synchronous circuit exchange
RACE	Research and Development of Advanced Communication in Europe
RAM	Random access memory
RI	Reference identifier
RTS	Residual time stamp
S-AAL	ATM adaptation layer for signalling
SAP	Service access point
SAR	Segmentation and reassembly
SDH	Synchronous digital hierarchy

SDU	Service data unit
SECAM	Système en Couleur avec Mémoire
SIR	Sustained information rate
SLMB	Subscriber line module broadband
SMDS	Switched multi-megabit data service
SMTP	Simple mail transfer protocol
SN	Sequence number
SNAP	Subnetwork attachment point
SNMP	Simple network management protocol
SNP	Sequence number protection
SOAP	Siemens optical ATM passive network
SOH	Section overhead
SONET	Synchronous optical network
SPID	Service profile identifier
SPN	Subscriber premises network
SRTS	Synchronous residual time stamp
SS7	Common channel signalling system no. 7
SSCF	Service-specific coordination function
SSCOP	Service-specific connection oriented protocol
SSCS	Service-specific convergence sublayer
SSM	Single-segment message
SSP	Service-specific part
ST	Segment type
STM	Synchronous transfer mode
STM-i	Synchronous transport module i
SVC	Signalling virtual channel
SVCI	Signalling virtual channel identifier
Tc	Committed rate measurement interval
TC	Transmission convergence sublayer
TCAP	Transaction capabilities application part
TCP	Transmission control protocol
TDM	Time division multiplexing
TE	Terminal equipment
TELNET	Remote login protocol
TMB	Trunk module broadband
TMN	Telecommunications management network
UDP	User datagram protocol
UME	UNI management entity
UNI	User–network interface
UPC	Usage parameter control
UPT	Universal personal telecommunications
UPTN	Universal personal telecommunication number
UU	CPCS user-to-user indication
VBR	Variable bit rate

VC	Virtual channel
VC-i	Virtual container i
VCC	Virtual channel connection
VCI	Virtual channel identifier
VP	Virtual path
VPC	Virtual path connection
VPCI	Virtual path connection identifier
VPI	Virtual path identifier
WAN	Wide area network
WDM	Wavelength division multiplexing

References

[1] ACAMPORA, A.S., KAROL, M.J.: An Overview of Lightwave Packet Networks. *IEEE Network*, vol. 3, no. 1, January 1989, pp. 29–40.

[2] ADAMS, J.L.: The Orwell Torus Communication Switch. *Proceedings of the GLSB Seminar on Broadband Switching*, Albufeira, 1987, pp. 215–224.

[3] AHMADI, H., DENZEL, W.E.: A Survey of Modern High-Performance Switching Techniques. *IEEE Journal on Selected Areas in Communications*, vol. 7, no. 7, September 1989, pp. 1091–1103.

[4] ANIDO, G.J., SEETO, A.W.: Multipath Interconnection: A Technique for Reducing Congestion within Fast Packet Switching Fabrics. *IEEE Journal on Selected Areas in Communications*, vol. 6, no. 9, December 1988, pp. 1480–1488.

[5] ANSI: ANSI Standard 'Hybrid Ring Control'. Revision 6, May 1990.

[6] ANSI: ANSI Standard T1.105-1988 'SONET Optical Interface Rates and Formats'. 1988.

[7] ARMBRÜSTER, H., ROTHAMEL, H.-J.: Breitbandanwendungen und -dienste – Qualitative und quantitative Anforderungen an künftige Netze. *Nachrichtentechnische Zeitschrift*, vol. 43, no. 3, March 1990, pp. 150–159.

[8] ARMBRÜSTER, H., SCHNEIDER H.: Phasing-in the Universal Broadband ISDN. Initial Trials for Examining ATM Applications and ATM Systems. *Proceedings of the International Conference on Integrated Broadband Services and Networks*, London, 1990, pp. 200–205.

[9] VAN AS, H.R., LEMPPENAU, W.W., ZAFIROPULO, P., ZURFLUH, E.: CRMA-II: A Gbit/s MAC Protocol for Ring and Bus Networks with Immediate Access Capability. *Proceedings of the European Fibre Optic and Local Area Networks Conference*, London, 1991, pp. 162–169.

[10] ATM-FORUM: ATM UNI-Specification (V3.0), 1993.

[11] ATM-FORUM: *Newsletter ('53 Bytes')*, vol. 2, no. 1, January 1994, pp. 2–3.

[12] BAIREUTHER, O.: Überlegungen zum Breitband-ISDN. *Der Fernmelde= Ingenieur*, vol. 45, no. 2/3, February/March 1991, pp. 1–62.

[13] BATCHER, K.E.: Sorting Networks and their Applications. *AFIPS Proceedings of the Spring Joint Computer Conference*, 1968, vol. 32, pp. 307–314.

[14] BARNSLEY, P.E., WICKES, H.J., WICKENS, G.E.: Switching in Future Ultra-high Capacity All-Optical Networks. *Proceedings of the XIV International Switching Symposium*, Yokohama, 1992, paper B10.1.

[15] BELLCORE: Technical Advisory TA-TSY-000772 'Generic System Requirements in Support of Switched Multi-Megabit Data Service'. Issue 3, October 1989.

[16] More Broadband For BellSouth. *Communications Weekly International*, 1990, p. 12.

[17] BENEŠ, V.: *Mathematical Theory of Connecting Networks*. Academic Press, New York, 1965.

[18] BESIER, H.A.: SPN (Subscriber Premises Network), An Essential Part of the Broadband Communication Network. *Proceedings of the GLOBECOM'88*, Hollywood, 1988, pp. 102–106.

[19] BIERSACK, E.: Principles of Network Interconnection. *Proceedings of the 7th European Fibre Optic Communications & Local Area Networks Exposition (EFOC/LAN)*, Amsterdam, 1989, pp. 37–43.

[20] BIOCCA, A., FRESCHI, G., FORCINA, A., MELEN, R.: Architectural Issues in the Interoperability between MANs and the ATM Network. *Proceedings of the XIII International Switching Symposium*, Stockholm, 1990, vol. II, pp. 23–28.

[21] BOCKER, P.: *ISDN – The Integrated Services Digital Network – Concepts, Methods, Systems*. Springer-Verlag, Berlin/Heidelberg/New York/London/Paris/Tokyo, 1992.

[22] BOULTER, R.A., POPPLE, G.W.: The Broadband User-Network Interface Projects within RACE. *Proceedings of the International Conference on Integrated Broadband Services and Networks*, London, 1990, pp. 11–16.

[23] BRACKETT, C.A., ACAMPORA, A.S., SWEITZER, J., TNAONAN, G., SMITH, M.T., LENNON, W., WANG, K.C., HOBBS, R.H.: A Scalable Multiwavelength Multihop Optical Network: A Proposal for Research on All-Optical Networks. *IEEE Journal of Lightwave Technology*, vol. 11, no. 5/6, May/June 1993, pp. 736–753.

[24] BREUER, H.-J., HELLSTRÖM, B.: Synchronous Transmission Networks. *Ericsson Review*, no. 2, 1990, pp. 60–71.

[25] BRILL, A., HUBER, M.N., PETRI, B.: Designing Signalling for Broadband. *Telecommunications*, July 1993, pp. 29–34.

[26] BROOKS, E.D.: A Butterfly-Memory Interconnection for a Vector Processing Environment. *Parallel Computing*, no. 4, 1987.

[27] BYRNE, W.R., KAFKA, H.J., LUDERER, G.W.R., NELSON, B.L., CLAPP, G.H.: Evolution of Metropolitan Area Networks to Broadband ISDN. *Proceedings of the XIII International Switching Symposium*, Stockholm, 1990, vol. II, pp. 15–22.

[28] CHEN, P.Y., LAWRIE, D.H., YEW, P.C., PADUA, D.A.: Interconnection Networks Using Shuffles. *IEEE Computer*, vol. 14, no. 12, December 1981, pp. 55–63.

[29] CHIDGEY, P.J., HILL, G.R., SAXTOFT, C.: Wavelength and Space Switched Optical Networks and Nodes. *Proceedings of the XIV International Switching Symposium*, Yokohama, 1992, paper B9.3.

[30] COUDREUSE, J.P., SERVEL, M.: PRELUDE: An Asynchronous Time-Division Switched Network. *Proceedings of the International Conference on Communications*, Seattle, 1987, paper 22.2.

[31] DAVID, R., FASTREZ, M., BAUWENS, J., DE VLEESCHOUWER, A., CHRISTIAENS, M., VAN VYVE, J.: A Belgian Broadband ATM Experiment. *Proceedings of the XIII International Switching Symposium*, Stockholm, 1990, vol. III, pp. 1–6.

[32] DEGAN, J.J., LUDERER, G.W.R., VAIDYA, A.K.: Fast Packet Technology for Future Switches. *AT&T Technical Journal*, vol. 68, no. 2, March/April 1989, pp. 36–50.

[33] DENZEL, W. E., LE BOUDEC, J.-H., PORT, E., TROUNG, H. L.: FALCON: A Switched-Based ATM LAN. *Proceedings of the European Fibre Optic Communications and Networks*, The Hague, 1993, pp. 72–77.

[34] DE PRYCKER, M., DE SOMER, M.: Performance of a Service Independent Switching Network with Distributed Control. *IEEE Journal on Selected Areas in Communications*, vol. 5, no. 8, October 1987, pp. 1293–1302.

[35] DE PRYCKER, M., VERBIEST, W., MESTAGH D.: ATM Passive Optical Networks: Preparing the Access Network for BISDN. *Proceedings of the XIV International Switching Symposium*, Yokohama, 1992, paper B4.1.

[36] DE SMEDT, A., DE VLEESCHOUWER A., THEEUWS R.: Subscribers' Premises Networks for the Belgian Broadband Experiment. *Proceedings of the XIII International Switching Symposium*, Stockholm, 1990, vol. VI, pp. 105–109.

[37] DIAS D.M., KUMAR M.: Packet Switching in $n \log n$ Multistage Networks. *Proceedings of the GLOBECOM'84*, Atlanta, 1984, pp. 114–120.

[38] DOBROWSKI, G.H., ESTES, G.H., SPEARS, D.R., WALTERS, S.M.: Implications of BISDN Services on Network Architecture and Switching. *Proceedings of the XIII International Switching Symposium*, Stockholm, 1990, vol. I, pp. 91–98.

[39] DU CHAFFAUT, G., BORGNE, M., COATANEA, P., BALLANCE, J.W., LEE, R.F., FAULKNER, D.W.: ATM PON based networks and related service requirements *Proceedings of IEEE Workshop on Local Optical Networks*, Versailles, September, 1992.

[40] Elrefaie, A.F.: Multiwavelength Survivable Ring Network Architecture. *Proceedings of the International Conference on Communications*, Geneva, 1993, pp. 1245–1251.

[41] ETSI: ETSI Sub Technical Committee NA5, Report of the Rome Meeting. March 1990.

[42] ETSI: ETR DE/NA-53203: 'Network Aspects (NA); CBDS over ATM', May 1993.

[43] FALCONER, R.M., ADAMS, J.L.: Orwell: A Protocol for an Integrated Service Local Network. *British Telecom Technology Journal*, vol. 3, no. 4, October 1985, pp. 27–35.

[44] FAULKNER, D.W., BALLANCE, J.W.: Passive Optical Networks for Local Telephony and Cable TV Provision. *International Journal of Digital and Analog Cabled Systems*, vol. 1, no. 3, July 1988, pp. 159–163.

[45] FISCHER, W., FUNDNEIDER, O., GOELDNER, E.-H., LUTZ, K.A.: A Scalable ATM Switching System Structure. *IEEE Journal on Selected Areas in Communications*, vol. 9, no. 8, October 1991, pp. 1299–1307.

[46] FISCHER, W., STIEFEL, R.: A Flexible ATM System Architecture for World-Wide Field Trials. *Proceedings of the International Conference on Communications*, Geneva, 1993, pp. 86–90.

[47] FRANTZEN, V., MAHER A., ESKE CHRISTENSEN, B.: Towards the Intelligent ISDN. *Proceedings of the International Conference on Intelligent Networks*, Bordeaux, 1989, pp. 152–156.

[48] FRANTZEN, V., HUBER, M.N., MAEGERL, G.: Evolutionary Steps from ISDN Signalling towards B-ISDN Signalling. *Proceedings of GLOBECOM'92*, Orlando, 1992, pp. 1161–1165.

[49] GARETTI, E., MELEN, R., ARNOLD, A., GALLASSI, G., SCOZZARI, G., FOX, A.L., FUNDNEIDER, O., GÖLDNER, E.H.: An Experimental ATM Switching Architecture for the Evolving B-ISDN Scenario. *Proceedings of the XIII International Switching Symposium*, Stockholm, 1990, vol. IV, pp. 15–22.

[50] GECHTER, J., O'REILLY, P.: Conceptual Issues for ATM. *IEEE Network*, vol. 3, no. 1, January 1989, pp. 14–16.

[51] GÖLDNER, E.H.: The Network Evolution towards B-ISDN: Applications, Network Aspects, Trials (e.g. BERKOM). *Proceedings of the International Conference on Communications*, Atlanta, 1990, paper 212.2.

[52] GOKE, L.R., LIPOVSKI, G.J.: Banyan Networks for Partitioning Multiprocessor Systems. *First Annual Symposium on Computer Architecture*, 1973, pp. 21–28.

[53] GREEN JR., P.E.: *Fibre Optic Networks*, Prentice Hall, Englewood Cliffs, New Jersey, 1993.

[54] HÄNDEL, R.: Evolution of ISDN towards Broadband ISDN. *IEEE Network*, vol. 3, no. 1, January 1989, pp. 7–13.

[55] HANDEL, R., HUBER, M.N.: Customer Network Configurations and Generic Flow Control. *International Journal of Digital and Analog Communication Systems*, vol. 4, 1991, pp. 117–122.

[56] HÄNDEL, R.: Operation and Maintenance Issues of ATM Networks. *Proceedings of the 1992 International Conference on Communication Technology*, Beijing, 1992, vol. 1, pp. 12.07.1–12.07.4.

[57] HAGENHAUS, L.: Gebührenerfassung bei ATM-Netzen. *Internal Siemens Report*, September 1990.

[58] HAGENHAUS, L., ÜBERLA, A.: Users' Bandwidth Needs Versus 155.520 Mbit/s Broadband Interface. *Proceedings of the X International Symposium on Subscriber Loops & Services*, Vancouver, 1993, pp. 44–49.

[59] HAUBER, C., WALLMEIER, E.: Blocking Probabilities in ATM Pipes Controlled by a Connection Acceptance Algorithm Based on Mean and Peak Bit Rates. *Proceedings of the XIII International Teletraffic Congress, ITC Workshops 'Queueing, Performance and Control in ATM'*, Copenhagen, 1991, pp. 137–142.

[60] HENRY, P.S.: High-Capacity Lightwave Local Area Networks. *IEEE Communications Magazine*, vol. 27, no. 10, October 1989, pp. 20–26.

[61] HINTON, H.S.: Photonics in Switching. *IEEE LTS The Magazine of Lightwave Telecommunication Systems*, vol. 3, no. 3, August 1992, pp. 26–35.

[62] HUANG, A., KNAUER, S.: STARLITE: A Wideband Digital Switch. *Proceedings of the GLOBECOM'84*, Atlanta, 1984, pp. 121–125.

[63] HUBER, M.N., RATHGEB, E.P., THEIMER T.H.: Self Routing Banyan Networks in an ATM-Environment.*Proceedings of the International Conference on Computer Communication*, Tel Aviv, 1988, pp. 167–174.

[64] HUBER, M.N., FRANTZEN, V., MAEGERL, G.: Proposed Evolutionary Paths for B-ISDN Signalling. *Proceedings of the XIV International Switching Symposium*, Yokohama, 1992, paper C3.3.

[65] HUBER, M.N., TEGTMEYER, V.H.: Bandwidth Management of Virtual Paths – Performance versus Control Aspects. *Tagungsband Messung, Modellierung und Bewertung von Rechen- und Kommunikationssystemen*, Aachen, 1993, pp. 226–238.

[66] HUBER, M.N., OSBORNE, R.: Architecture of an All-Optical Ring Network. To appear in *Proceedings of the European Fibre Optic Communications and Networks*, Heidelberg, 1994.

[67] HUI, J.Y.: Resource Allocation for Broadband Networks. *IEEE Journal on Selected Areas in Communications*, vol. 6, no. 9, December 1988, pp. 1598–1608.

[68] IEEE: IEEE Std 802.2 - 1989: 'Information Processing Systems – Local Area Networks – Part 2: Logical Link Control'.

[69] IEEE: IEEE Std 802.6 - 1991: 'Distributed Queue Dual Bus (DQDB) Subnetwork of a Metropolitan Area Network (MAN)'.

[70] INTERNET ENGINEERING TASK FORCE (IETF): Internet Protocol and Transmission Control Protocol *RFCs 791 and 793*, September 1981.

[71] INTERNET ENGINEERING TASK FORCE (IETF): TCP Extensions for High Performance *RFC 1323*, May 1992.

[72] INTERNET ENGINEERING TASK FORCE (IETF): Multiprotocol Encapsulation over ATM Adaptation Layer 5 *RFC 1483*, July 1993.

[73] ISO: ISO 7498 - 1984: 'Information Processing Systems – Open System Interconnection – Basic Reference Model'. American National Standards Association, New York.

[74] ISO: ISO 8802-3 - 1990: 'Carrier Sense Multiple Access with Collision Detection (CSMA/CD) Access Method and Physical Layer Specifications'. American National Standards Association, New York.

[75] ISO: ISO 8802-4 - 1990: 'Token-passing Bus Access Method and Physical Layer Specifications'. American National Standards Association, New York.

[76] ISO: ISO 8802-5 - 1991: 'Token Ring Access Method'. American National Standards Association, New York.

[77] ISO: ISO 9314-1,-2,-3: 'Fibre Distributed Data Interface (FDDI)'. American National Standards Association, New York.

[78] ITU-T: COM XVIII-228-E, Geneva, March, 1984.

[79] ITU-T: COM XVIII-D1109, Hamburg, July 1987.

[80] ITU-T: COM XVIII-R41-E, Geneva, June 1990.

[81] ITU-T: Recommendation E.164: 'Numbering Plan for the ISDN Era'. Rev. 1, Geneva, 1991.

[82] ITU-T: Recommendation G.114. 'One-way Propagation Time'. Rev. 1, Geneva, 1993.

[83] ITU-T: Recommendation G.131. 'Stability and Echo'. *Blue Book*, Fascicle III.1, Geneva, 1989.

[84] ITU-T: Recommendation G.652. 'Characteristics of a Single-Mode Optical Fibre Cable'. Rev. 1, Geneva, 1993.

[85] ITU-T: Recommendation G.702. 'Digital Hierarchy Bit Rates'. *Blue Book*, Fascicle III.4, Geneva, 1988.

[86] ITU-T: Recommendation G.703. 'Physical/Electrical Characteristics of Hierarchical Digital Interfaces'. Rev. 1, Geneva, 1991.

[87] ITU-T: Recommendation G.704. 'Synchronous Frame Structures Used at Primary and Secondary Hierarchical Levels'. Rev. 1, Geneva, 1991.

[88] ITU-T: Recommendation G.707. 'Synchronous Digital Hierarchy Bit Rates'. Rev. 2, Geneva, 1993.

[89] ITU-T: Recommendation G.708. 'Network Node Interface for the Synchronous Digital Hierarchy'. Rev. 2, Geneva, 1993.

[90] ITU-T: Recommendation G.709. 'Synchronous Multiplexing Structure'. Rev. 2, Geneva, 1993.

[91] ITU-T: Draft Recommendation G.804. 'ATM Cell Mapping into Plesiochronous Digital Hierarchy (PDH)'. Geneva, 1993.

[92] ITU-T: Recommendation G.811. 'Timing Requirements at the Outputs of Primary Reference Clocks suitable for Plesiochronous Operation of International Digital Links'. *Blue Book*, Fascicle III.5, Geneva, 1988.

[93] ITU-T: Recommendation G.821. 'Error Performance of an International Digital Connection forming Part of an Integrated Services Digital Network'. *Blue Book*, Fascicle III.5, Geneva, 1988.

[94] ITU-T: Recommendation G.822. 'Controlled Slip Rate Objectives on an International Digital Connection'. *Blue Book*, Fascicle III.5, Geneva, 1988.

[95] ITU-T: Recommendation G.823. 'The Control of Jitter and Wander within Digital Networks which are based on the 2048 kbit/s Hierarchy'. Rev. 1, Geneva, 1993.

[96] ITU-T: Recommendation G.824. 'The Control of Jitter and Wander within Digital Networks which are based on the 1544 kbit/s Hierarchy'. Rev. 1, Geneva, 1993.

[97] ITU-T: Draft Recommendation G.832. 'Transport of SDH Elements on PDH Networks: Frame and Multiplexing Structures'. Geneva, 1993.

[98] ITU-T: Recommendation G.957. 'Optical Interfaces for Equipments and Systems Relating to the Synchronous Digital Hierarchy'. Rev. 1, Geneva, 1993.

[99] ITU-T: Recommendation I.113. 'Vocabulary of Terms for Broadband Aspects of ISDN'. Rev. 1, Geneva, 1991.

[100] ITU-T: Recommendation I.120. 'Integrated Services Digital Networks (ISDNs)'. Rev. 1, Geneva, 1993.

[101] ITU-T: Recommendation I.121. 'Broadband Aspects of ISDN'. Rev. 1, Geneva, 1991.

[102] ITU-T: Recommendation I.150. 'B-ISDN ATM Functional Characteristics'. Rev. 1, Geneva, 1993.

[103] ITU-T: Recommendation I.211. 'B-ISDN Service Aspects'. Rev. 1, Geneva, 1993.

[104] ITU-T: Recommendation I.233. 'Frame Mode Bearer Services'. Geneva, 1991.

[105] ITU-T: Recommendation I.311. 'B-ISDN General Network Aspects'. Rev. 1, Geneva, 1993.

[106] ITU-T: Recommendation I.320. 'ISDN Protocol Reference Model'. *Blue Book*, Fascicle III.8, Geneva, 1988.

[107] ITU-T: Recommendation I.321. 'B-ISDN Protocol Reference Model and its Application'. Geneva, 1991.

[108] ITU-T: Recommendation I.327. 'B-ISDN Functional Architecture'. Rev. 1, Geneva, 1993.

[109] ITU-T: Recommendation I.356. 'B-ISDN ATM Layer Cell Transfer Performance', Geneva, 1993.

[110] ITU-T: Recommendation I.361. 'B-ISDN ATM Layer Specification'. Rev. 1, Geneva, 1993.

[111] ITU-T: Recommendation I.362. 'B-ISDN ATM Adaptation Layer (AAL) Functional Description'. Rev. 1, Geneva, 1993.

[112] ITU-T: Recommendation I.363. 'B-ISDN ATM Adaptation Layer Specification'. Rev. 1, Geneva, 1993.

[113] ITU-T: Recommendation I.371. 'Traffic Control and Congestion Control in B-ISDN'. Geneva, 1993.

[114] ITU-T: Recommendation I.373. 'Network Capabilities to Support Universal Personal Telecommunication'. Geneva, 1993.

[115] ITU-T: Recommendation I.411. 'ISDN User–Network Interfaces – Reference Configurations'. Rev. 1, Geneva, 1993.

[116] ITU-T: Recommendation I.412. 'ISDN User–Network Interfaces – Interface Structures and Access Capabilities'. *Blue Book*, Fascicle III.8, Geneva, 1988.

[117] ITU-T: Recommendation I.413. 'B-ISDN User–Network Interface'. Rev. 1, Geneva, 1993.

[118] ITU-T: Recommendation I.430. 'Basic User–Network Interface – Layer 1 Specification'. Rev. 1, Geneva, 1993.

[119] ITU-T: Recommendation I.431. 'Primary Rate User–Network Interface – Layer 1 Specification'. Rev. 1, Geneva, 1993.

[120] ITU-T: Recommendation I.432. 'B-ISDN User–Network Interface – Physical Layer Specification'. Rev. 1, Geneva, 1993.

[121] ITU-T: Draft Recommendation I.555. 'Frame Relay Bearer Service Interworking'. Geneva, 1993.

[122] ITU-T: Recommendation I.601. 'General Maintenance Principles of ISDN Subscriber Access and Subscriber Installation'. *Blue Book*, Fascicle III.9, Geneva, 1988.

[123] ITU-T: Recommendation I.610. 'B-ISDN Operation and Maintenance Principles and Functions'. Rev. 1, Geneva, 1993.

[124] ITU-T: Recommendation M.20. 'Maintenance Philosophy for Telecommunications Networks'. Rev. 1, Geneva, 1992.

[125] ITU-T: Recommendation M.60. 'Maintenance Terminology and Definitions'. Rev. 1, Geneva, 1993.

[126] ITU-T: Recommendation M.3010. 'Principles for a Telecommunications Management Network'. Rev. 1, Geneva, 1992.

[127] ITU-T: Recommendation M.3600. 'Principles for the Management of ISDNs'. Rev. 1, Geneva, 1992.

[128] ITU-T: Draft Recommendation Q.73. 'Basic Call Handling with Separation of Call Control and Connection Control'. Geneva, 1992.

[129] ITU-T: Recommendation Q.704. 'Signalling Network Functions and Messages'. Rev. 1, Geneva, 1993.

[130] ITU-T: Recommendation Q.761. 'Functional Description of the ISDN User Part of Signalling System No. 7'. Rev. 1, Geneva, 1993.

[131] ITU-T: Recommendation Q.762. 'General Functions of Messages and Signals'. Rev. 1, Geneva, 1993.

[132] ITU-T: Recommendation Q.763. 'Formats and Codes'. Rev. 1, Geneva, 1993.

[133] ITU-T: Recommendation Q.764. 'Signalling Procedures'. Rev. 1, Geneva, 1993.

[134] ITU-T: Recommendation Q.922. 'ISDN Data Link Layer Specification for Frame Mode Bearer Services'. Geneva, 1992.

[135] ITU-T: Recommendation Q.931. 'ISDN User–Network Interface Layer 3 Specification for Basic Call Control'. Rev. 1, Geneva, 1993.

[136] ITU-T: Recommendation Q.940. 'ISDN User–Network Interface Protocol for Management – General Aspects'. *Blue Book*, Fascicle VI.11, Geneva, 1988.

[137] ITU-T: Draft Recommendation Q.1400. 'Architecture Framework for the Development of Signalling and Organisation, Administration and Maintenance Protocols Using OSI Concepts'. Geneva, 1993.

[138] ITU-T: Draft Recommendation Q.2010. 'General Introduction to Signalling in B-ISDN'. Geneva, 1993.

[139] ITU-T: Draft Recommendation Q.2100. 'B-ISDN Signalling ATM Adaptation Layer (SAAL) Overview Description'. Geneva, 1993.

[140] ITU-T: Draft Recommendation Q.2110. 'B-ISDN Signalling ATM Adaptation Layer (SAAL) – Service Specific Connection Oriented Protocol (SSCOP)'. Geneva, 1993.

[141] ITU-T: Draft Recommendation Q.2120. 'B-ISDN Meta-signalling Protocol'. Geneva, 1993.

[142] ITU-T: Draft Recommendation Q.2130. 'B-ISDN Signalling ATM Adaptation Layer (SAAL) – Service Specific Coordination Function for support of Signalling at the User-to-Network Interface (SSCF at UNI)'. Geneva, 1993.

[143] ITU-T: Draft Recommendation Q.2140. 'B-ISDN Signalling ATM Adaptation Layer (SAAL) – Service Specific Coordination Function for support of Signalling at the Network–Node Interface (SSCF at NNI)'. Geneva, 1993.

[144] ITU-T: Draft Recommendation Q.2761. 'Functional Description of the B-ISDN User Part of Signalling System No. 7'. Geneva, 1993.

[145] ITU-T: Draft Recommendation Q.2762. 'General Functions of Messages and Signals'. Geneva, 1993.

[146] ITU-T: Draft Recommendation Q.2763. 'Formats and Codes'. Geneva, 1993.

[147] ITU-T: Draft Recommendation Q.2764. 'Signalling Procedures'. Geneva, 1993.

[148] ITU-T: Draft Recommendation Q.2931. 'B-ISDN User–Network Interface Layer 3 Protocol'. Geneva, 1993.

[149] ITU-T: Recommendation X.1. 'International User Classes of Service in Public Data Networks and Integrated Services Digital Networks '. Rev. 1, Geneva, 1993.

[150] ITU-T: Recommendation X.25. 'Interface between Data Terminal Equipment (DTE) and Data Circuit-terminating Equipment (DCE) for Terminals Operating in the Packet Mode and Connected to Public Data Networks by Dedicated Circuit'. Rev. 1, Geneva, 1993.

[151] ITU-T: Recommendation X.28. 'DTE/DCE Interface for a Start-Stop Mode Data Terminal Equipment accessing the Packet Assembly/Disassembly Facility (PAD) in a Public Data Network situated in the same Country'. Rev. 1, Geneva, 1993.

[152] ITU-T: Recommendation X.200. 'Reference Model of Open Systems Interconnection for CCITT Applications'. *Blue Book*, Fascicle VIII.4, Geneva, 1988.

[153] ITU-T: Recommendation X.208. 'Specification of Abstract Syntax Notation One (ASN.1)'. *Blue Book*, Fascicle VIII.4, Geneva, 1988.

[154] JANNIELLO, F.J., RAMASWAMI, R., STEINBERG, D.G.: A Prototype Circuit-Switched Multi-Wavelength Optical Metropolitan-Area Network. *IEEE Journal of Lightwave Technology*, vol. 11, no. 5/6, May/June 1993, pp. 777–782.

[155] JOHANSSON, S., LINDBLOM, M., BUHRGARD, M., GRANESTRAND, P., LAGERSTRÖM, B., THYLÉN, L., WOSINSKA, L.: Photonic Switching in High Capacity Transport Networks. *Proceedings of the XIV International Switching Symposium*, Yokohama, 1992, paper B9.1.

[156] JTC: JTC1/SC6 WG6 N71: 'Specification of the Asynchronous Transfer Mode Ring (ATMR) Protocol', Japanese National Body, Japan, 1990.

[157] KAROL, M.J., HLUCHYI, M.G., MORGAN, S.P.: Input versus Output Queueing on a Space-division Packet Switch. *IEEE Transactions on Communications*, vol. 35, no. 12, December 1987, pp. 1347–1356.

[158] KAMMERL, A.: Contribution on Echo Control. Submitted to CEPT/NA5 Meeting in Madeira, October 1988.

[159] KELLER, H., GLADE, B., HARTL, B., HORBACH, C.: Optical Broadband Access using ATM on a Passive Optical Network. *International Journal of Digital and Analog Communication Systems*, vol. 6, 1993, pp. 143–149.

[160] KOLJONEN, J.: HDSL Boosts the Value of the Copper-Based Network. *Discovery*, vol. 27, 1992, pp. 34–37.

[161] KRÖNER, H.: Comparative Performance Study of Space Priority Mechanisms for ATM Networks. *Proceedings of the INFOCOM'90*, San Francisco, 1990, pp. 1136–1143.

[162] KUEHN, P.J.: From ISDN to IBCN (Integrated Broadband Communication Network). *Proceedings of the World Computer Congress IFIP'89*, San Francisco, 1989, pp. 479–486.

[163] LAMPE, D.: Transfer Delay Deviation of Packets in ATD Switching Matrices and its Effect on Dimensioning a Depacketizer Buffer. *Proceedings of the International Conference on Computer Communication*, Tel Aviv, 1988, pp. 55–60.

[164] LEA, C.T.: Multi-log$_2$ N Self-Routing Networks and their Applications in High Speed Electronic and Photonic Switching Systems. *Proceedings of the INFOCOM'89*, Ottawa, 1989, pp. 877–886.

[165] LEMPPENAU, W.W., GOETZER, M., SEIBOLT, W.: Access Protocols for High-Speed LANs and MANs. *Proceedings of the European Fibre Optic Communications and Networks*, The Hague, 1993, pp. 253–259.

[166] LUDERER, G.W.R., KNAUER, S.C.: The Evolution of Space Division Packet Switches. *Proceedings of the XIII International Switching Symposium*, Stockholm, 1990, vol. V, pp. 211–216.

[167] LUTZ, K.A.: Considerations on ATM Switching Techniques. *International Journal of Digital and Analog Cabled Systems*, vol. 1, no. 4, October 1988, pp. 237–243.

[168] LYLES, B., SWINEHART, D.: The Emerging Gigabit Environment and the Role of Local ATM, *IEEE Communications Magazine*, vol. 30, no. 4, April 1992, pp. 52–58.

[169] MCMAHON, D.H.: Doing Wavelength-Division Multiplexing with Today's Technology. *IEEE LTS The Magazine of Lightwave Telecommunication Systems*, vol. 3, no. 1, February 1992, pp. 40–50.

[170] MÖHRMANN, K.H.: Kupfer oder Glasfaser zum Teilnehmer – Wettbewerb oder Ergänzung? *Tagungsband zur VDI/VDE-Tagung Verbindungstechnik'91*, Karlsruhe 1991.

[171] MOLLENAUER, J.F: Standards of Metropolitan Area Networks. *IEEE Communications Magazine*, vol. 26, no. 4, April 1988, pp. 15–19.

[172] MÜLLER, H.R., NASSEHI, M.M., WONG, J.W., ZURFLUH, E., BUX, W., ZAFIROPULO, P.: DQMA and CRMA: New Access Schemes for Gbit/s LANs and MANs. *Proceedings of the INFOCOM'90*, San Francisco, 1990, pp. 185–191.

[173] NEWMAN, P: ATM Technology for Corporate Networks, *IEEE Communications Magazine*, vol. 30, no. 4, April 1992, pp. 90–101.

[174] NEWMAN, R.M., BUDRIKIS, Z.L., HULLETT J.L.: The QPSX MAN. *IEEE Communications Magazine*, vol. 26, no. 4, April 1988, pp. 20–28.

[175] NUSSBAUM, E.: Communication Network Needs and Technologies – A Place for Photonic Switching? *IEEE Journal on Selected Areas in Communications*, vol. 6, no. 7, August 1988, pp. 1036–1043.

[176] OIE, Y., MURATA, M., KUBOTA, K., MIYAHARA, H.: Effect of Speedup in Nonblocking Packet Switches. *Proceedings of the International Conference on Communications*, Boston, 1989, pp. 410–414.

[177] PARTRIDGE, C.: *Gigabit Networking*. Addison-Wesley Publishing Company, Wokingham, 1994.

[178] PATEL, J.H.: Performance of Processor-Memory Interconnection for Multi-processors. *IEEE Transactions on Computers*, vol. 30, no. 10, October 1981, pp. 771–780.

[179] POPESCU-ZELETIN, R., EGLOFF, P., BUTSCHER, B.: BERKOM – A Broadband ISDN Project. *Proceedings of the International Zurich Seminar*, Zürich, 1988, paper B5.

[180] RACE: RACE Project R1044/2.10 Broadband User/Network Interface BUNI, 4th Deliverable 'Interface Specification – Draft A and Rationale'. *British Telecom Research Laboratories*, Martlesham Heath, November 1989.

[181] RAMASWAMI, R.: Multiwavelength Lightwave Networks for Computer Communication. *IEEE Communications Magazine*, vol. 31, no. 2, February 1993, pp. 78–88.

[182] RATHGEB, E.P., THEIMER, T.H., HUBER, M.N.: Buffering Concepts for ATM Switching Networks. *Proceedings of the GLOBECOM'88*, Hollywood, 1988, pp. 1277–1281.

[183] RATHGEB, E.P., THEIMER, T.H., HUBER, M.N.: ATM Switches – Basic Architectures and their Performance. *International Journal of Digital and Analog Cabled Systems*, vol. 2, no. 4, October 1989, pp. 227–236.

[184] RATHGEB, E.P.: Policing Mechanisms for ATM Networks – Modelling and Performance Comparison. *Proceedings of the 7th International Teletraffic Congress Seminar on 'Broadband Technologies: Architectures, Applications, Control and Performance'*, Morristown, 1990, paper 10.1.

[185] RENGER, T., BRIEM, U.: Leistungsuntersuchung von ATM Adaptation Layer Protokollen für Signalisierung, *private communication*.

[186] ROSE, M.T.: *The Simple Book – An Introduction to Internet Management*, Prentice Hall, Englewood Cliffs, 1993.

[187] ROTHERMEL, K., SEEGER, D.: Traffic Studies of Switching Networks for Asynchronous Tranfer Mode (ATM). *Proceedings of the 12th International Teletraffic Congress*, Torino, 1988, paper 1.3A.5.

[188] SATO, K., OKAMATO, S., HADAMA, H.: Optical Path Layer Technologies to Enhance B-ISDN Performance. *Proceedings of the International Conference on Communications*, Geneva, 1993, pp. 1300–1307.

[189] SCHAFFER, B.: ATM Switching in the Developing Telecommunication Network. *Proceedings of the XIII International Switching Symposium*, Stockholm, 1990, vol. I, pp. 105–110.

[190] SCHOUTE, F.C.: Simple Decision Rules for Acceptance of Mixed Traffic Streams. *Proceedings of the 12th International Teletraffic Congress*, Torino, 1988, paper 4.2A.5.

[191] SIEBENHAAR, R., BAUSCHERT, T.: Vergleich von Algorithmen zur Verbindungsannahme in ATM-Netzen. *Tagungsband zur ITG/GI-Fachtagung Kommunikation in Verteilten Systemen*, Munich, 1993, pp. 114–128.

[192] SIEMENS: The Intelligent Integrated Broadband Network – Telecommunications in the 1990s. Siemens, Munich, 1989.

[193] SUNSHINE, C.A.: Network Interconnection and Gateways. *IEEE Journal on Selected Areas in Communications*, vol. 8, no. 1, December 1990, pp. 4–11.

[194] THEIMER, T.H.: Performance Comparison of Routing Strategies in ATM Switches. *Proceedings of the XIII International Teletraffic Congress*, Copenhagen, 1991, pp. 923–928.

[195] TOBAGI, F.A.: Fast Packet Switch Architectures for Broadband Integrated Services Digital Networks. *Proceedings of the IEEE*, vol. 78, no. 1, January 1990, pp. 133–167.

[196] TOLMIE, D., RENWICK, J.: HIPPI: Simplicity Yields Success. *IEEE Network Magazine*, vol. 7, no. 1, January 1993, pp. 28–33.

[197] TURNER, J.S.: Design of a Broadcast Packet Switching Network. *IEEE Transactions on Communications*, vol. 36, no. 6, June 1987, pp. 734–743.

[198] VORSTERMANS, J.P., DE VLEESCHOUWER, A.P.: Layered ATM Systems and Architectural Concepts for Subscribers' Premises Networks. *IEEE Journal on Selected Areas in Communications*, vol. 6, no. 9, December 1988, pp. 1545–1555.

[199] WATSON, G., OOI, S., SKELLERN, D., CUNNIGHAM, D.: HANGMAN Gb/s Network. *IEEE Network*, vol, 6, no. 4, July 1992, pp. 10–18.

[200] WIEST, G.: More Intelligence and Flexibility for Communication Network – Challenges for Tomorrow's Switching Systems. *Proceedings of the XIII International Switching Symposium*, Stockholm, 1990, vol. V, pp. 201–204.

[201] WU, C.L., FENG, T.Y.: On a Class of Multistage Interconnection Networks. *IEEE Transactions on Computers*, vol. 29, no. 8, August 1980, pp. 694–702.

[202] ZITZEN, W.: Metropolitan Area Networks: Taking LANs into the Public Network. *Telecommunications*, June 1990, pp. 53–60.

Index